THE AMAZING REMARKABLE MONSIEUR LEOTARD

THE AMAZING REMARKABLE
MONSIEUR LEOTARD

A NOVEL

with typographical acrobatics and illustrational feats
in an ideal production of entirely new tricks,
statuesque acts, and performances.

Story by **EDDIE CAMPBELL** and **DAN BEST**
Art by **EDDIE CAMPBELL**

First Second
NEW YORK & LONDON

First Second

New York & London

Copyright © 2008 by Eddie Campbell and Dan Best

Published by First Second
First Second is an imprint of Roaring Brook Press,
a division of Holtzbrinck Publishing Holdings Limited Partnership
175 Fifth Avenue, New York, NY 10010

Distributed in Canada by H. B. Fenn and Company Ltd.
Distributed in the United Kingdom by Macmillan Children's Books,
a division of Pan Macmillan.

Design by Danica Novgorodoff

Cataloging-in-Publication Data is on file at the Library of Congress.

ISBN-13: 978-1-59643-301-4
ISBN-10: 1-59643-301-9

First Second books are available for special promotions and premiums.
For details, contact: Director of Special Markets, Holtzbrinck Publishers.

First Edition September 2008
Printed in China

1 3 5 7 9 10 8 6 4 2

"man is a rope fastened
between animal and superman,
a rope over an abyss.
A dangerous going-over,
a dangerous wayfaring,
a dangerous looking-back
a dangerous shuddering
and staying-still."
        – Friedrich Nietzsche

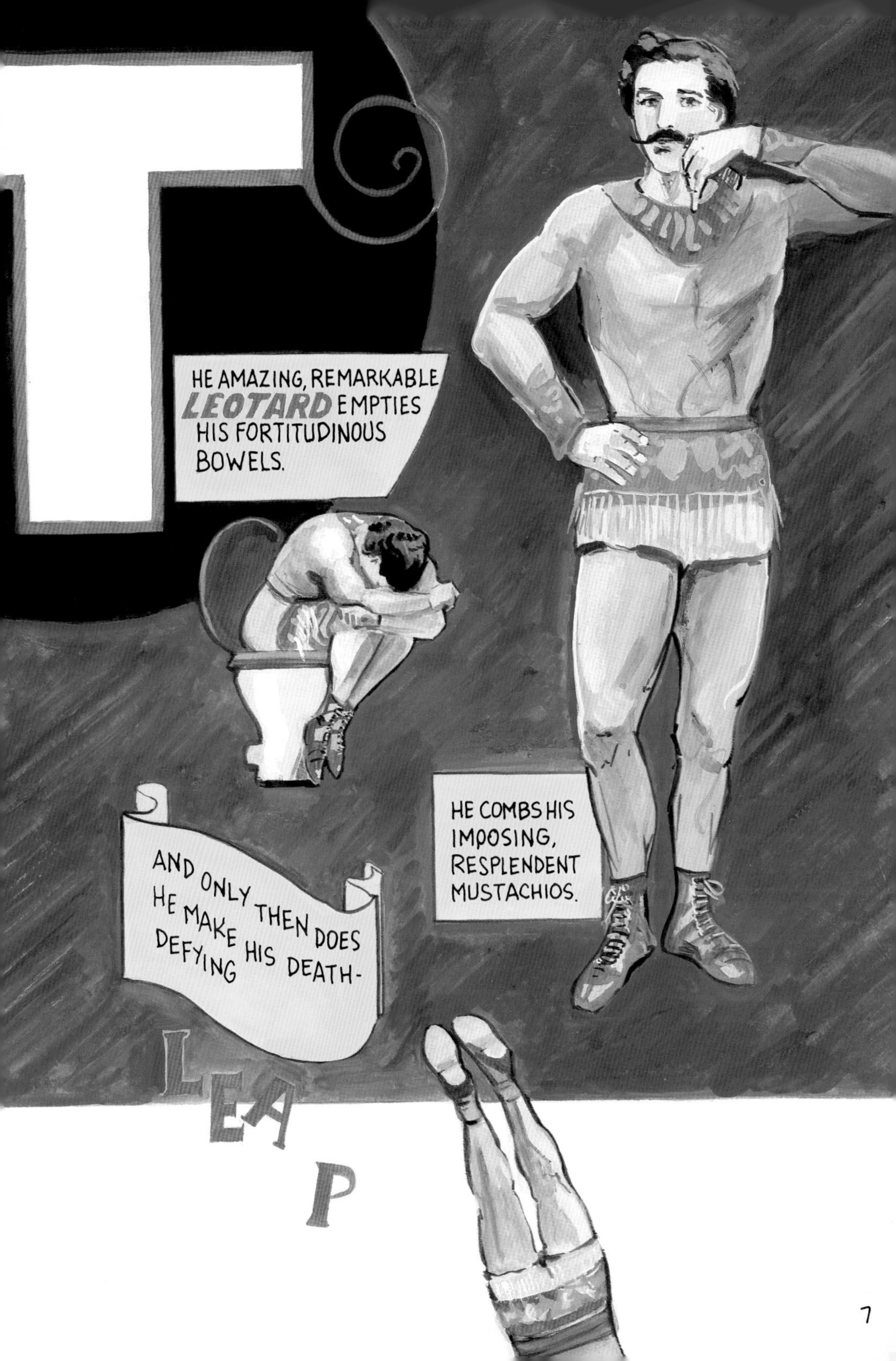
T
HE AMAZING, REMARKABLE LEOTARD EMPTIES HIS FORTITUDINOUS BOWELS.
HE COMBS HIS IMPOSING, RESPLENDENT MUSTACHIOS.
AND ONLY THEN DOES HE MAKE HIS DEATH-DEFYING
LEAP

BIRD'S-EYE VIEWS

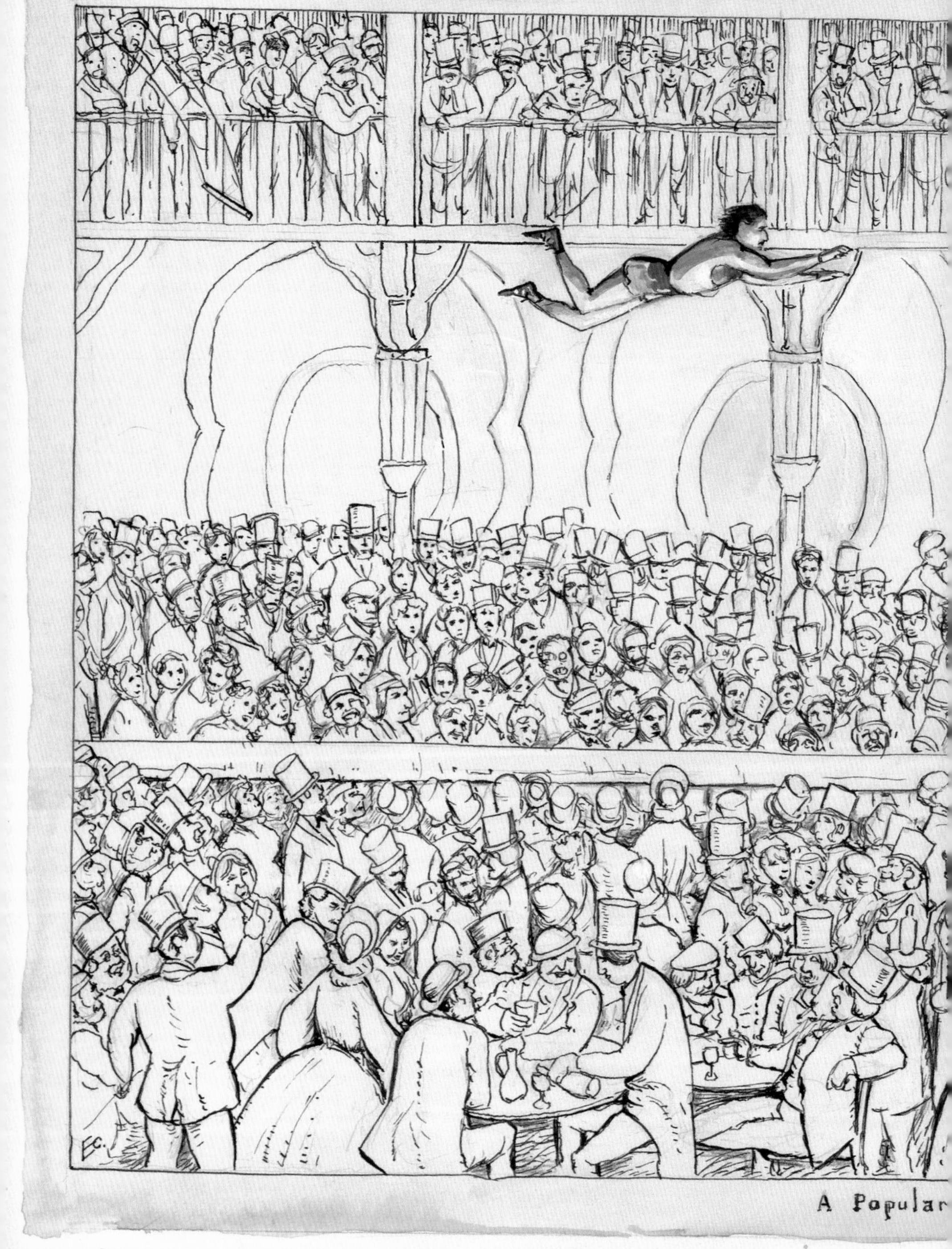
E.C.

A Popular

SOCIETY No IX

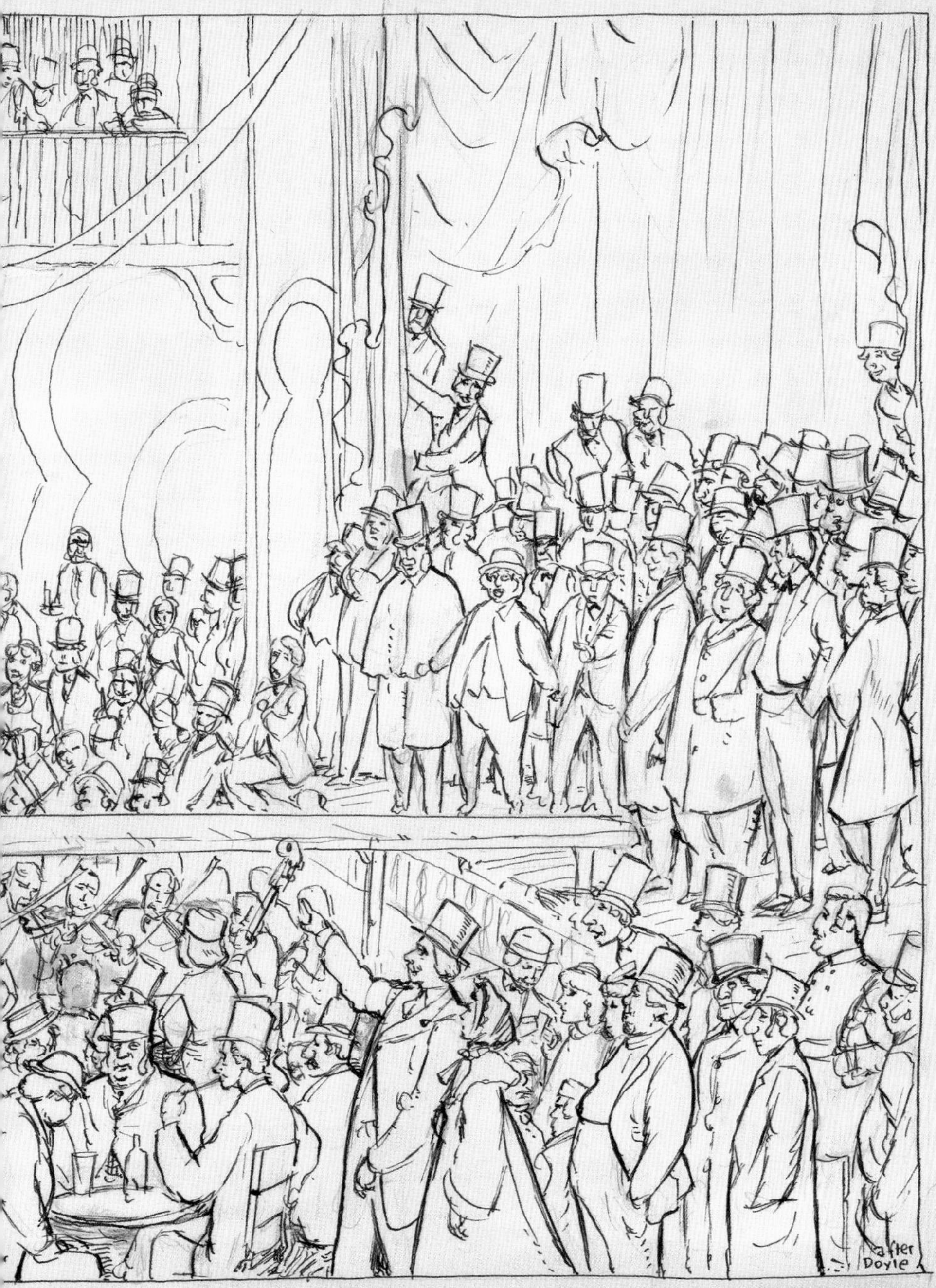
after
Doyle

ntertainment

THE MAN ON THE FLYING TRAPEZE

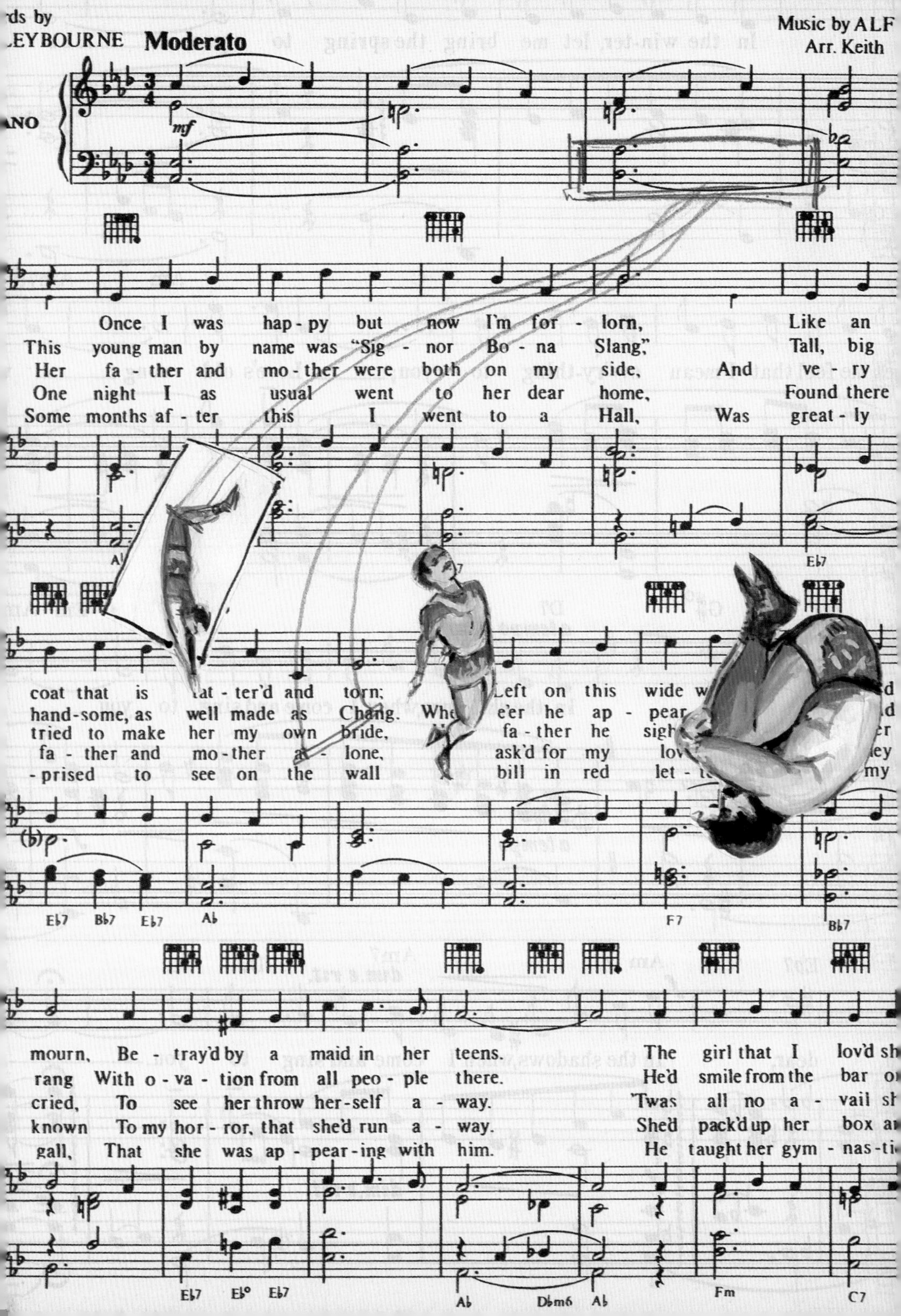

ds by
LEYBOURNE
Moderato
Music by ALF
Arr. Keith
NO
mf
Once I was hap - py but now I'm for - lorn, Like an
This young man by name was "Sig - nor Bo - na Slang," Tall, big
Her fa - ther and mo - ther were both on my side, And ve - ry
One night I as usual went to her dear home, Found there
Some months af - ter this I went to a Hall, Was great - ly
Ab
Eb7
coat that is tat - ter'd and torn; Left on this wide w
hand-some, as well made as Chang. Whe e'er he ap - pear
tried to make her my own bride, fa - ther he sigh
fa - ther and mo - ther a - lone, ask'd for my lov
- prised to see on the wall bill in red let - te
Eb7 Bb7 Eb7 Ab
F7
Bb7
mourn, Be - tray'd by a maid in her teens. The girl that I lov'd sh
rang With o - va - tion from all peo - ple there. He'd smile from the bar o
cried, To see her throw her-self a - way. 'Twas all no a - vail sh
known To my hor - ror, that she'd run a - way. She'd pack'd up her box a
gall, That she was ap - pear - ing with him. He taught her gym - nas - ti
Eb7 Eb° Eb7
Ab Dbm6 Ab
Fm
C7

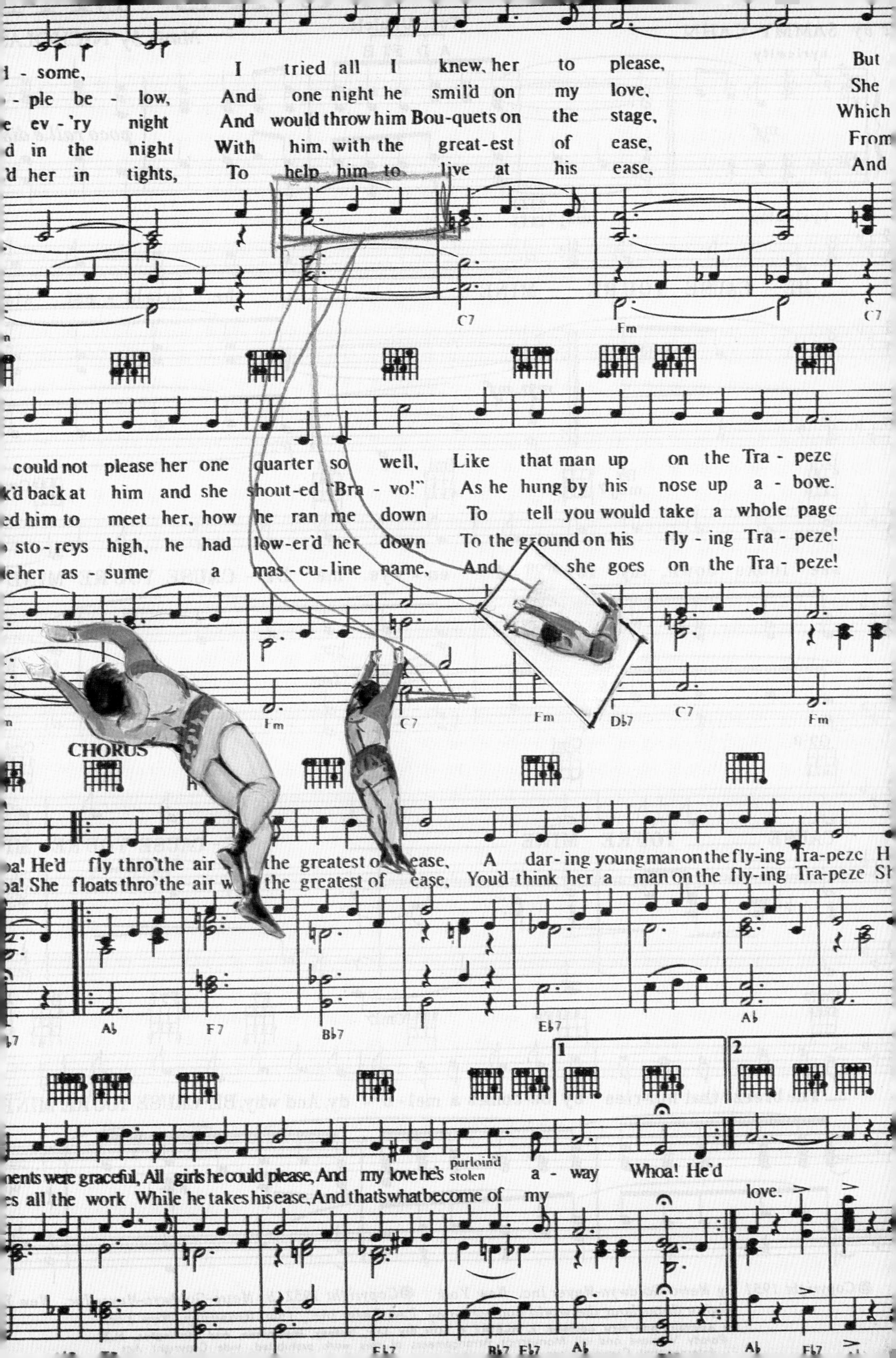

-some, I tried all I knew, her to please, But
-ple be-low, And one night he smil'd on my love, She
e ev-'ry night And would throw him Bou-quets on the stage, Which
d in the night With him, with the great-est of ease, From
'd her in tights, To help him to live at his ease, And
C7
Fm
C7
could not please her one quarter so well, Like that man up on the Tra-peze
k'd back at him and she shout-ed "Bra-vo!" As he hung by his nose up a-bove.
ed him to meet her, how he ran me down To tell you would take a whole page
sto-reys high, he had low-er'd her down To the ground on his fly-ing Tra-peze!
e her as-sume a mas-cu-line name, And she goes on the Tra-peze!
Fm
C7
Fm
Db7
C7
Fm
CHORUS
oa! He'd fly thro' the air the greatest of ease, A dar-ing young man on the fly-ing Tra-peze H
oa! She floats thro' the air the greatest of ease, You'd think her a man on the fly-ing Tra-peze Sh
Ab
F7
Bb7
Eb7
Ab
1
2
nents were graceful, All girls he could please, And my love he's purloin'd stolen a-way Whoa! He'd
es all the work While he takes his ease, And that's what become of my love.
Eb7
Bb7
Eb7
Ab
Ab
Eb7

THE INTREPID, MAJESTIC
BLONDIN
THE EMINENT, FASHIONABLE
LORD GEORGE SANGER
THE UNSURPASSABLE, INDEFATIGABLE
Barnum
THE PRODIGIOUS, STUPENDOUS
PABLO FANQUE
But you cannot die! The Amazing Remarkable Leotard has only just begun-
You were the hero of the London Alhambra. You have inspired a popular song.
In Paris they fought for seats at your last performance.
Everyone is wearing the Leotard cravat, using the Leotard walking stick, and all the dancers are now dressing in the tight-fitting costume.
Who-?
Zany-It's me; Useless Etienne.

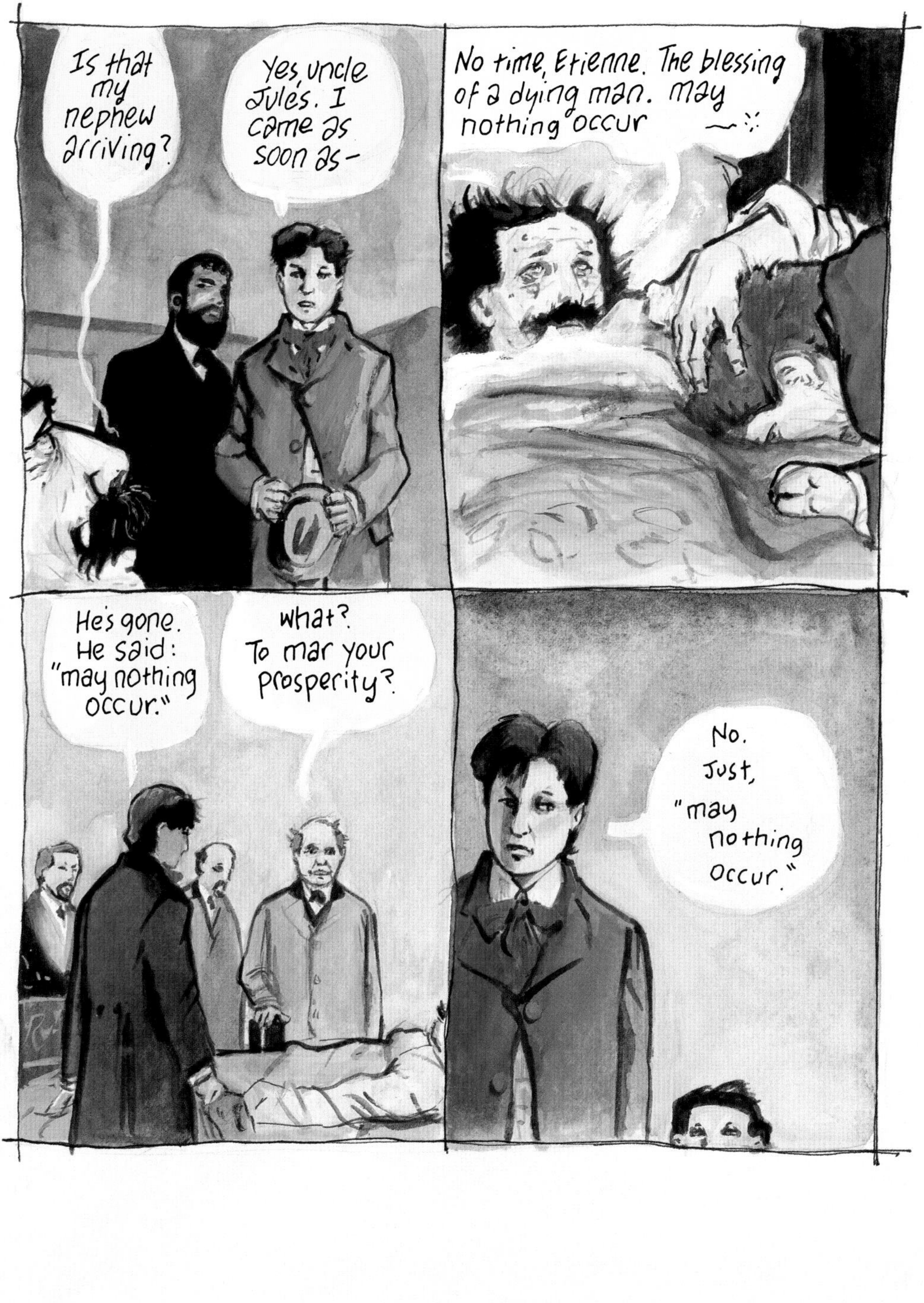
Is that my nephew arriving?
Yes, uncle Jules. I came as soon as-
No time, Etienne. The blessing of a dying man. May nothing occur
He's gone. He said: "may nothing occur."
What? To mar your prosperity?
No. Just, "may nothing occur."

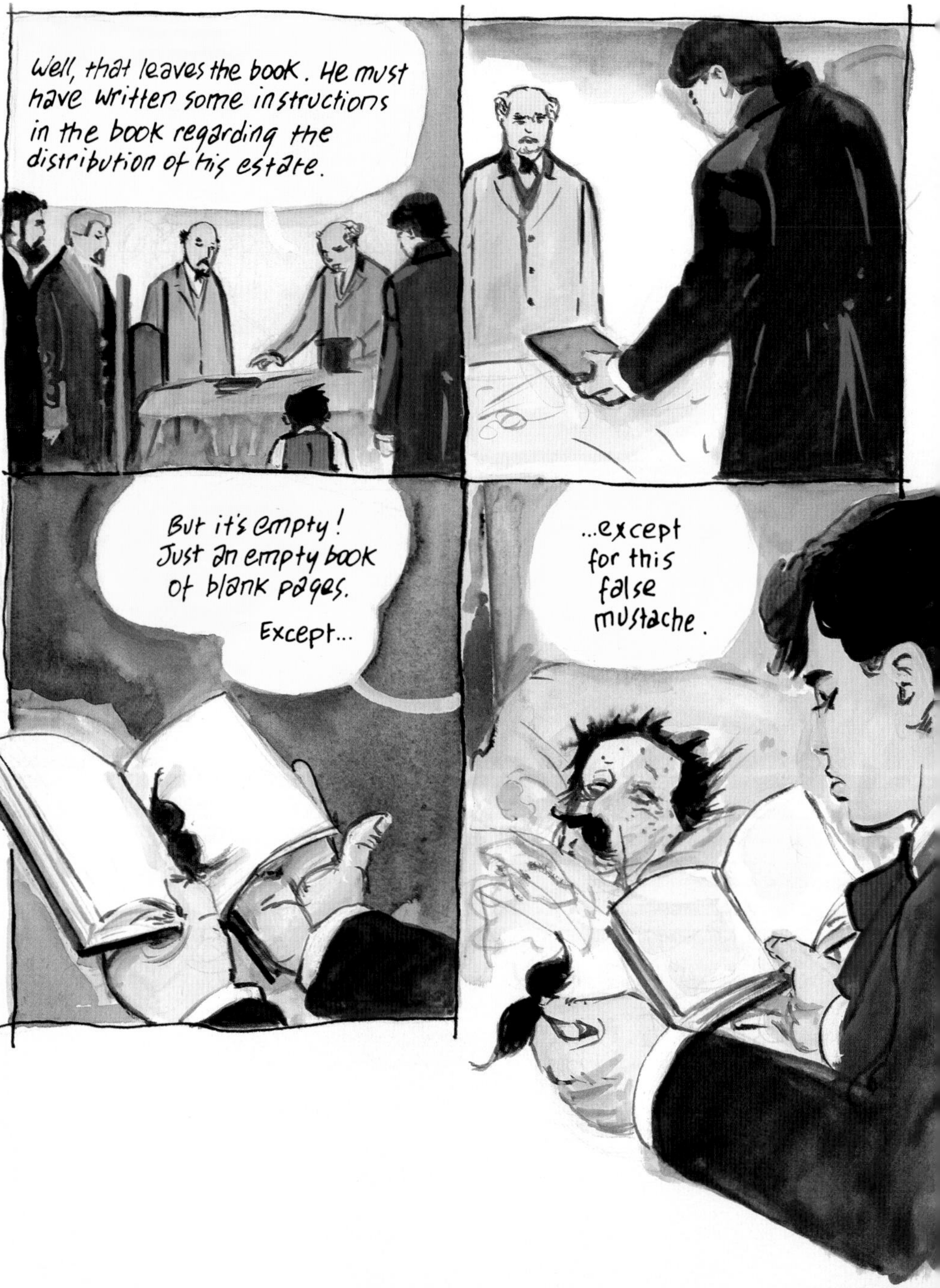
Well, that leaves the book. He must have written some instructions in the book regarding the distribution of his estate.
But it's empty! Just an empty book of blank pages.
Except...
...except for this false mustache.

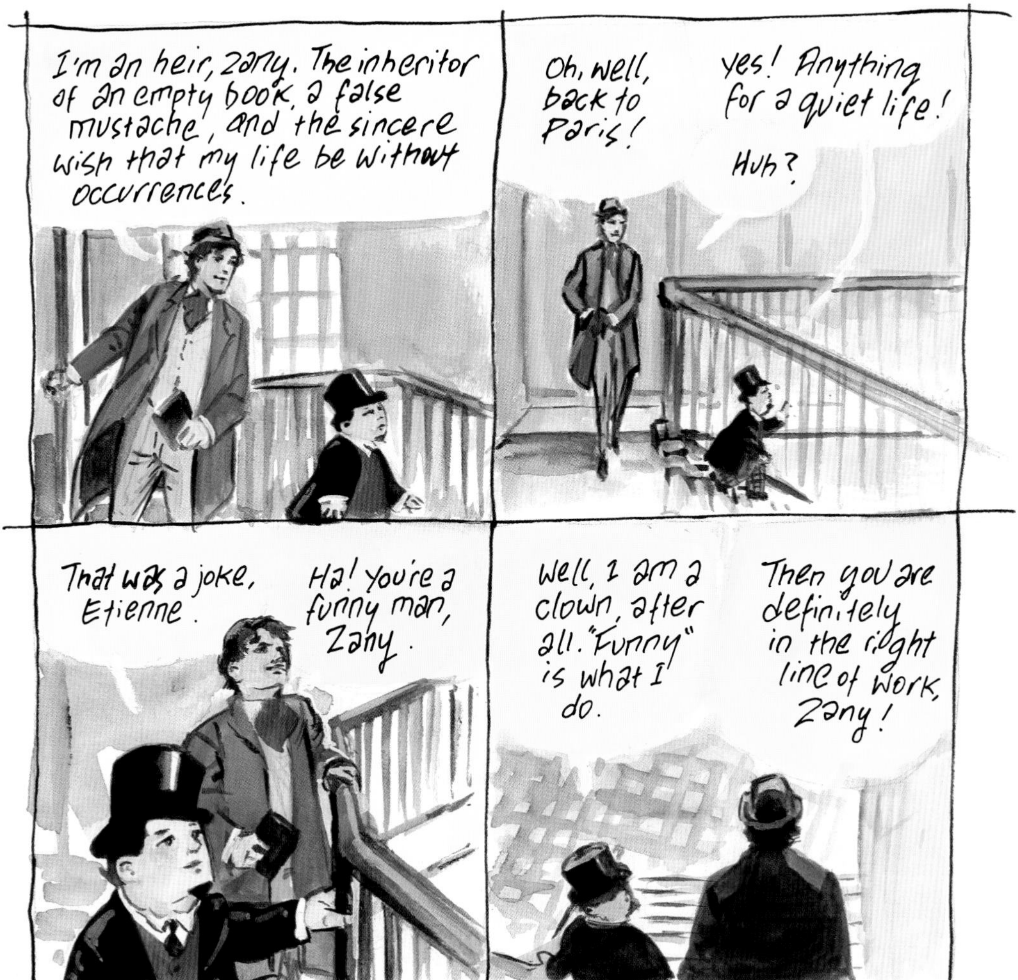
I'm an heir, Zany. The inheritor of an empty book, a false mustache, and the sincere wish that my life be without occurrences.
Oh, well, back to Paris!
Yes! Anything for a quiet life!
Huh?
That was a joke, Etienne.
Ha! You're a funny man, Zany.
Well, I am a clown, after all. "Funny" is what I do.
Then you are definitely in the right line of work, Zany!

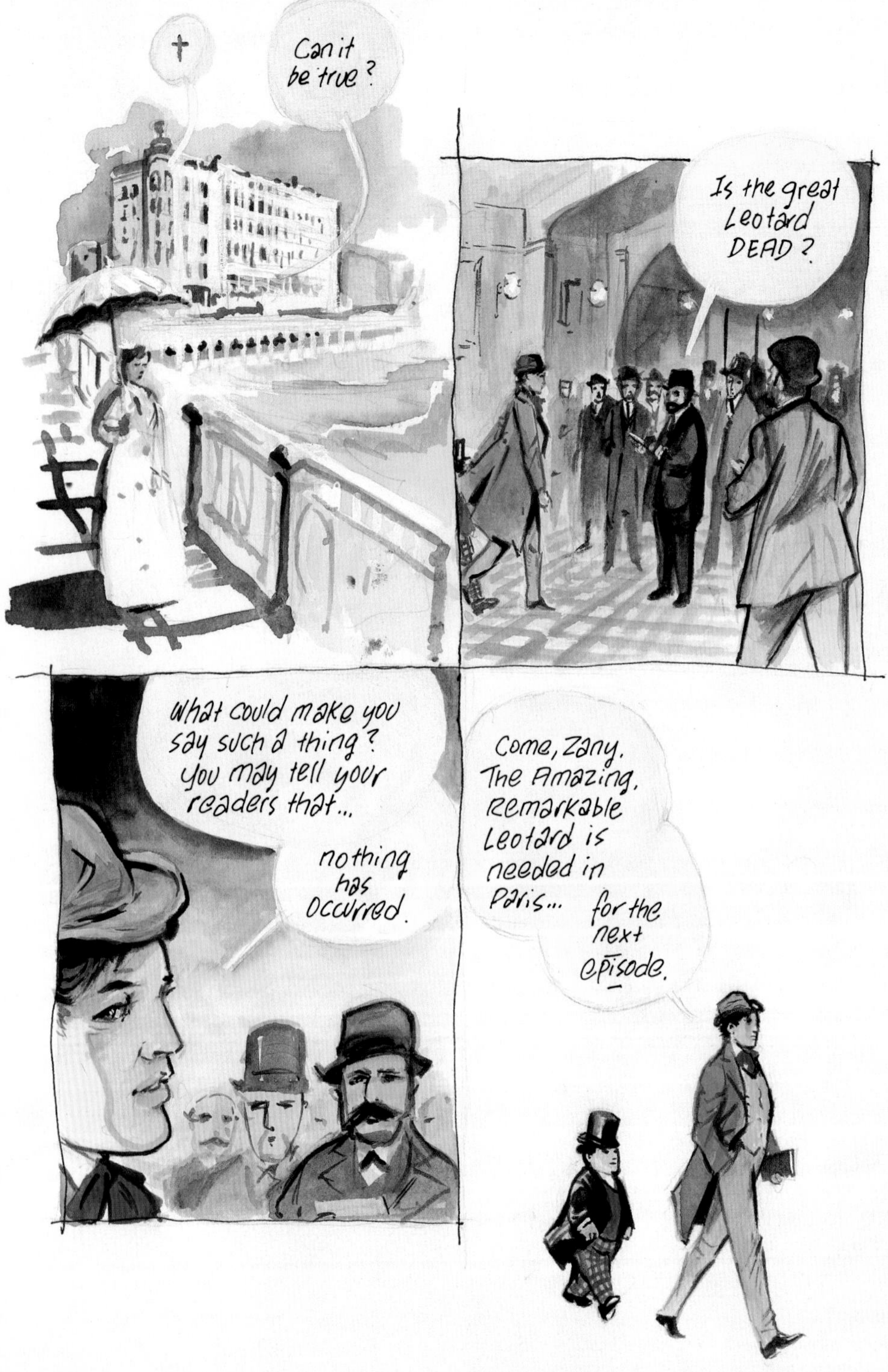
Can it be true?
Is the great Leotard DEAD?
What could make you say such a thing? You may tell your readers that...
nothing has occurred.
Come, Zany. The Amazing, Remarkable Leotard is needed in Paris...
for the next episode.

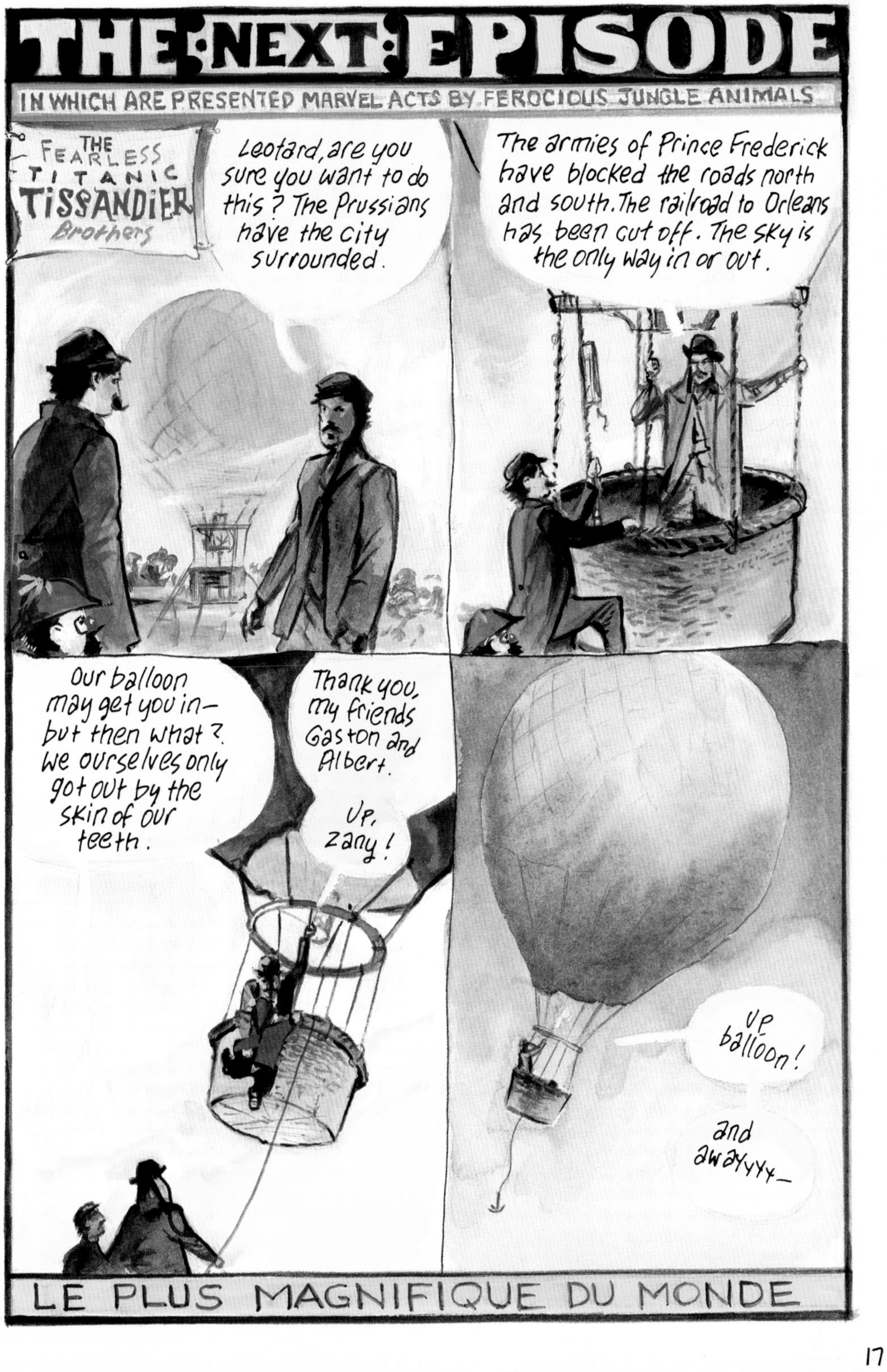
THE NEXT EPISODE
IN WHICH ARE PRESENTED MARVEL ACTS BY FEROCIOUS JUNGLE ANIMALS
THE FEARLESS TITANIC TISSANDIER Brothers
Leotard, are you sure you want to do this? The Prussians have the city surrounded.
The armies of Prince Frederick have blocked the roads north and south. The railroad to Orleans has been cut off. The sky is the only way in or out.
Our balloon may get you in- but then what? We ourselves only got out by the skin of our teeth.
Thank you, my friends Gaston and Albert.
Up, zany!
Up balloon!
and awayyyy-
LE PLUS MAGNIFIQUE DU MONDE

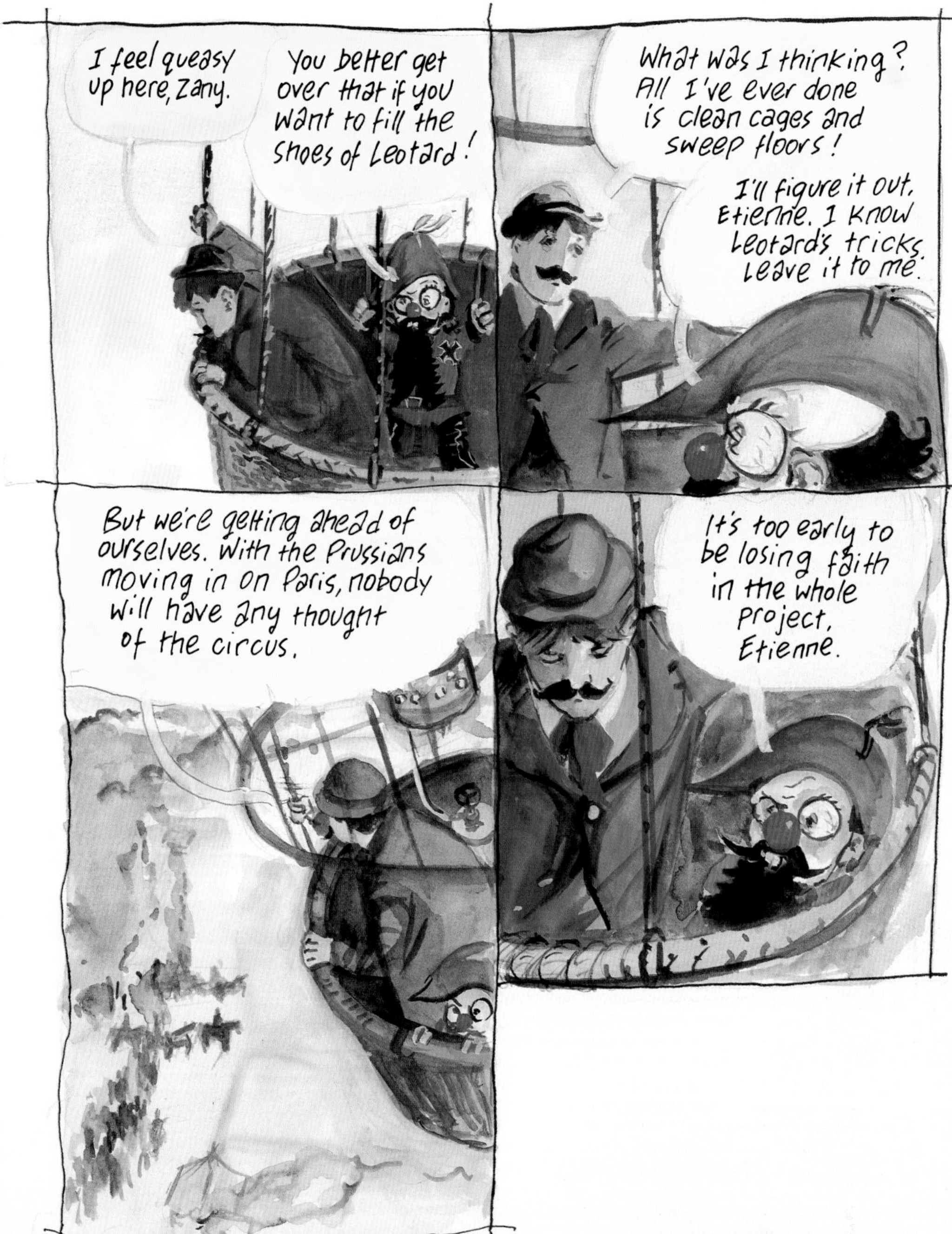
I feel queasy up here, Zany.
You better get over that if you want to fill the shoes of Leotard!
What was I thinking? All I've ever done is clean cages and sweep floors!
I'll figure it out, Etienne. I know Leotard's tricks. Leave it to me.
But we're getting ahead of ourselves. With the Prussians moving in on Paris, nobody will have any thought of the circus.
It's too early to be losing faith in the whole project, Etienne.

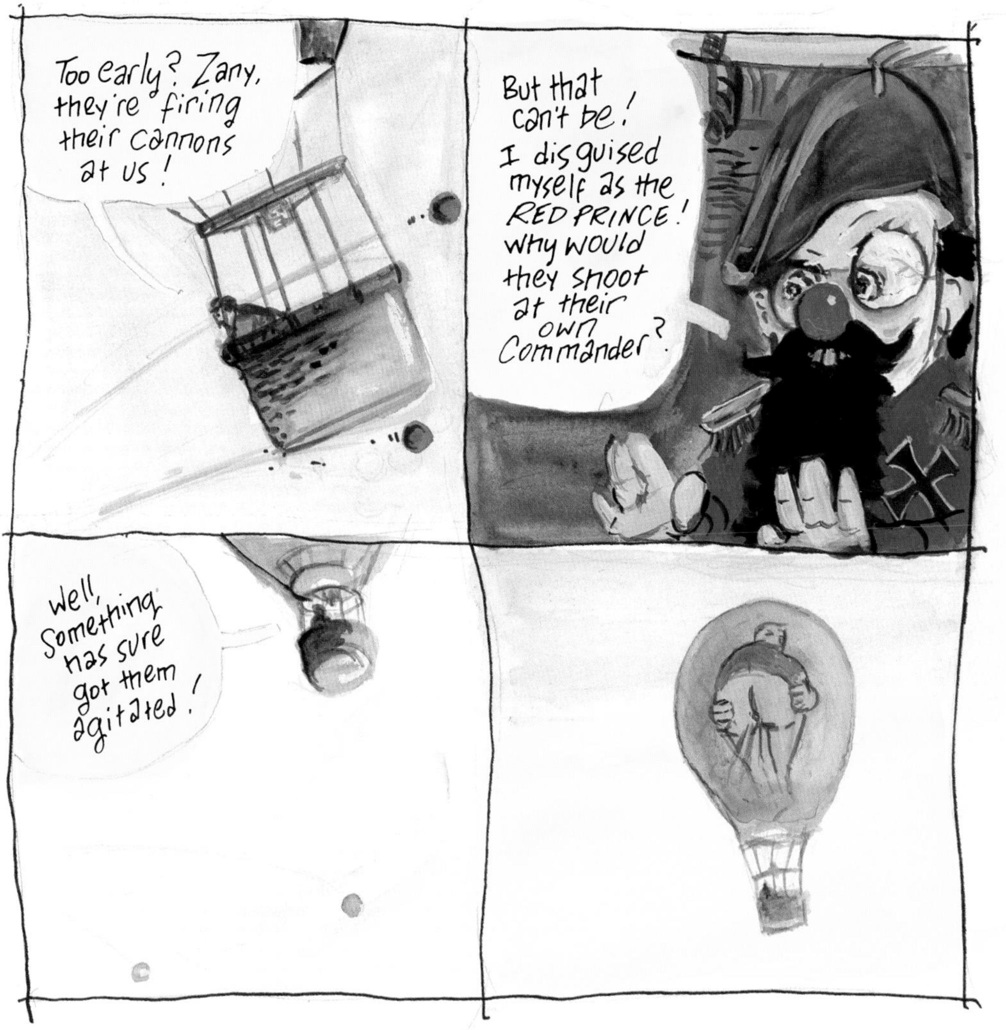
Too early? Zany, they're firing their cannons at us!
But that can't be! I disguised myself as the RED PRINCE! Why would they shoot at their own Commander?
Well, Something has sure got them agitated!

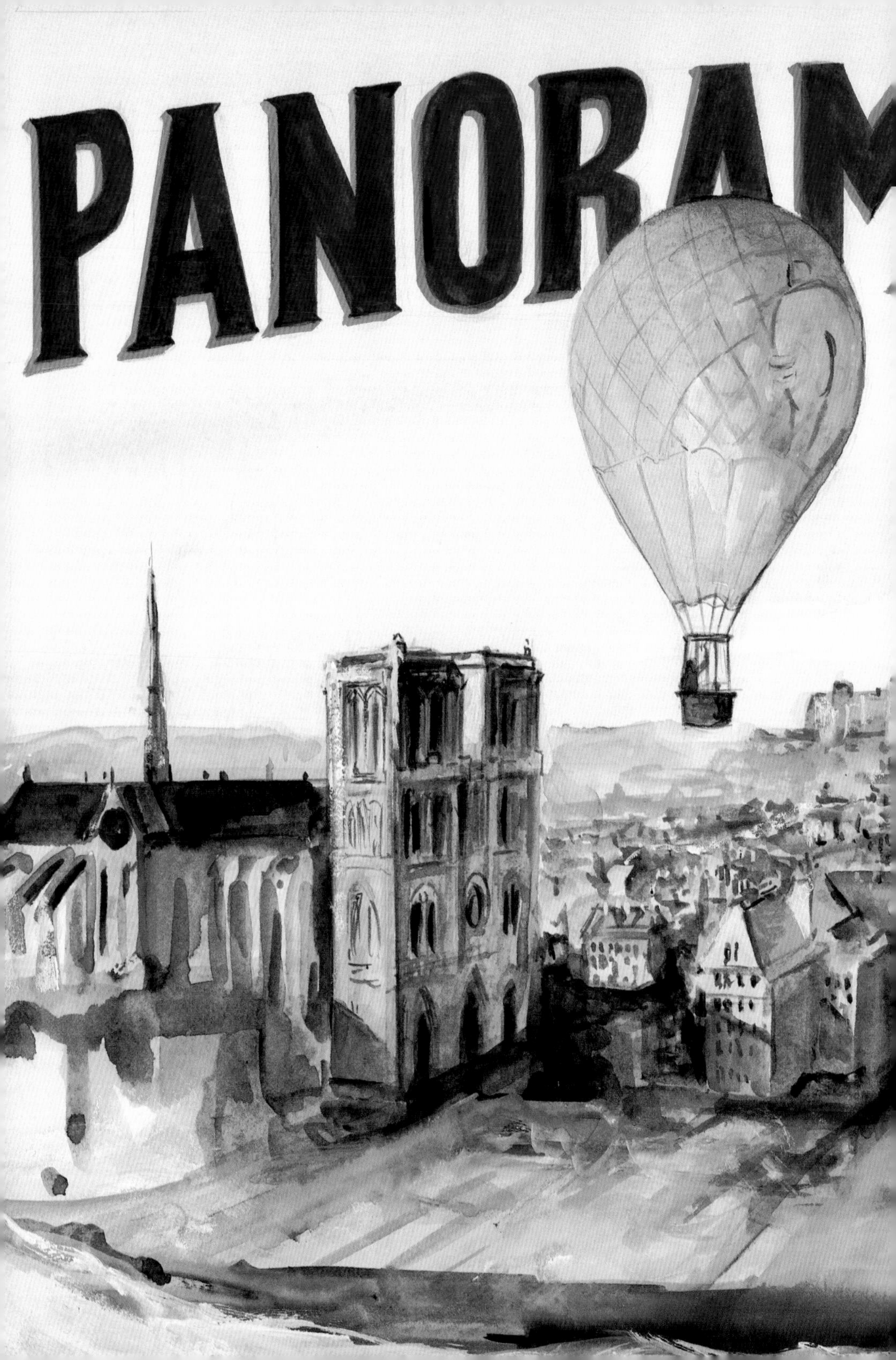
PANORAM

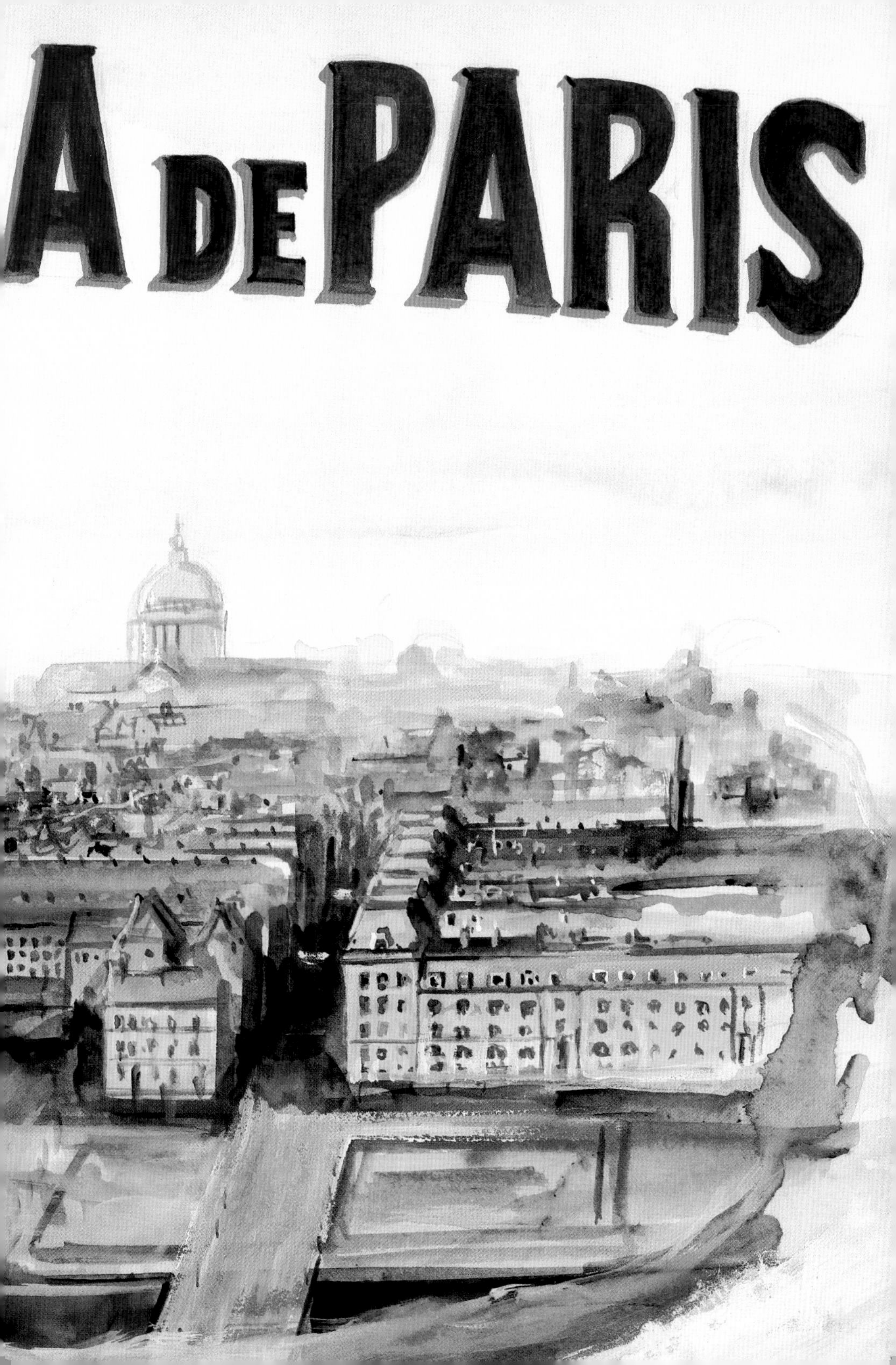
A DE PARIS

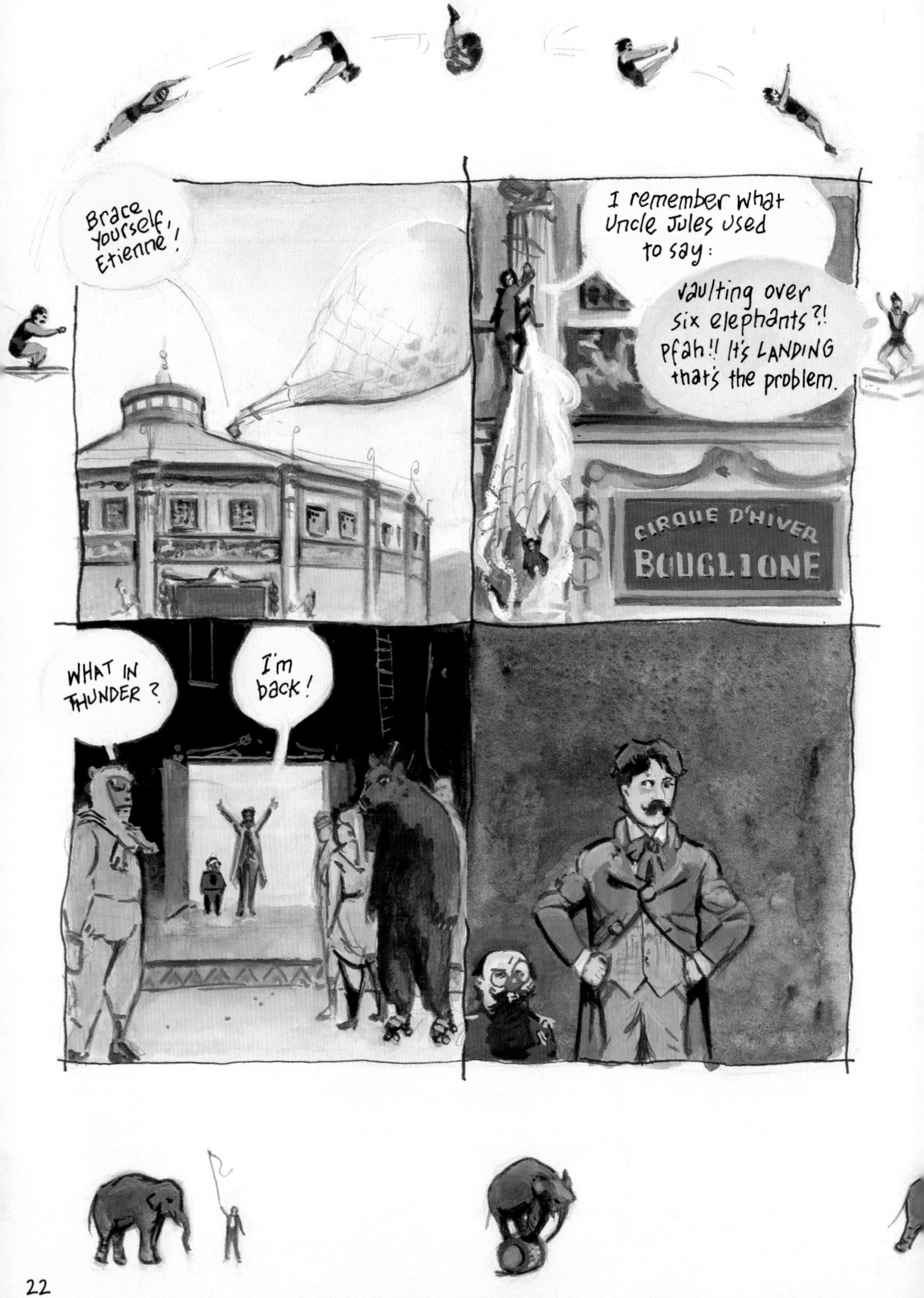
Brace yourself, Etienne!
I remember what Uncle Jules used to say:
Vaulting over six elephants?! Pfah!! It's LANDING that's the problem.
CIRQUE D'HIVER
BOUGLIONE
WHAT IN THUNDER?
I'm back!

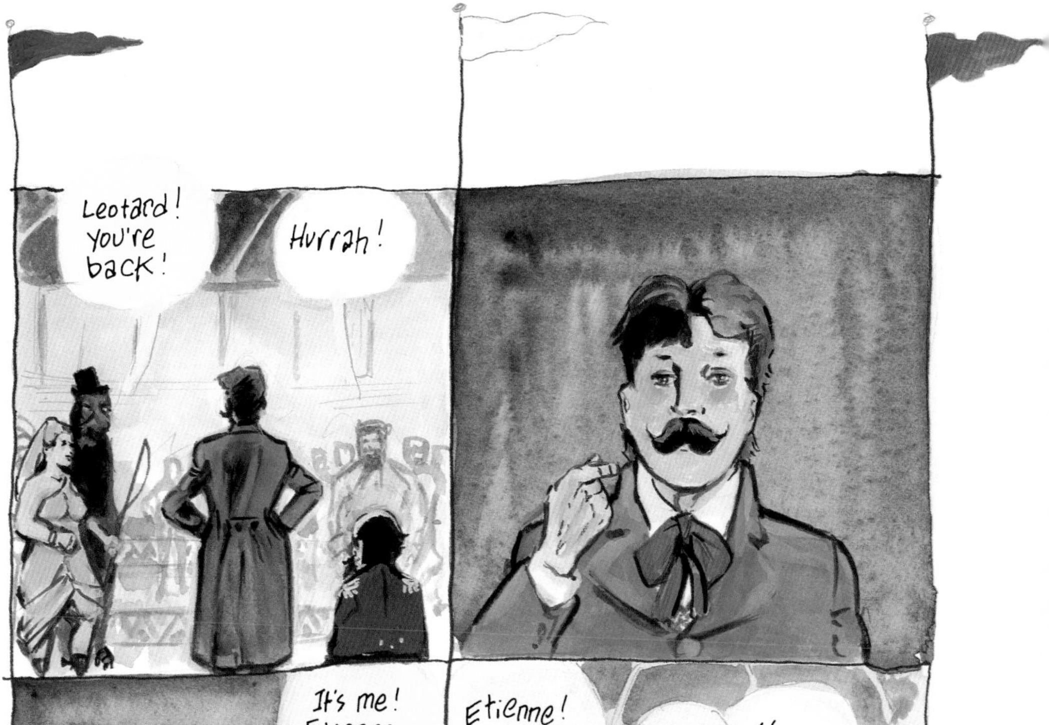
Leotard! You're back!
Hurrah!
It's me! Etienne.
Etienne! You're back. How wonderful.
Yay!
Hurrah!

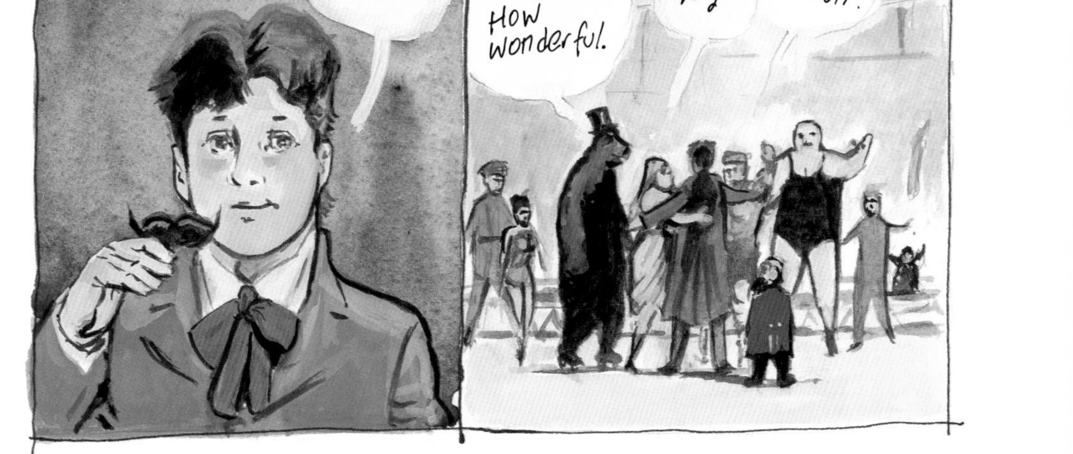
POOF!

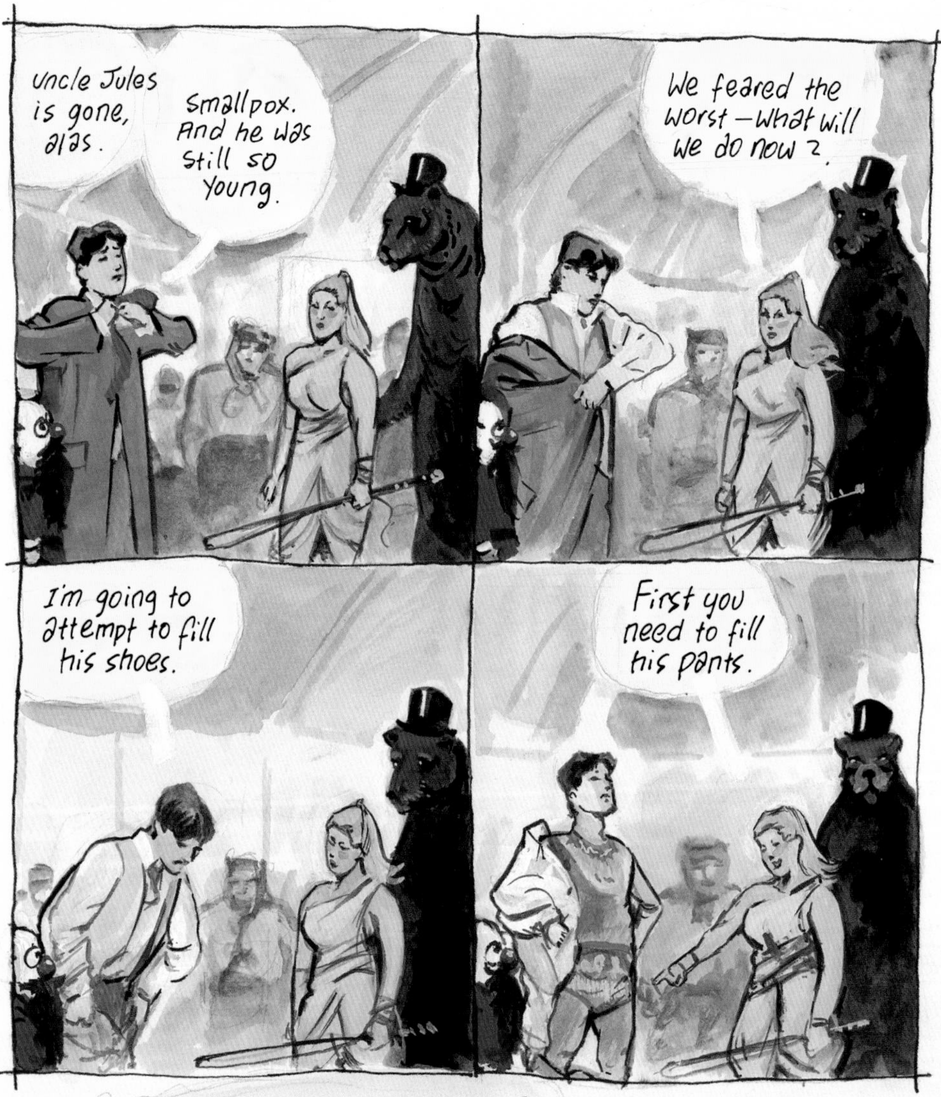

Uncle Jules is gone, alas.
Smallpox. And he was still so young.
We feared the worst — what will we do now ?
I'm going to attempt to fill his shoes.
First you need to fill his pants.
"Do you want to be adored by the ladies ? A trapeze is not required, but instead of draping yourself in unflattering clothes, invented by ladies, and which give us the air of ridiculous mannequins, put on a more natural garb, which does not hide your best features."

"I have eaten the flesh of elephants, wolves, cassowaries, porcupines, bears, kangaroos, rats, cats and horses. The proprietor of the English butcher-shop, M. Debos, supplied most of these strange dishes, for he bought nearly all the animals from the zoological Gardens at tremendous prices. The elephants were sold to M. Debos for 27,000 francs."

– Memoir, An Englishman in Paris, Albert D. Vandam, quoted in *Schott's Food and Drink Miscellany*, 2003.

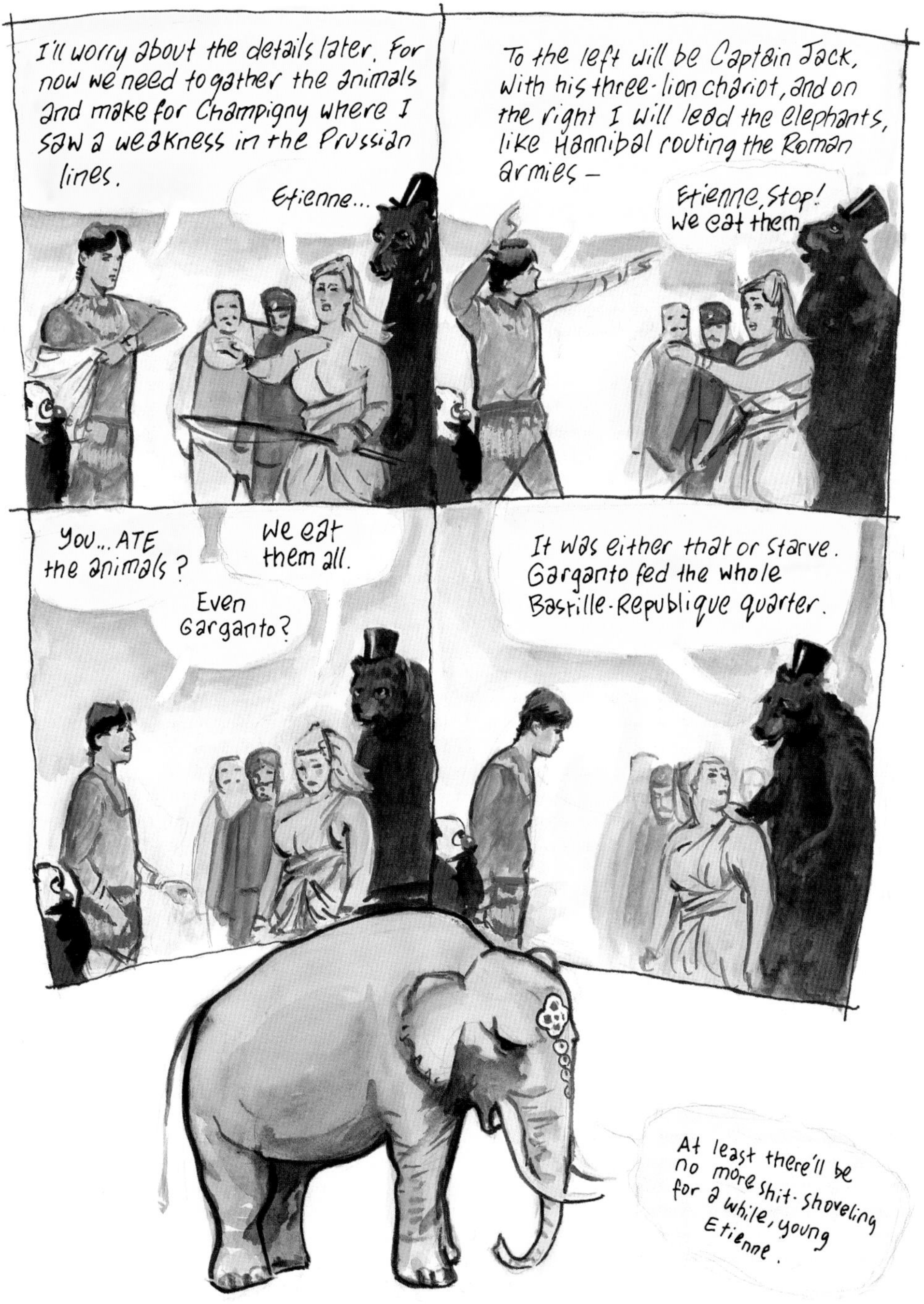

I'll worry about the details later. For now we need to gather the animals and make for Champigny where I saw a weakness in the Prussian lines.
Etienne...
To the left will be Captain Jack, with his three-lion chariot, and on the right I will lead the elephants, like Hannibal routing the Roman armies –
Etienne, Stop! We eat them.
You... ATE the animals?
We eat them all.
Even Garganto?
It was either that or starve. Garganto fed the whole Bastille-Republique quarter.
At least there'll be no more shit-shoveling for a while, young Etienne.

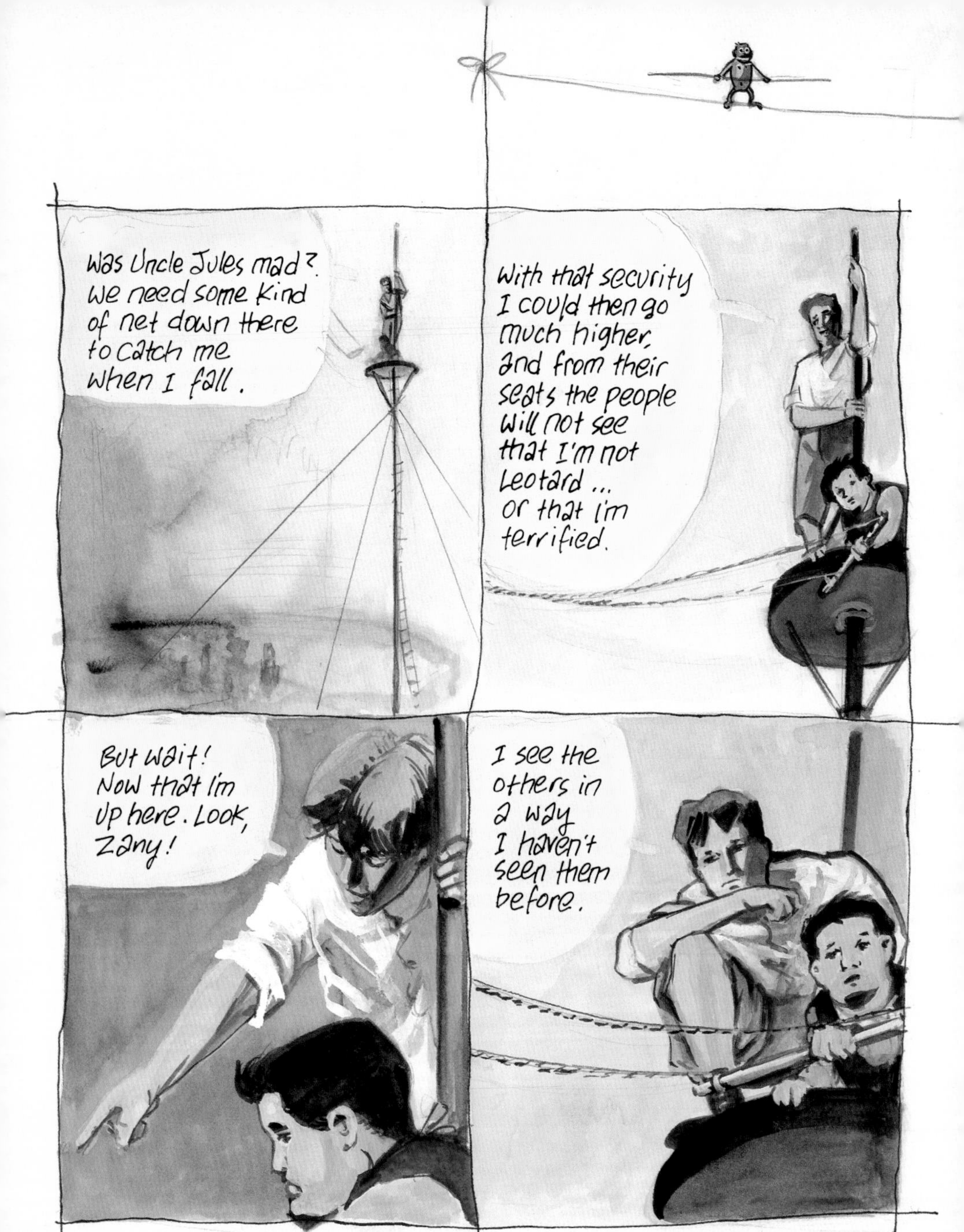
Was Uncle Jules mad? We need some kind of net down there to catch me when I fall.
With that security I could then go much higher, and from their seats the people will not see that I'm not Leotard ... or that I'm terrified.
But wait! Now that I'm up here. Look, Zany!
I see the others in a way I haven't seen them before.

Pull yourselves together, friends. We're going to perform once more.
But half our troupe is dead or gone to join the Guards.
No matter. We will construct a show such as no one has seen before, using unusual combinations of our talents.
You, Juan Tempestade, with your fire; Morris, the india-rubber man; Ernst, the strong man–
And Hilde, the girl who disappears in the magician's cabinet– Together you will be the Quartette Fantastique!

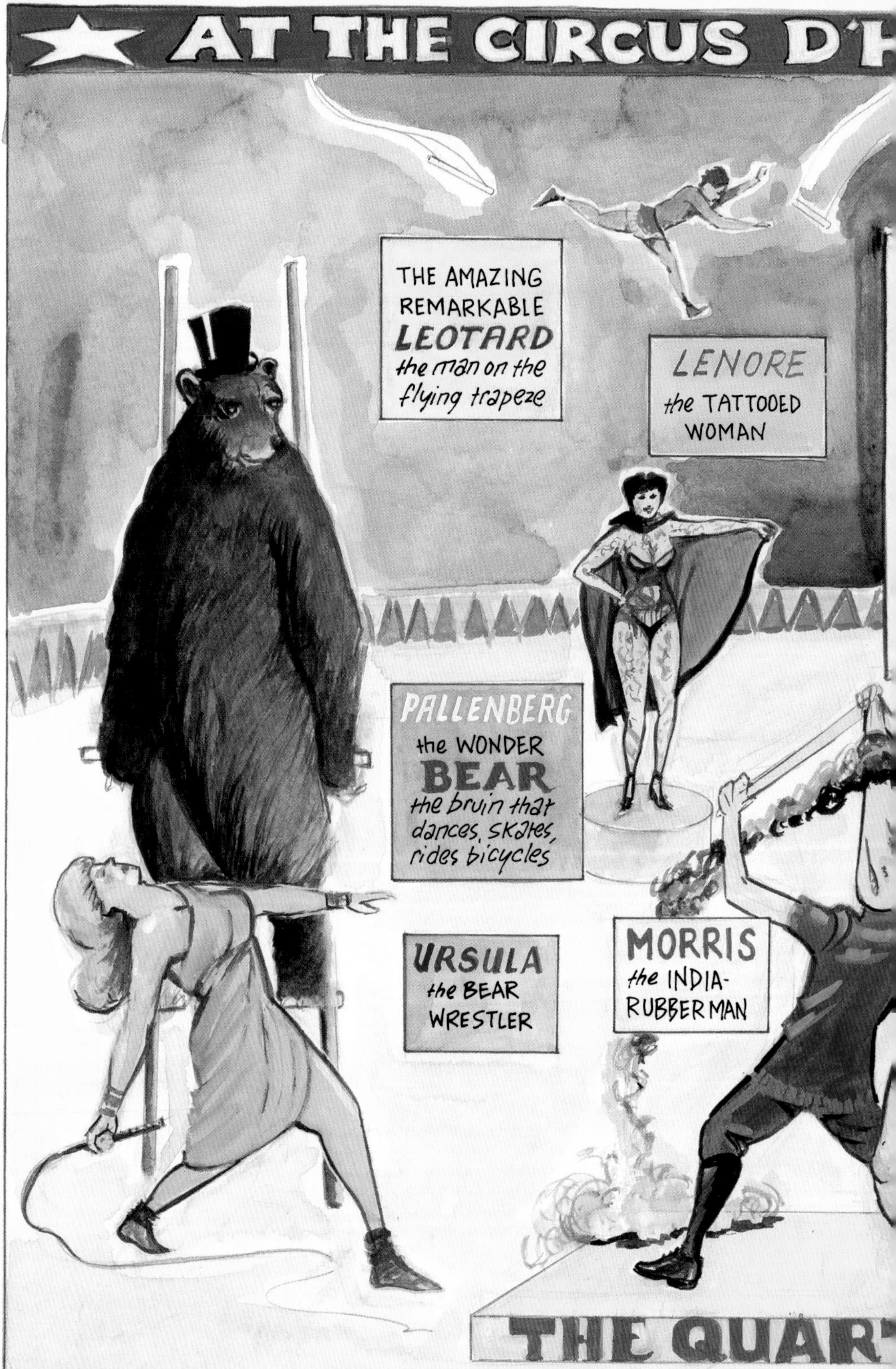
AT THE CIRCUS D'H
THE AMAZING REMARKABLE LEOTARD the man on the flying trapeze
LENORE the TATTOOED WOMAN
PALLENBERG the WONDER BEAR the bruin that dances, skates, rides bicycles
URSULA the BEAR WRESTLER
MORRIS the INDIA-RUBBER MAN
THE QUART

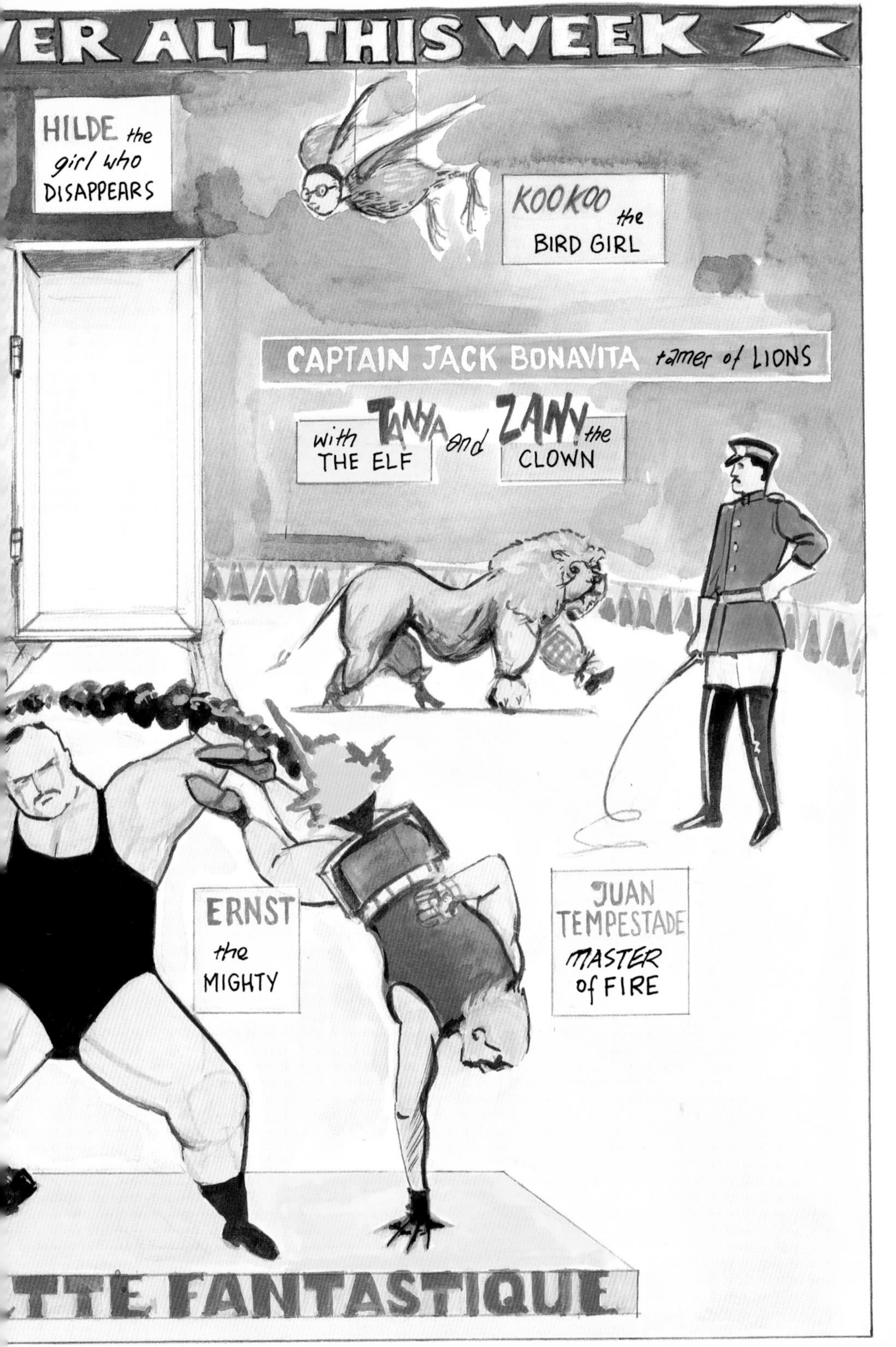

ER ALL THIS WEEK
HILDE the girl who DISAPPEARS
KOOKOO the BIRD GIRL
CAPTAIN JACK BONAVITA tamer of LIONS
with TANYA THE ELF and ZANY the CLOWN
ERNST the MIGHTY
JUAN TEMPESTADE MASTER of FIRE
TTE FANTASTIQUE

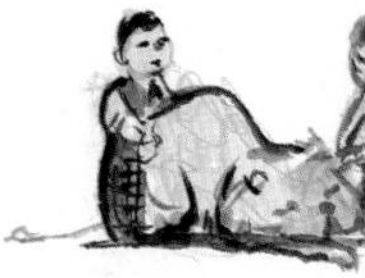

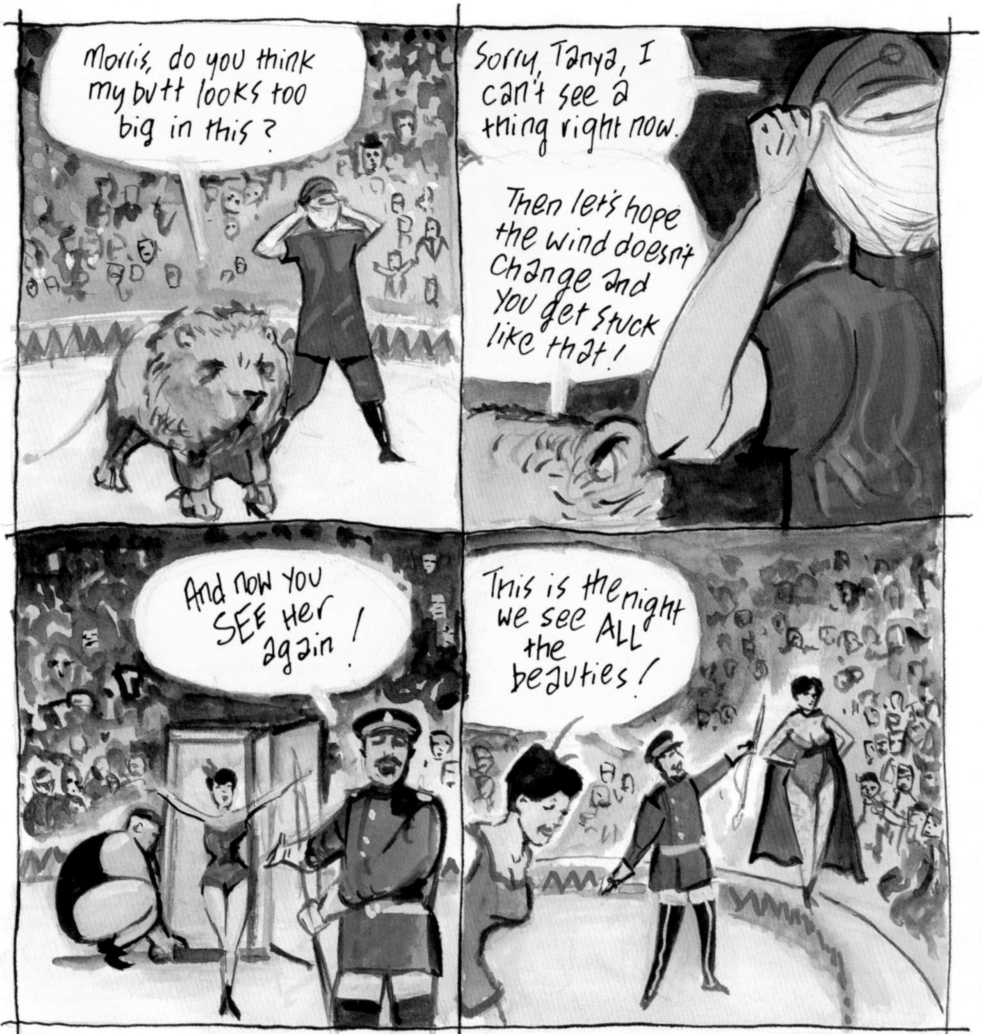
Morris, do you think my butt looks too big in this?
Sorry, Tanya, I can't see a thing right now.
Then let's hope the wind doesn't change and you get stuck like that!
And now you SEE her again!
This is the night we see ALL the beauties!

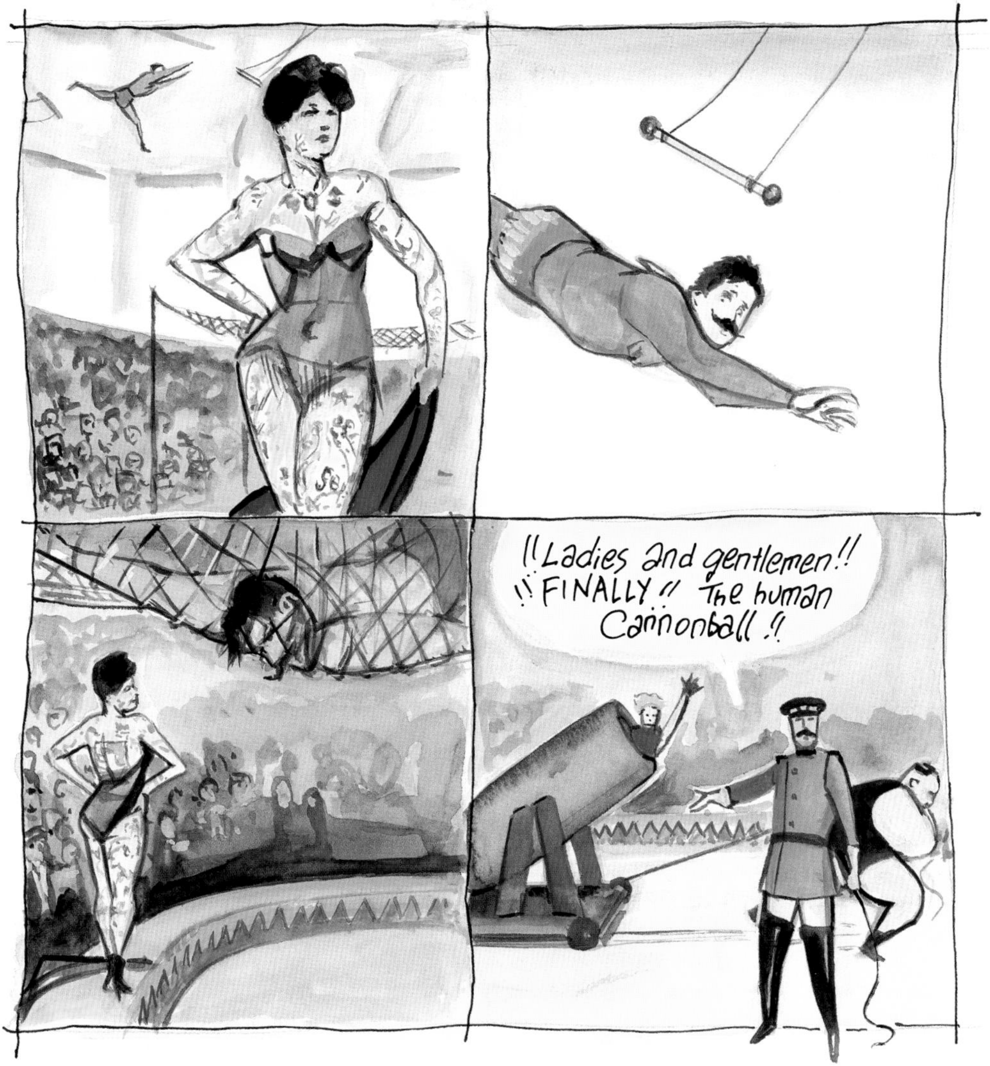
!!Ladies and gentlemen!!
!!FINALLY!! The human
Cannonball!!

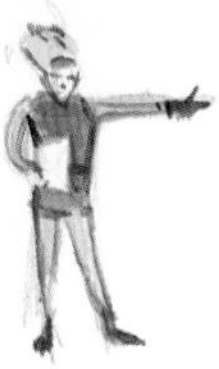

Terminal velocity for a person in cannonball formation is about 200 mph (can be between 160 and 320 in standing-up-straight formation). Assuming a 45 degree declination angle and no air friction

vx = 200 * .707 = 141.4 mph
viy = 200 * .707 = 141.4 mph
time in air = 2 * viy / g = 2 * 141.4 mph / 32.2 ft/s/s
tia = 2 * 207.4 ft/s / 32.2 ft/s/s = 12.88 seconds
x = vx * tia = 12.88 s * 207.4 ft/s
x = 2671.3 feet = .506 miles

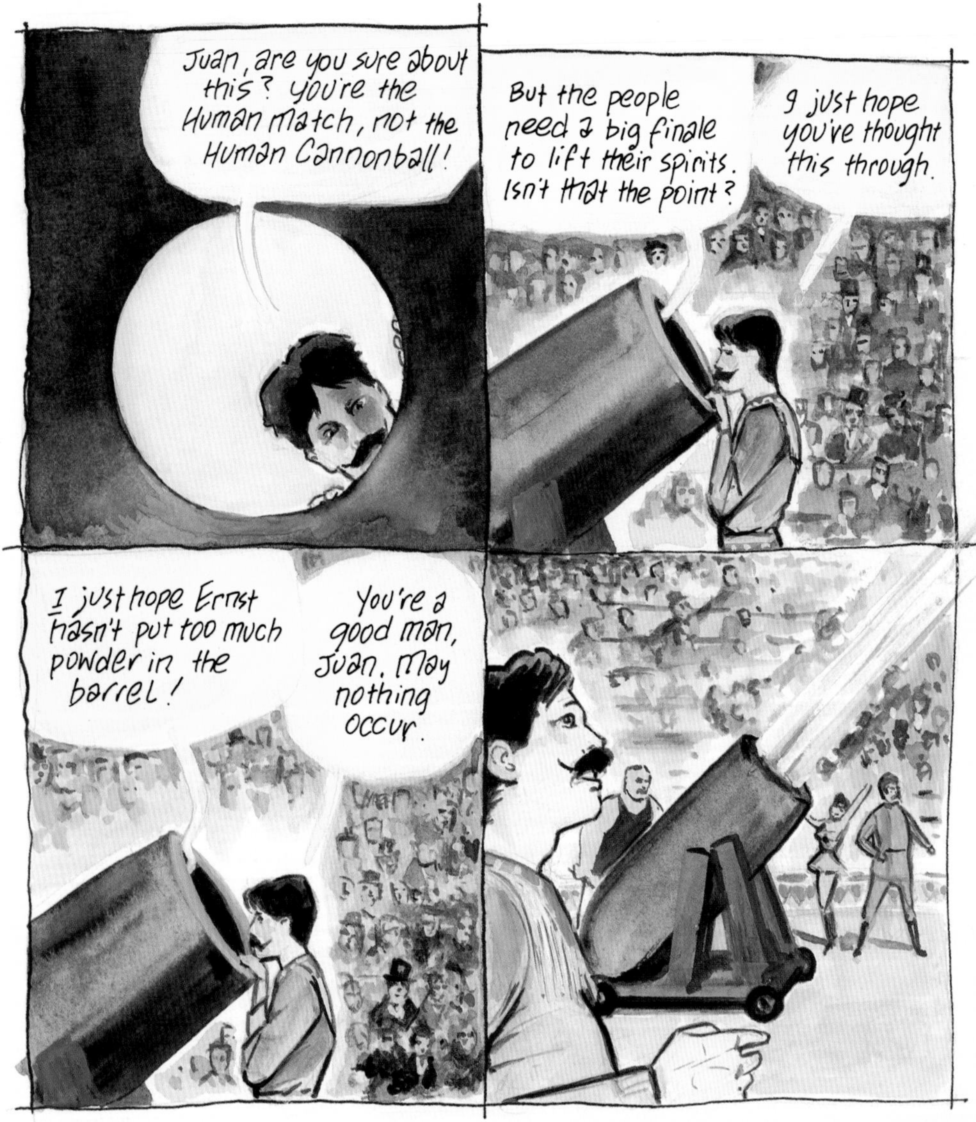
Juan, are you sure about this? You're the Human Match, not the Human Cannonball!
But the people need a big finale to lift their spirits. Isn't that the point?
I just hope you've thought this through.
I just hope Ernst hasn't put too much powder in the barrel!
You're a good man, Juan. May nothing occur.

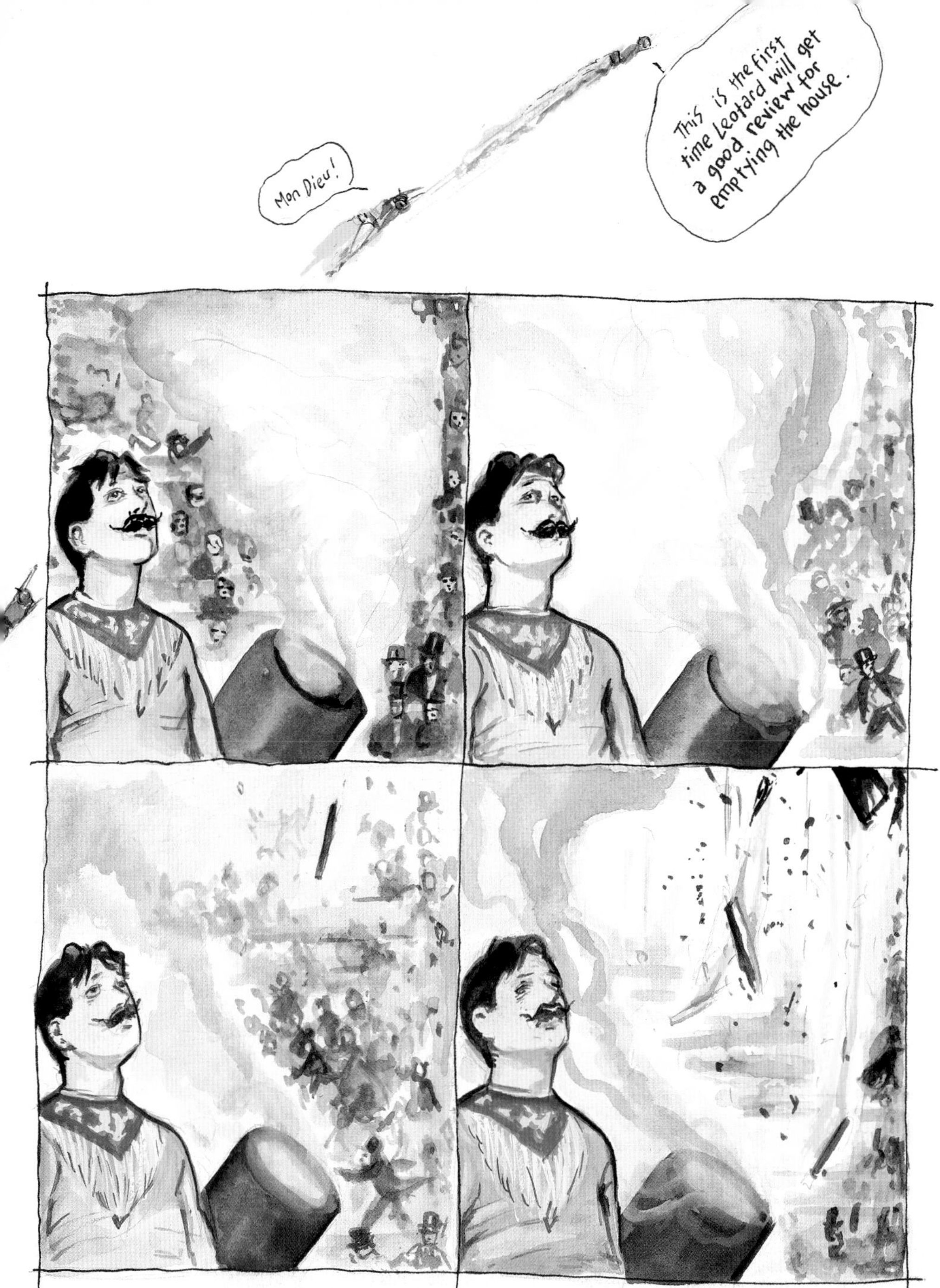

Mon Dieu!
This is the first time Leotard will get a good review for emptying the house.

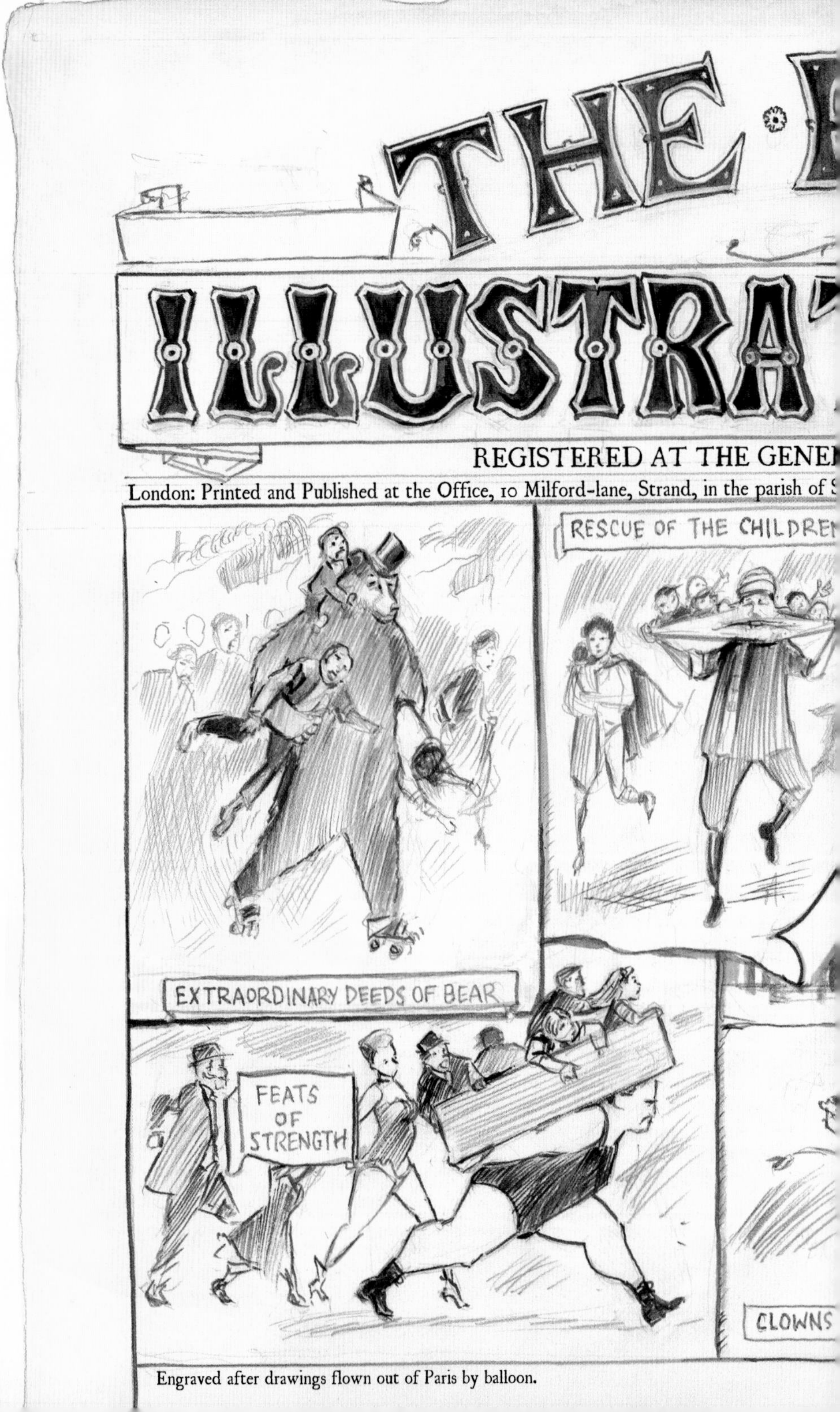
THE
ILLUSTRA
REGISTERED AT THE GENE
London: Printed and Published at the Office, 10 Milford-lane, Strand, in the parish of S
RESCUE OF THE CHILDRE
EXTRAORDINARY DEEDS OF BEAR
FEATS OF STRENGTH
CLOWNS
Engraved after drawings flown out of Paris by balloon.

ENNY ED·PAPER

ST-OFFICE AS A NEWSPAPER

Danes, in the county of Middlesex, by Thomas Fox, Milford-lane, Strand, aforesaid.

FAMOUS BUILDING SAVED BY RAIN

THEIR METTLE

Dramatic rescue in Paris

A circus performance designed to lift the morale of besieged Parisians nearly turned to tragedy after a devastating fire broke out at the famous Parisian Cirque de Hiver at half-past two in the afternoon of Wednesday, and raged uninterruptedly throughout that afternoon and was not finally mastered till the evening. We read exciting accounts of how understudy "Human Cannonball" Juan Tempestade, in a tragic miscalculation, was shot through the roof of the circus, setting the famous building on fire as he flew into the stratosphere. It is difficult to imagine anything more terrible than the spectacle as onlookers were shocked at Tempestade's fiery end and the rapidity with which the flames spread, sweeping from the rafters into the audience below.

More remarkable is the dramatic rescue of the audience from certain death. We can imagine how, as the flames spread, the frightened people panicked, hurrying hither and thither in doubtful hope of finding an exit or place of safety for them. If not for the bravery of the "Amazing Remarkable Leotard" and his band of performers, many lives would have been lost. Speculation is rife that this is the same Jules Leotard rumoured to have died some months past. Nevertheless, witnesses praised "Leotard" and his troupe, who, in spite of what some describe as an "underwhelming performance" prior to the fire, managed to rescue all from an untimely end.

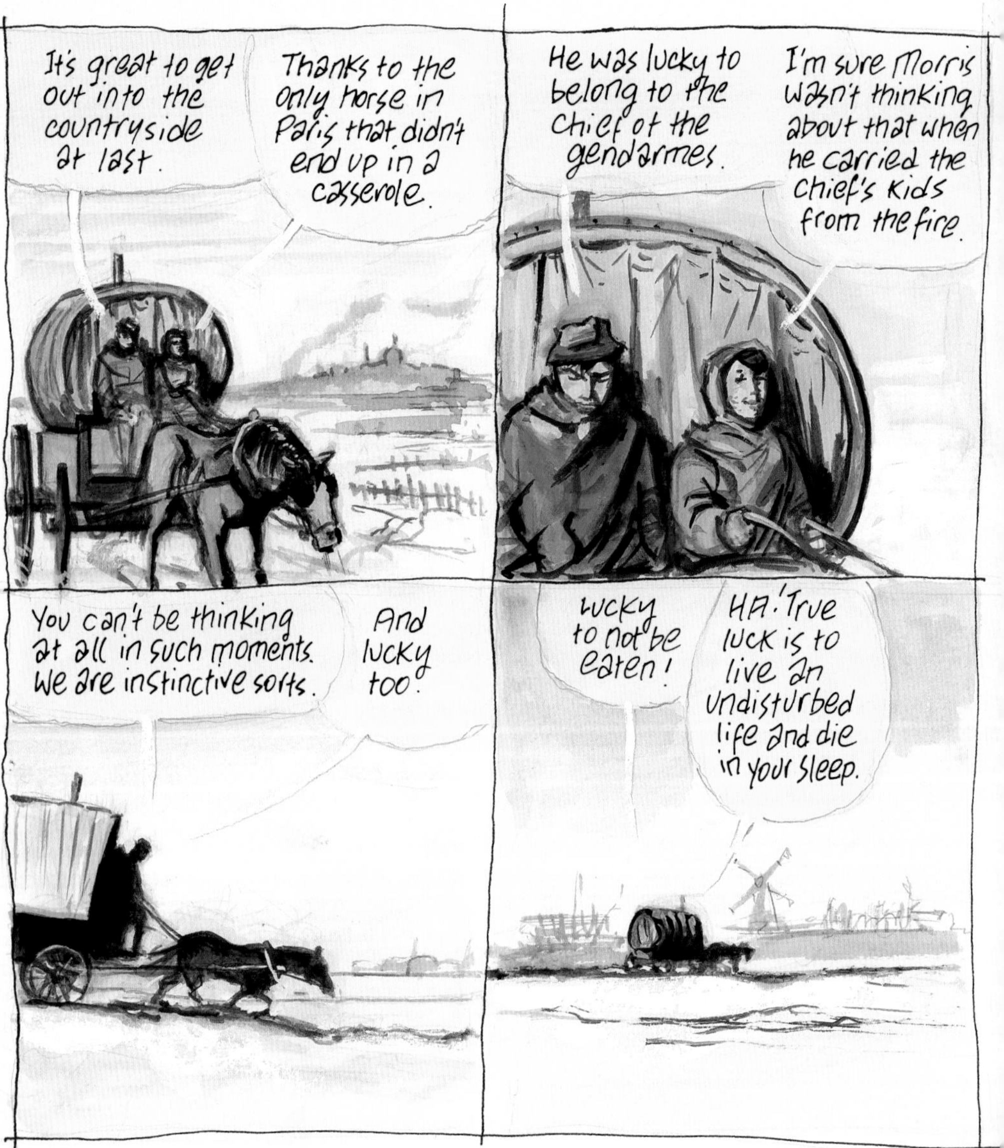
It's great to get out into the countryside at last.
Thanks to the only horse in Paris that didn't end up in a casserole.
He was lucky to belong to the chief of the gendarmes.
I'm sure Morris wasn't thinking about that when he carried the chief's kids from the fire.
You can't be thinking at all in such moments. We are instinctive sorts.
And lucky too.
Lucky to not be eaten!
HA! True luck is to live an undisturbed life and die in your sleep.

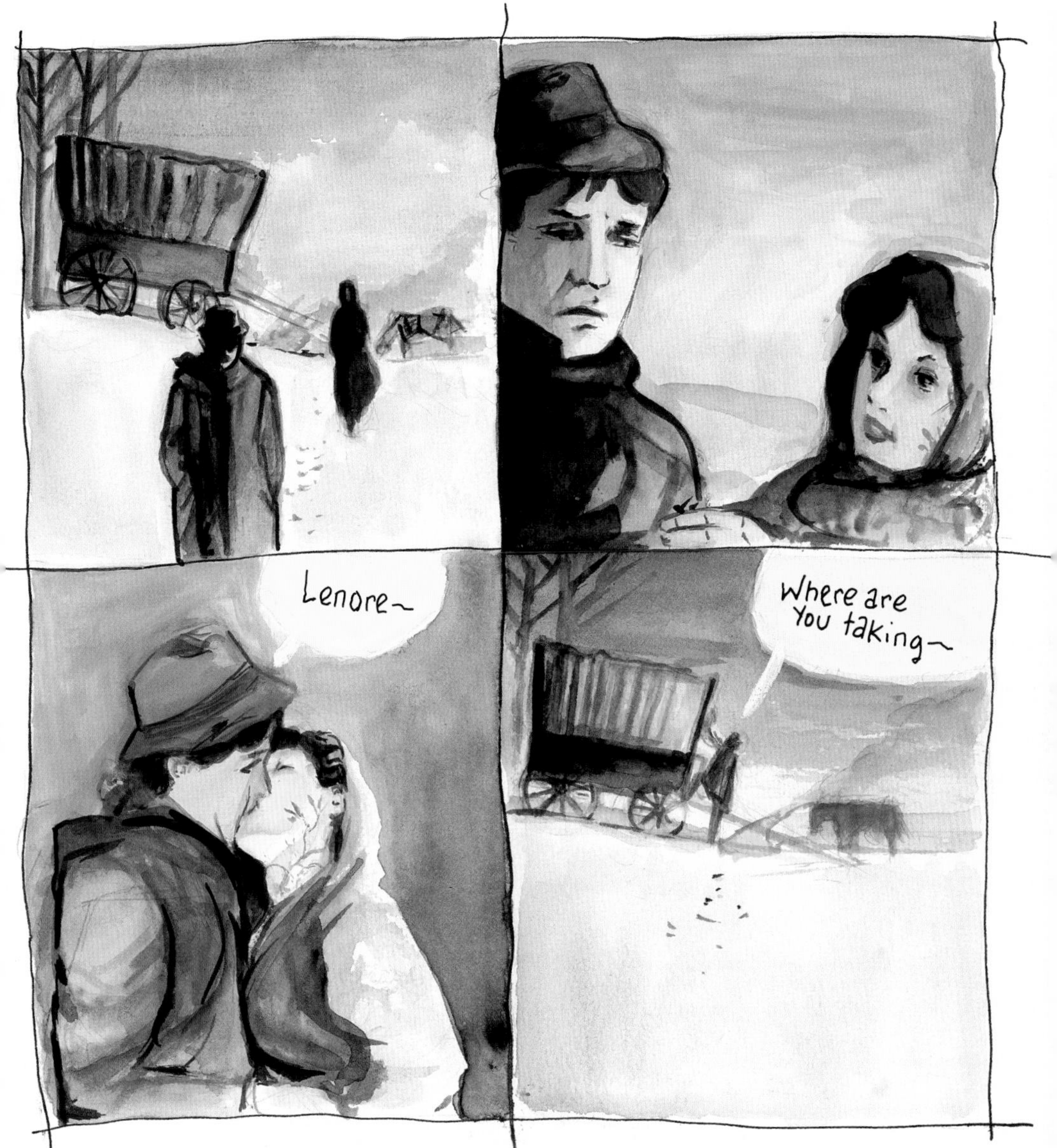
Lenore~
Where are you taking~

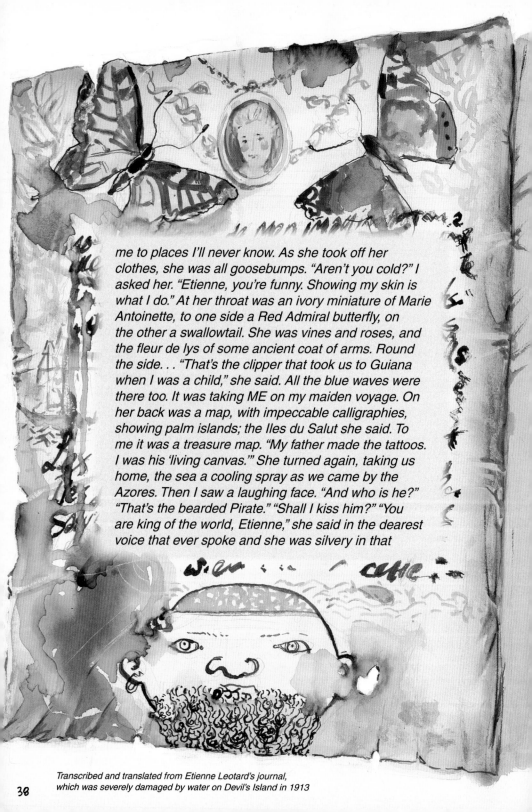

me to places I'll never know. As she took off her clothes, she was all goosebumps. "Aren't you cold?" I asked her. "Etienne, you're funny. Showing my skin is what I do." At her throat was an ivory miniature of Marie Antoinette, to one side a Red Admiral butterfly, on the other a swallowtail. She was vines and roses, and the fleur de lys of some ancient coat of arms. Round the side. . . "That's the clipper that took us to Guiana when I was a child," she said. All the blue waves were there too. It was taking ME on my maiden voyage. On her back was a map, with impeccable calligraphies, showing palm islands; the Iles du Salut she said. To me it was a treasure map. "My father made the tattoos. I was his 'living canvas.'" She turned again, taking us home, the sea a cooling spray as we came by the Azores. Then I saw a laughing face. "And who is he?" "That's the bearded Pirate." "Shall I kiss him?" "You are king of the world, Etienne," she said in the dearest voice that ever spoke and she was silvery in that

Transcribed and translated from Etienne Leotard's journal, which was severely damaged by water on Devil's Island in 1913

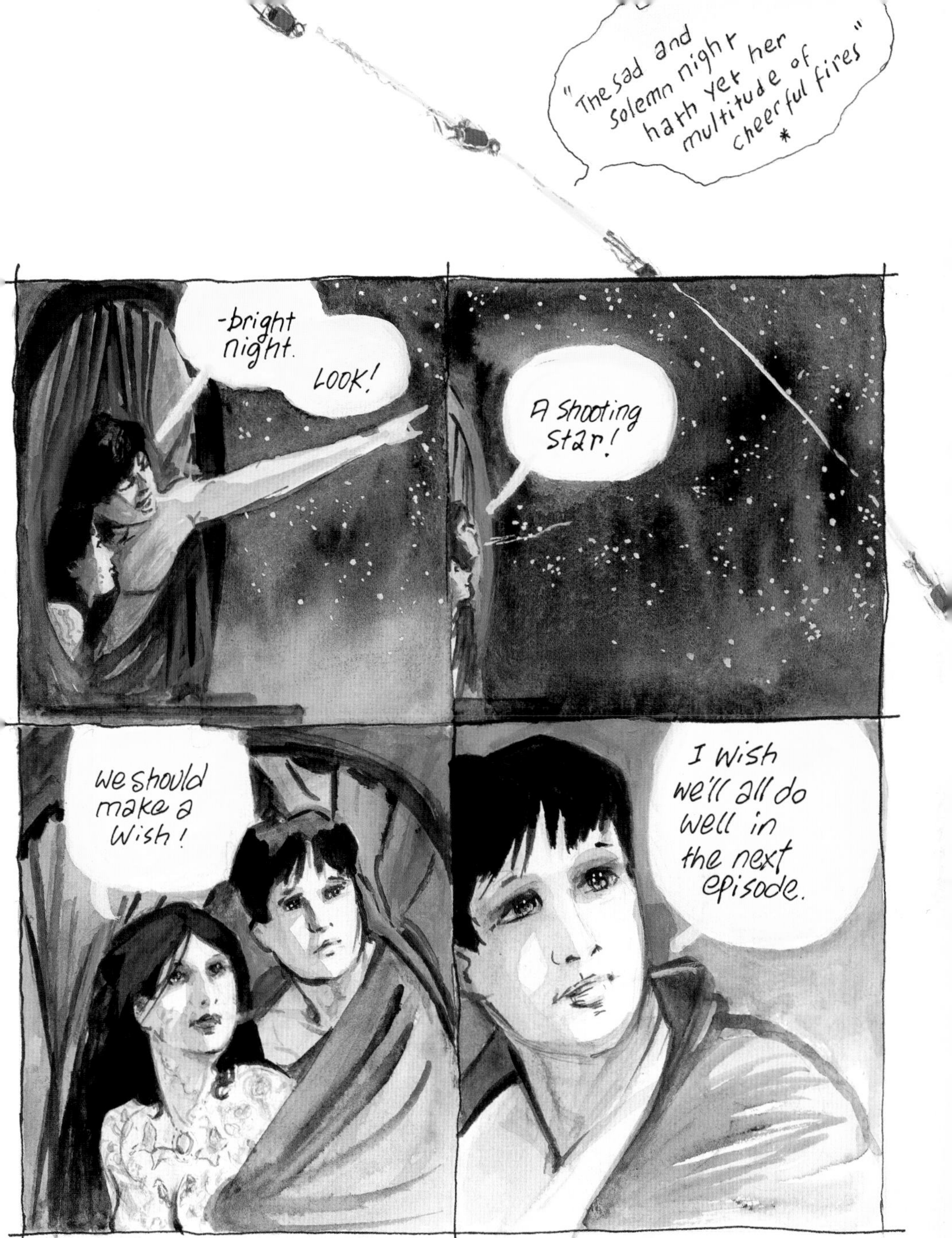
"The sad and solemn night hath yet her multitude of cheerful fires" *
-bright night.
LOOK!
A shooting star!
We should make a wish!
I wish we'll all do well in the next episode.

"The sad and solemn night hath yet her multitude of cheerful fires,
The glorious host of light walk the dark hemisphere till she retires,
All through her silent watches, gliding slow,
Her constellations come, and climb the heavens, and go."
– William Cullen Bryant, "Hymn to the North Star"

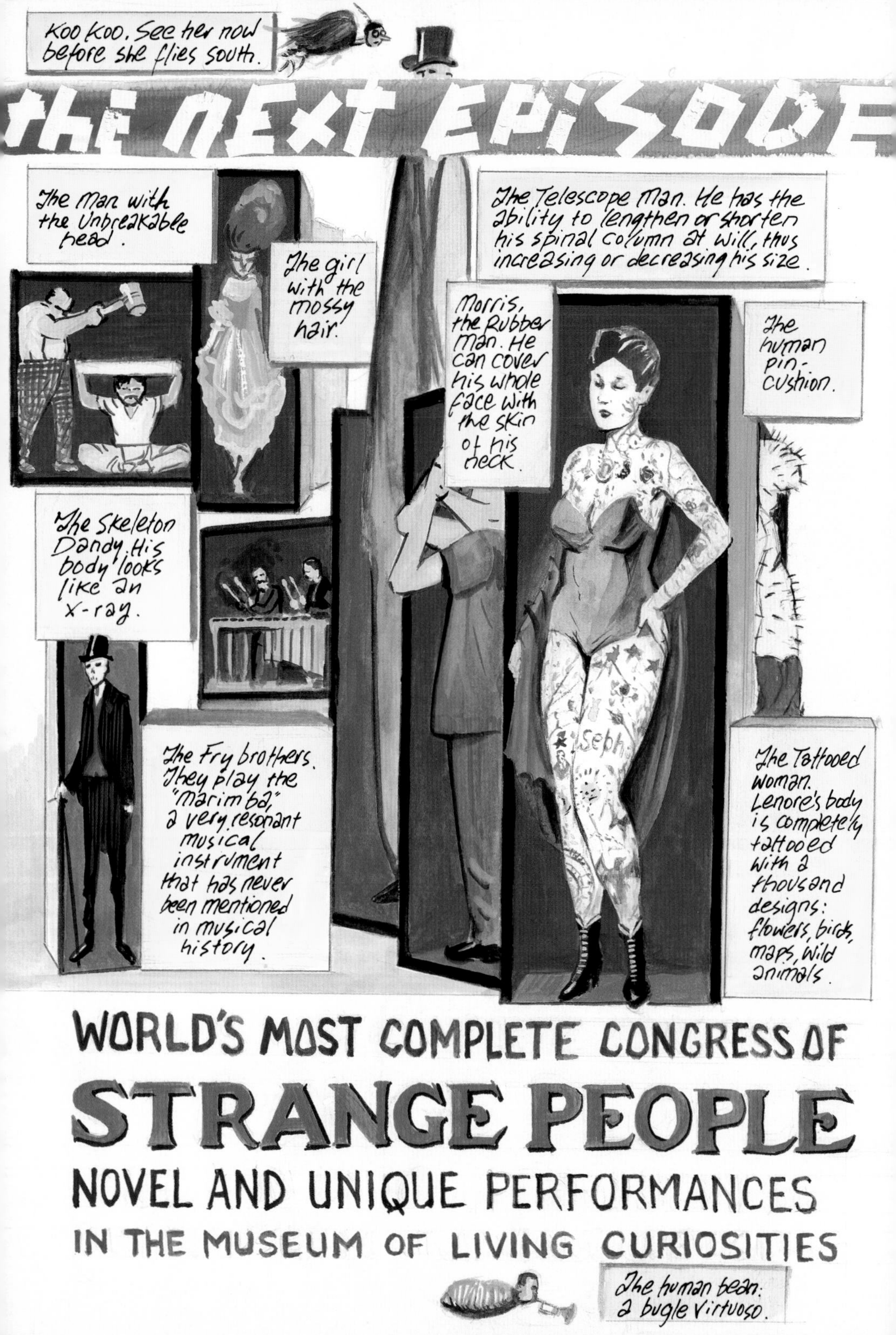
Koo Koo. See her now before she flies south.
the next episode
The man with the unbreakable head.
The girl with the mossy hair.
The Telescope Man. He has the ability to lengthen or shorten his spinal column at will, thus increasing or decreasing his size.
Morris, the Rubber Man. He can cover his whole face with the skin of his neck.
The human pin-cushion.
The Skeleton Dandy. His body looks like an x-ray.
The Fry brothers. They play the "marimba," a very resonant musical instrument that has never been mentioned in musical history.
The Tattooed woman. Lenore's body is completely tattooed with a thousand designs: flowers, birds, maps, wild animals.
WORLD'S MOST COMPLETE CONGRESS OF
STRANGE PEOPLE
NOVEL AND UNIQUE PERFORMANCES
IN THE MUSEUM OF LIVING CURIOSITIES
The human bean: a bugle virtuoso.

The Eminent, Fashionable

LORD GEORGE SANGER

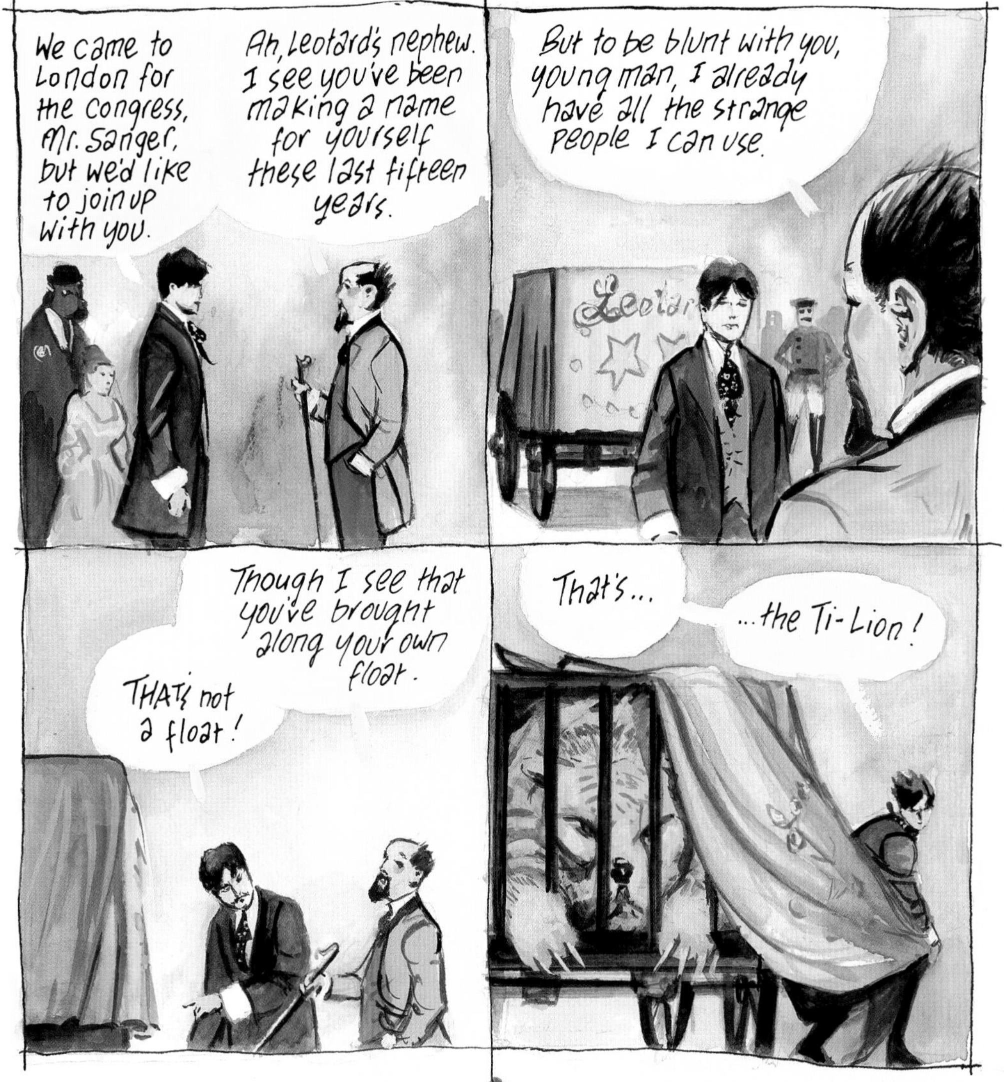
We came to London for the congress, Mr. Sanger, but we'd like to join up with you.
Ah, Leotard's nephew. I see you've been making a name for yourself these last fifteen years.
But to be blunt with you, young man, I already have all the strange people I can use.
Leotar
Though I see that you've brought along your own float.
THAT's not a float!
That's...
...the Ti-Lion!

** Despite the title, George Sanger was no Lord. Rumor has it that early in his career Sanger became embroiled in litigation against one William F. "Buffalo Bill" Cody. During the highly publicized trial, Cody, as was his manner, was quite flamboyant and prone to outbursts of embellished recountings of his own career. To add insult to injury, Cody's legal counsel, when addressing Cody or making submissions to the court, constantly referred to him as "the Honorable Mr. Cody." Sanger, not to be outdone by Cody, and tired of his theatrics, took to the witness stand and proclaimed. . . "If he's Honorable then I am a Lord, you may address me as Lord George Sanger!"*

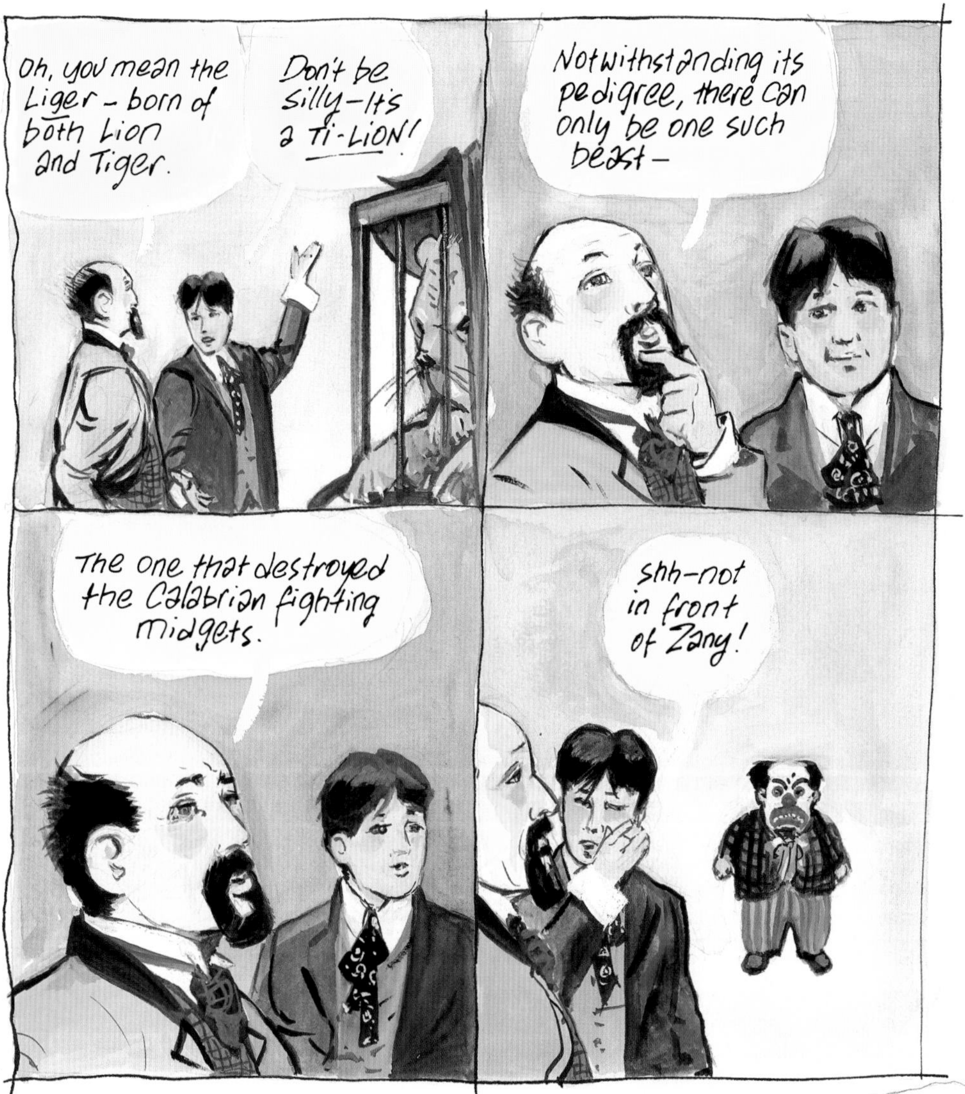
Oh, you mean the Liger - born of both Lion and Tiger.
Don't be silly-It's a TI-LION!
Notwithstanding its pedigree, there can only be one such beast-
The one that destroyed the Calabrian fighting midgets.
shh-not in front of Zany!

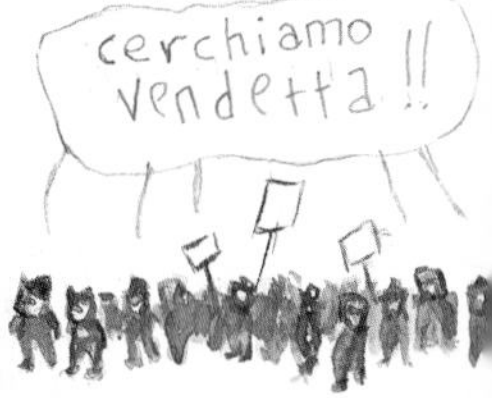
cerchiamo vendetta!!

Leoni's Fighting Dwarves made their debut in 1865 when the 19 pint-size pugilists defeated Antonio Canzoneri, the Calabrian prizefighter and baker, who was supported by a gang of street-toughs.

In Britain they beat the select of the London Boxing Academy in a notorious melee in which a man was killed. However, the introduction of the Queensbury Rules in 1867 made it difficult for the dwarves to continue in competition there.

In Austria, a squad of dragoons armed with sabers met ignominious defeat at their hands wielding only kitchen pans.

No team of equal number could best them, and Leoni's dwarves were undefeated on that fateful day in Sardinia in 1869. In Cagliari, Leoni was approached by circus owner, and known shyster, Vittorio Lazzari, who wagered the equivalent of 200,000 dollars of today's money, that his LION, which he said was captured in Africa the previous year, could rout the famous team. Whether Leoni was motivated by greed, or by genuine pride in his little warriors, will never be known, but the wager was accepted.

The event was staged in the ruins of the town's ancient amphitheater before a 5,000-strong crowd, and many a large bet was laid that day. Suddenly a stunned silence fell on the spectators as the huge cat was let into the arena. It was neither LION nor TIGER, but the progeny of BOTH and bigger than the combined size of its parents. It was 12 feet long and weighed 1200 pounds. Within ten minutes all but one of the dwarves had been savaged. Leoni and the single surviving dwarf fled Italy in shame, and Lazzari sold the beast to a traveling circus for a princely sum.

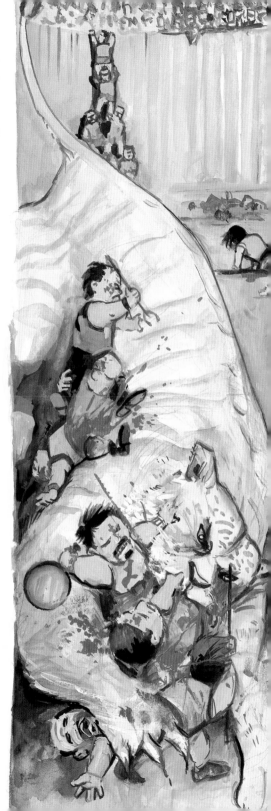

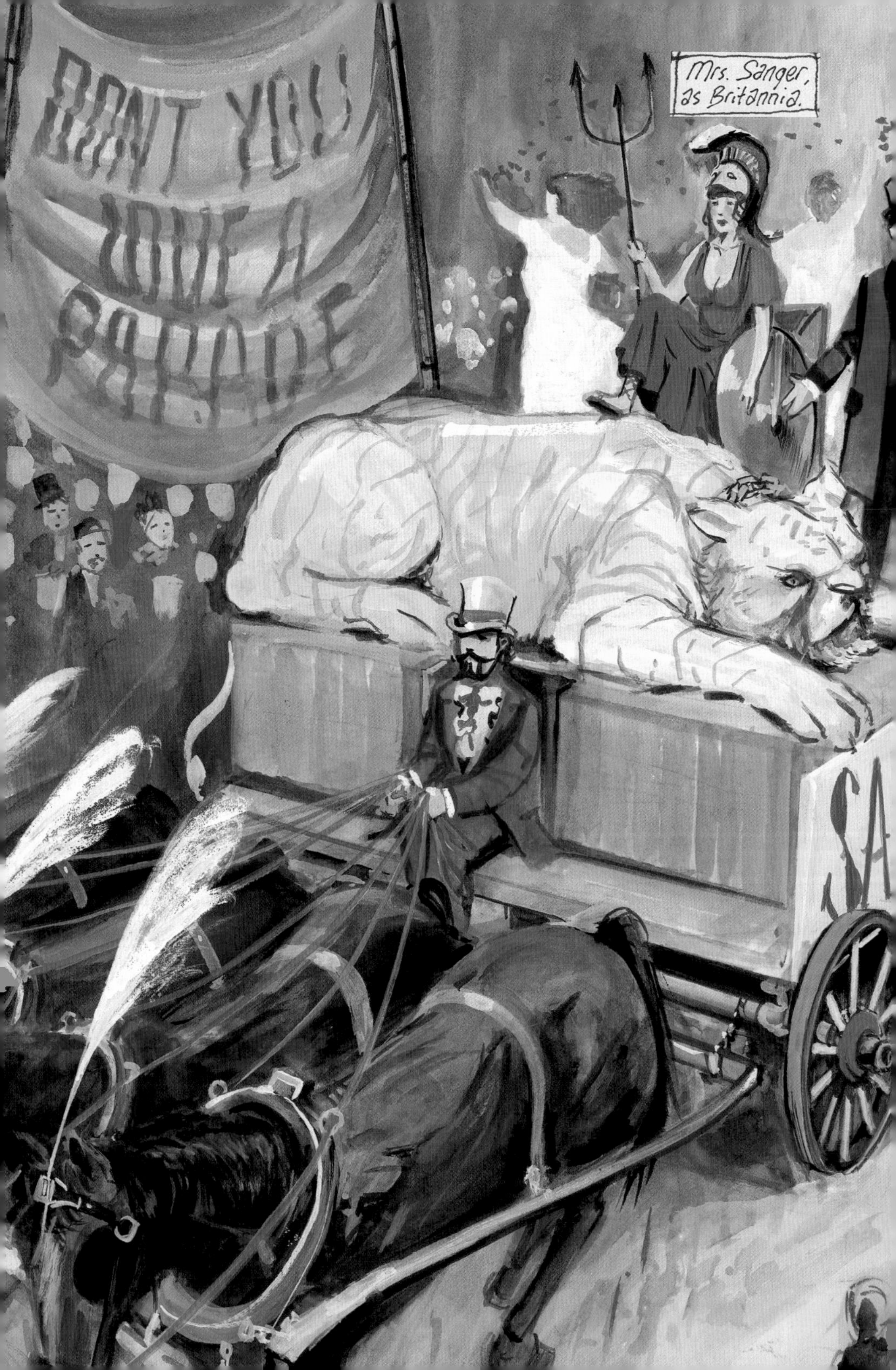
Mrs. Sanger, as Britannia.
DON'T YOU LOVE A PARADE
SA

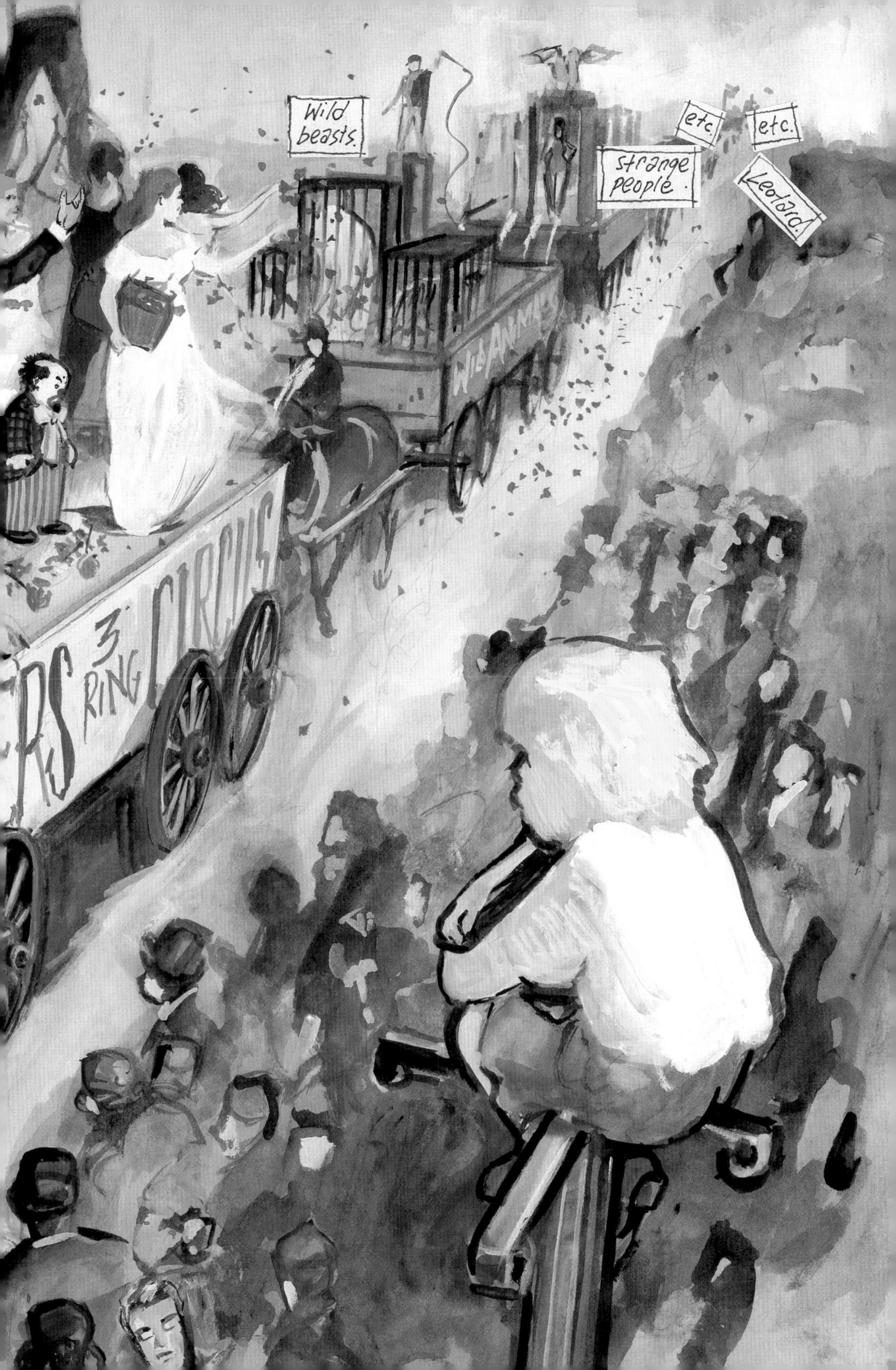

Wild beasts.
strange people.
etc.
etc.
Leotard.
3 RING CIRCUS

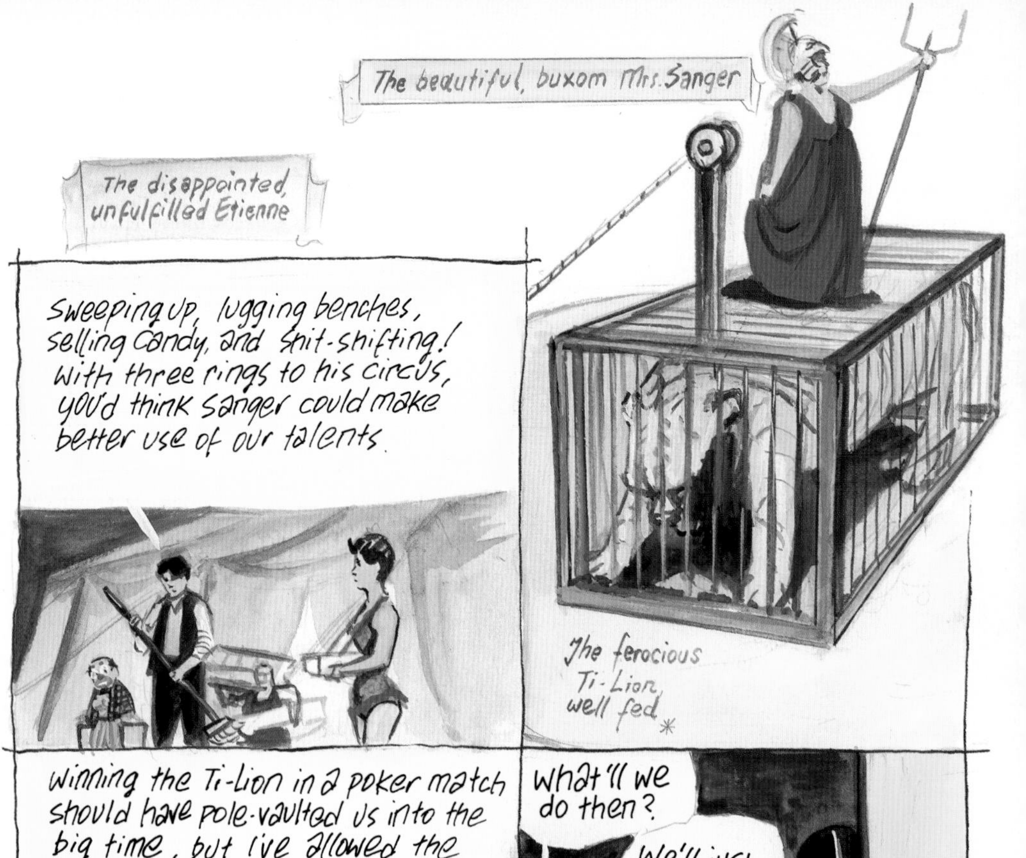
The beautiful, buxom Mrs. Sanger
The disappointed, unfulfilled Etienne
Sweeping up, lugging benches, selling candy, and shit-shifting! With three rings to his circus, you'd think Sanger could make better use of our talents.
The ferocious Ti-Lion, well fed *
Winning the Ti-Lion in a poker match should have pole-vaulted us into the big time, but I've allowed the situation to take control of us instead of vice versa.
What'll we do then?
We'll just have to boggle the ring-master! Ready, Zany?

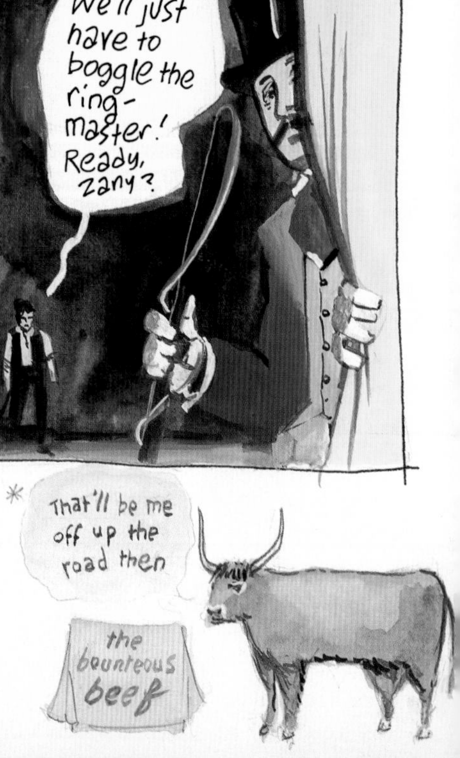
* That'll be me off up the road then
the bounteous beef

Lord George was a perfectionist when it came to live entertainment, always striving to bring the best to his audience. It is reputed that it was Lord George who had introduced the concept of the three-ring circus so as to keep the audience's attention at all times.

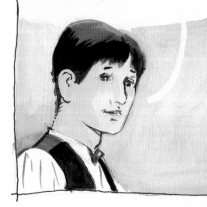

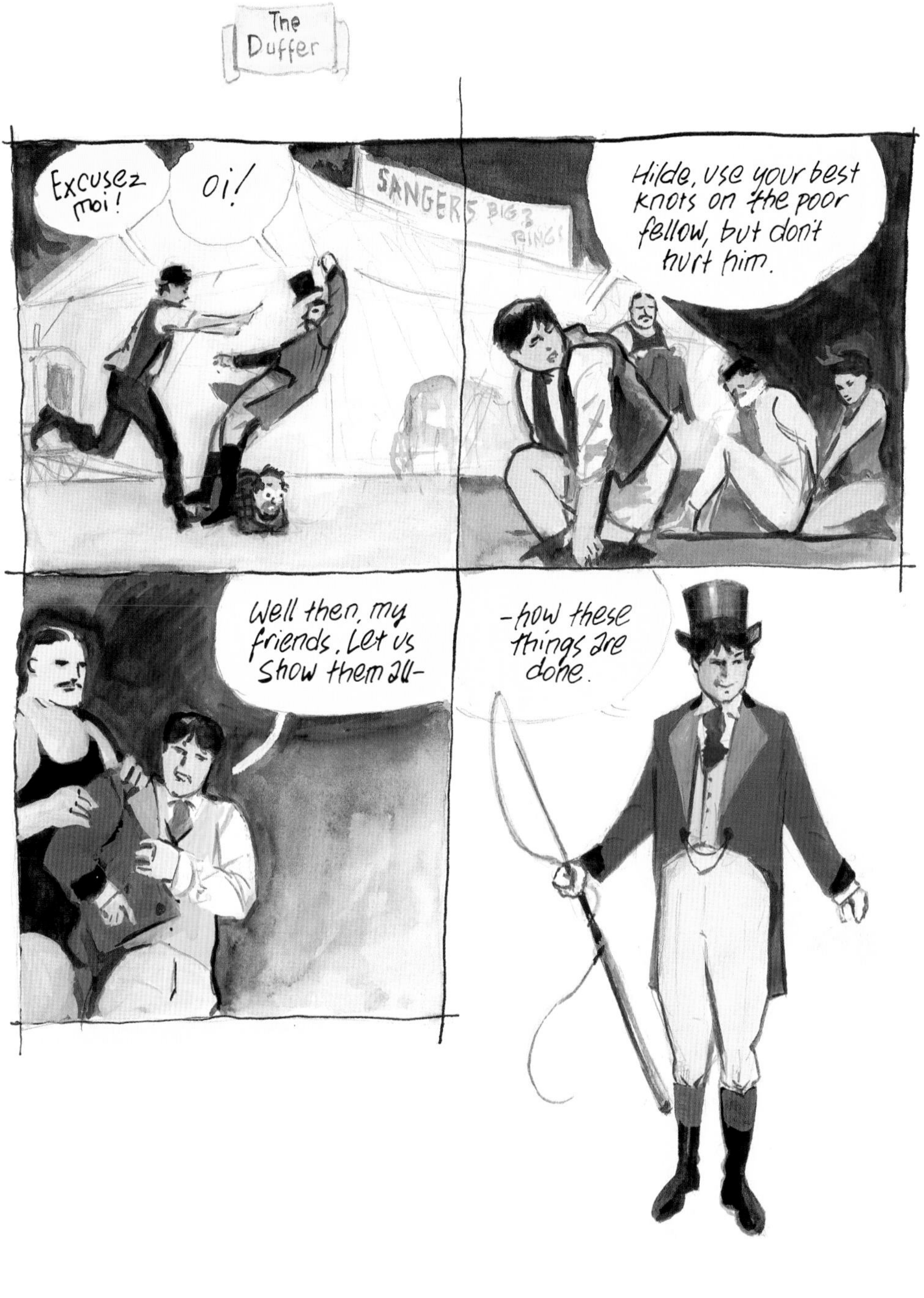
The Duffer
Excusez moi!
Oi!
SANGERS BIG 3 RINGS
Hilde, use your best knots on the poor fellow, but don't hurt him.
Well then, my friends. Let us show them all-
-how these things are done.

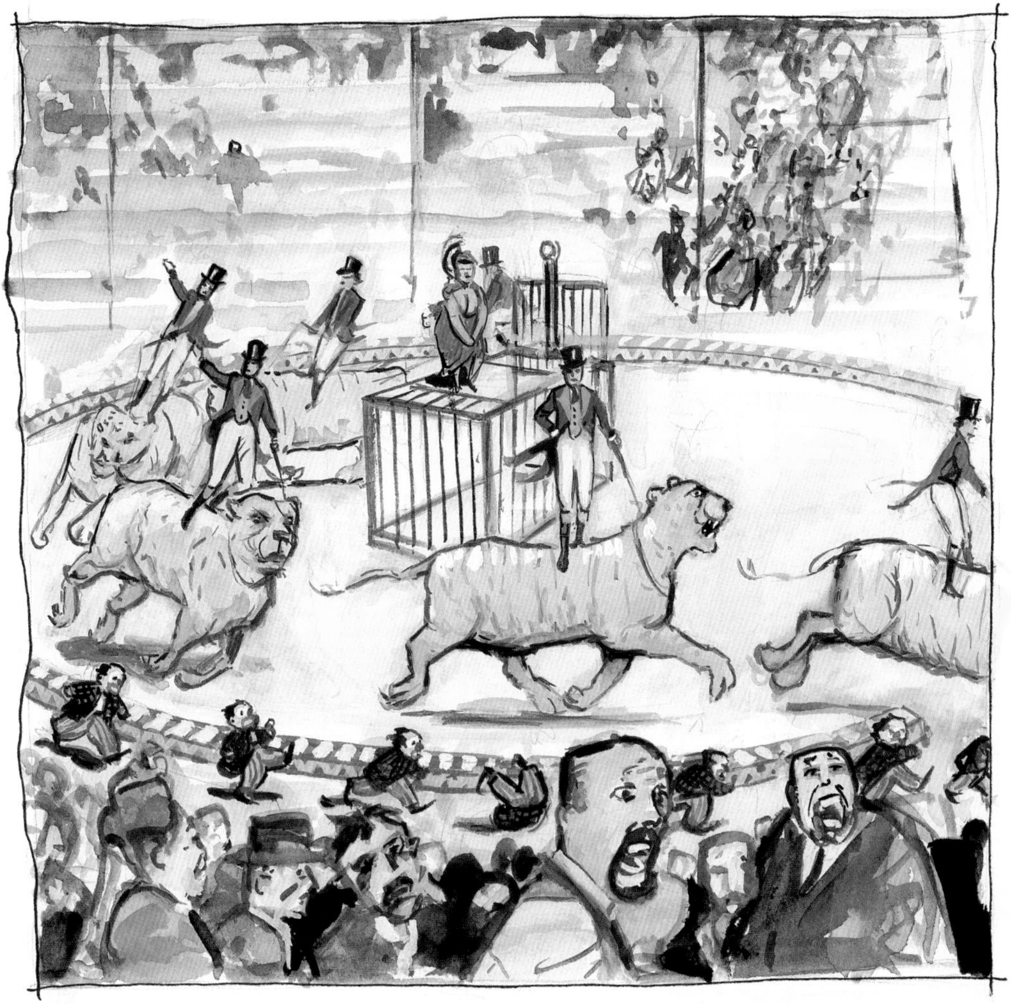

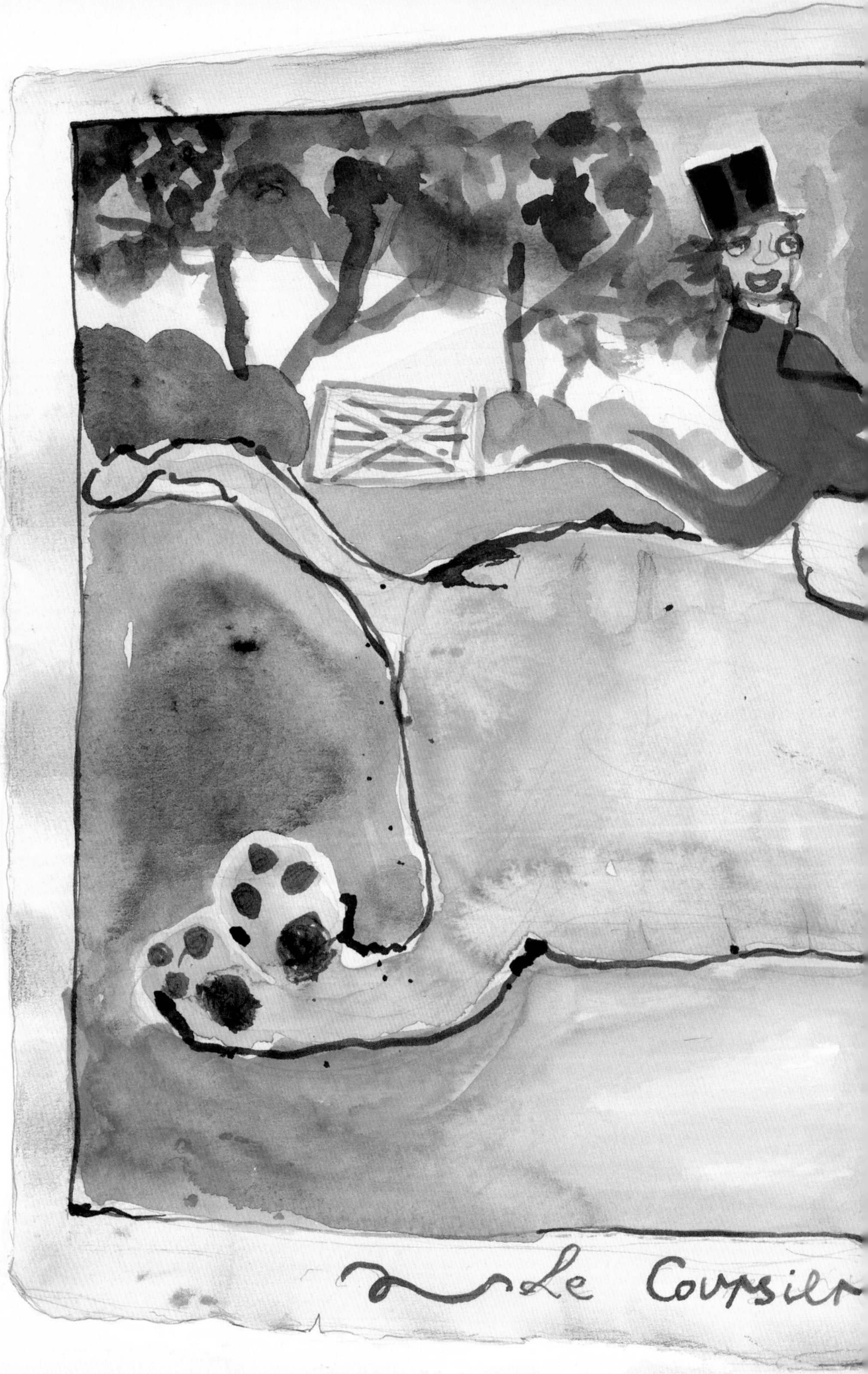
Le Coursier

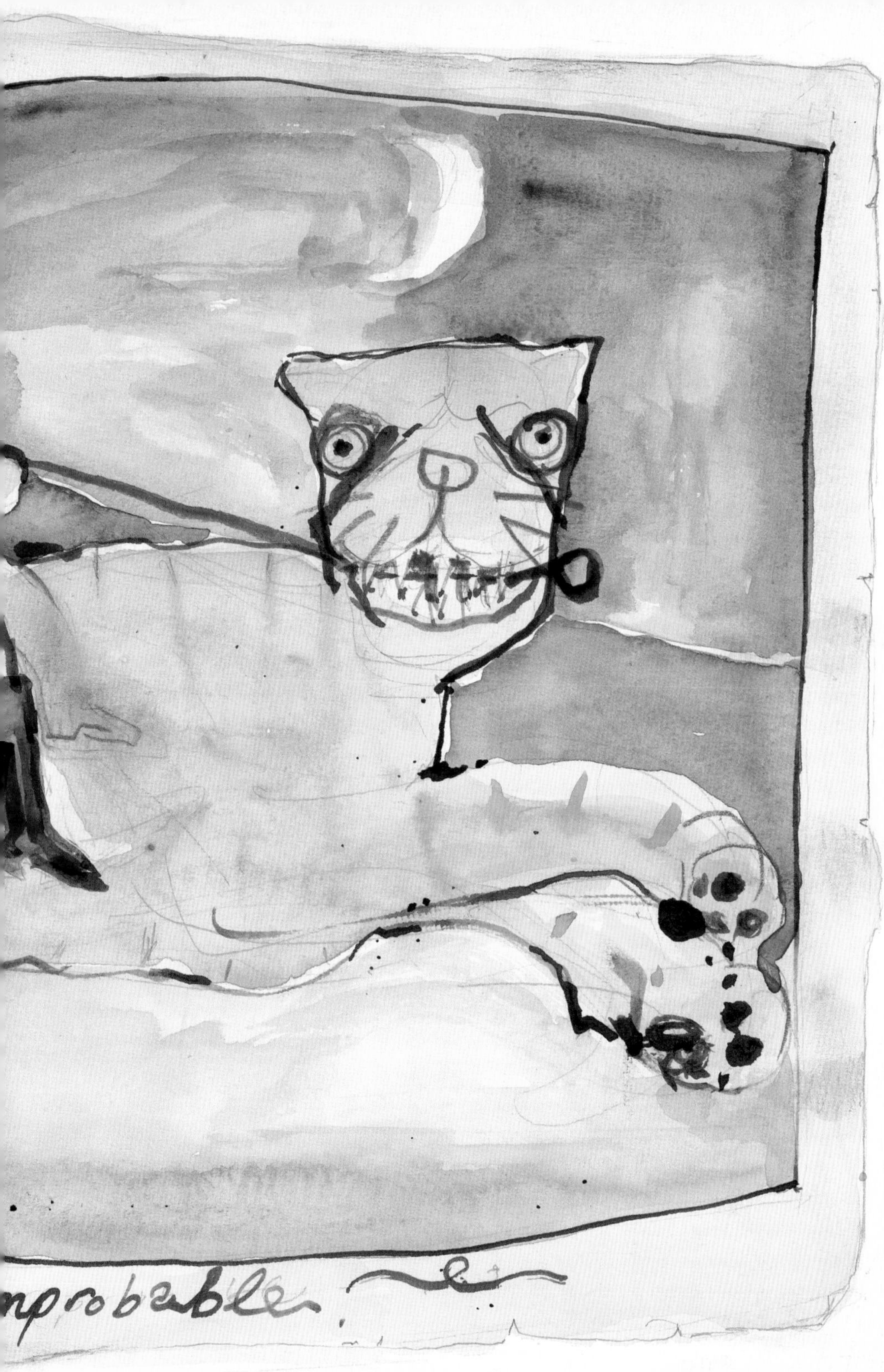
nprobable.

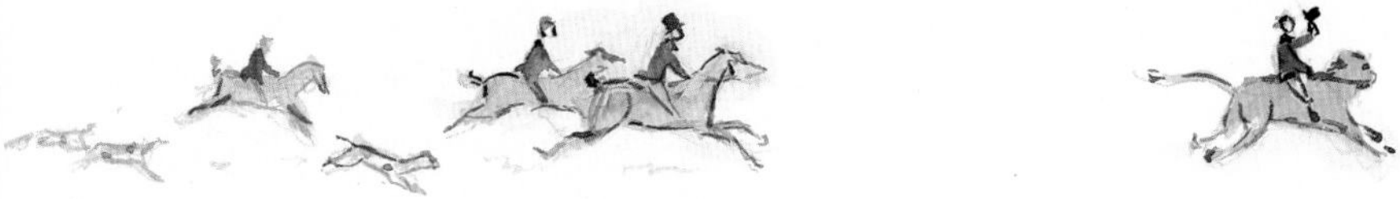

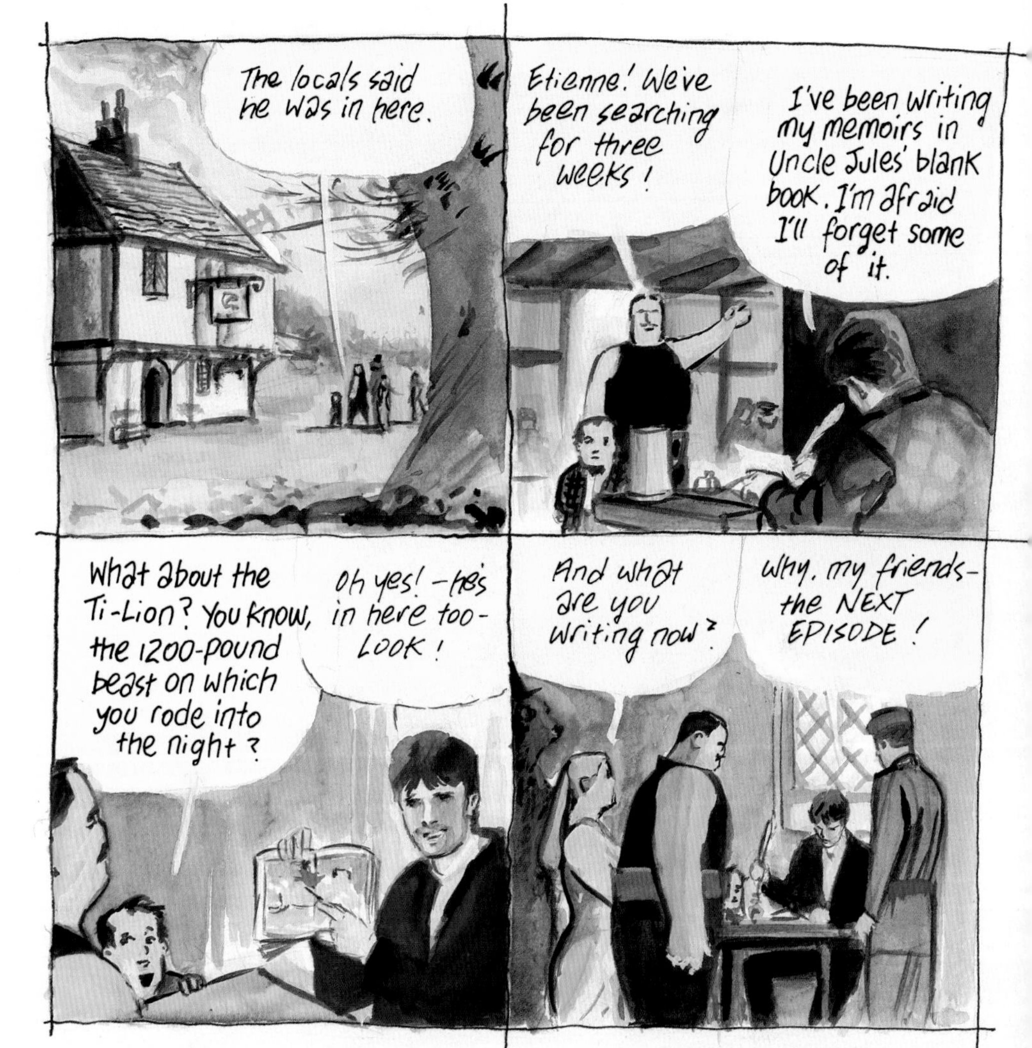

The locals said he was in here.
Etienne! We've been searching for three weeks!
I've been writing my memoirs in Uncle Jules' blank book. I'm afraid I'll forget some of it.
What about the Ti-Lion? You know, the 1200-pound beast on which you rode into the night?
Oh yes! —he's in here too— LOOK!
And what are you writing now?
Why, my friends— the NEXT EPISODE!

Le Prochain épisode

All about the shoes I invented, which could have made my name a household familiarity were it not for the fact that I have spent my life using somebody else's name.

Tout sur les chaussures que j'ai inventée, qui auraient pu rendre mon nom familier à tous, si je n'avais pas passé ma vie à utiliser celui de quelqu'un d'autre.

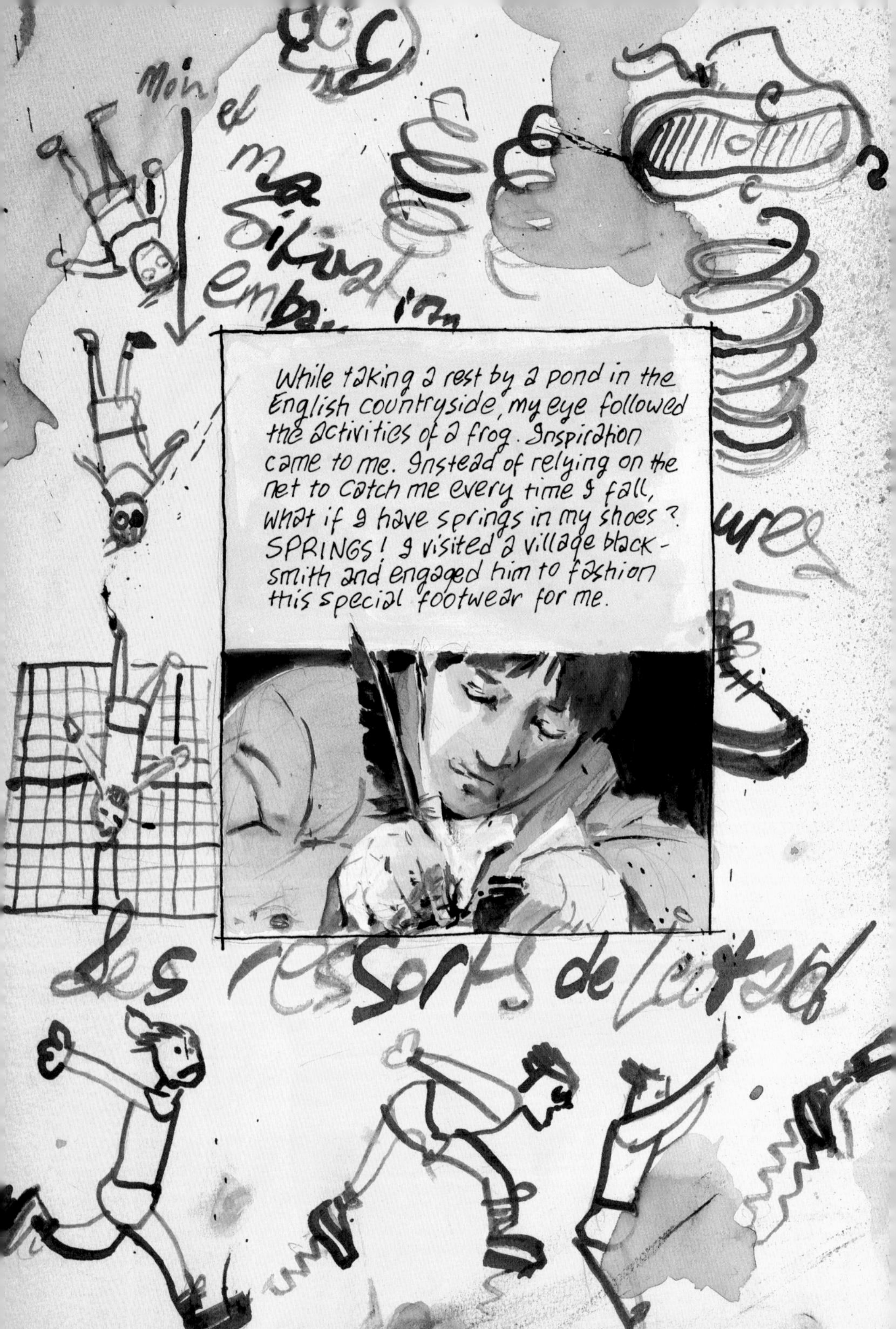
While taking a rest by a pond in the English countryside, my eye followed the activities of a frog. Inspiration came to me. Instead of relying on the net to catch me every time I fall, what if I have springs in my shoes? SPRINGS! I visited a village black-smith and engaged him to fashion this special footwear for me.
Les ressorts de

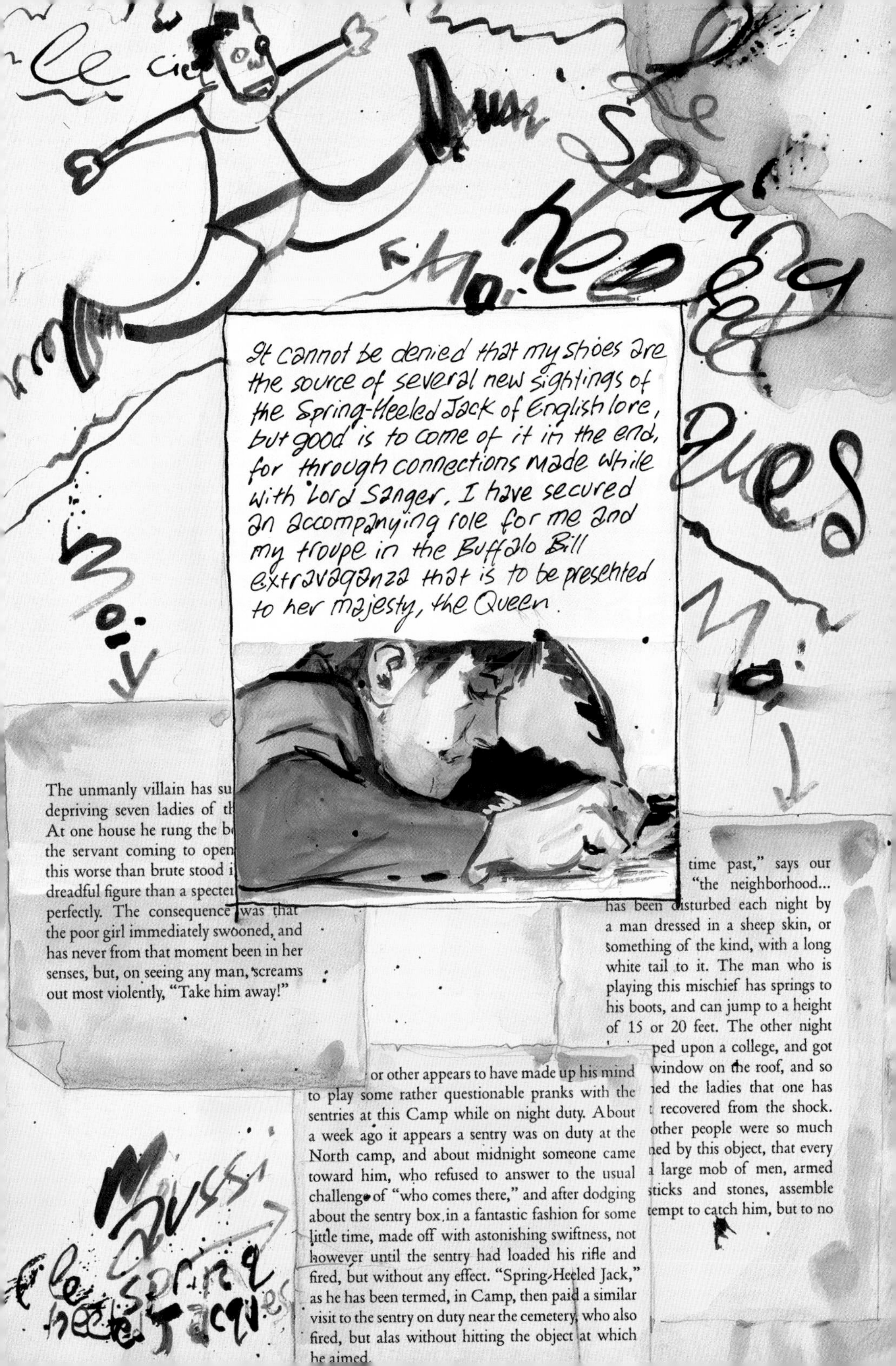
It cannot be denied that my shoes are the source of several new sightings of the Spring-Heeled Jack of English lore, but good is to come of it in the end, for through connections made while with Lord Sanger, I have secured an accompanying role for me and my troupe in the Buffalo Bill extravaganza that is to be presented to her majesty, the Queen.
Le Spring Heeled Jacques
Moi
Moi
Moi
Moi aussi
le spring heeled Jacques
The unmanly villain has su
depriving seven ladies of th
At one house he rung the b
the servant coming to open
this worse than brute stood i
dreadful figure than a specter
perfectly. The consequence was that
the poor girl immediately swooned, and
has never from that moment been in her
senses, but, on seeing any man, screams
out most violently, "Take him away!"
time past," says our
"the neighborhood...
has been disturbed each night by
a man dressed in a sheep skin, or
something of the kind, with a long
white tail to it. The man who is
playing this mischief has springs to
his boots, and can jump to a height
of 15 or 20 feet. The other night
ped upon a college, and got
window on the roof, and so
ned the ladies that one has
recovered from the shock.
other people were so much
ned by this object, that every
a large mob of men, armed
sticks and stones, assemble
tempt to catch him, but to no
or other appears to have made up his mind
to play some rather questionable pranks with the
sentries at this Camp while on night duty. About
a week ago it appears a sentry was on duty at the
North camp, and about midnight someone came
toward him, who refused to answer to the usual
challenge of "who comes there," and after dodging
about the sentry box in a fantastic fashion for some
little time, made off with astonishing swiftness, not
however until the sentry had loaded his rifle and
fired, but without any effect. "Spring-Heeled Jack,"
as he has been termed, in Camp, then paid a similar
visit to the sentry on duty near the cemetery, who also
fired, but alas without hitting the object at which
he aimed.

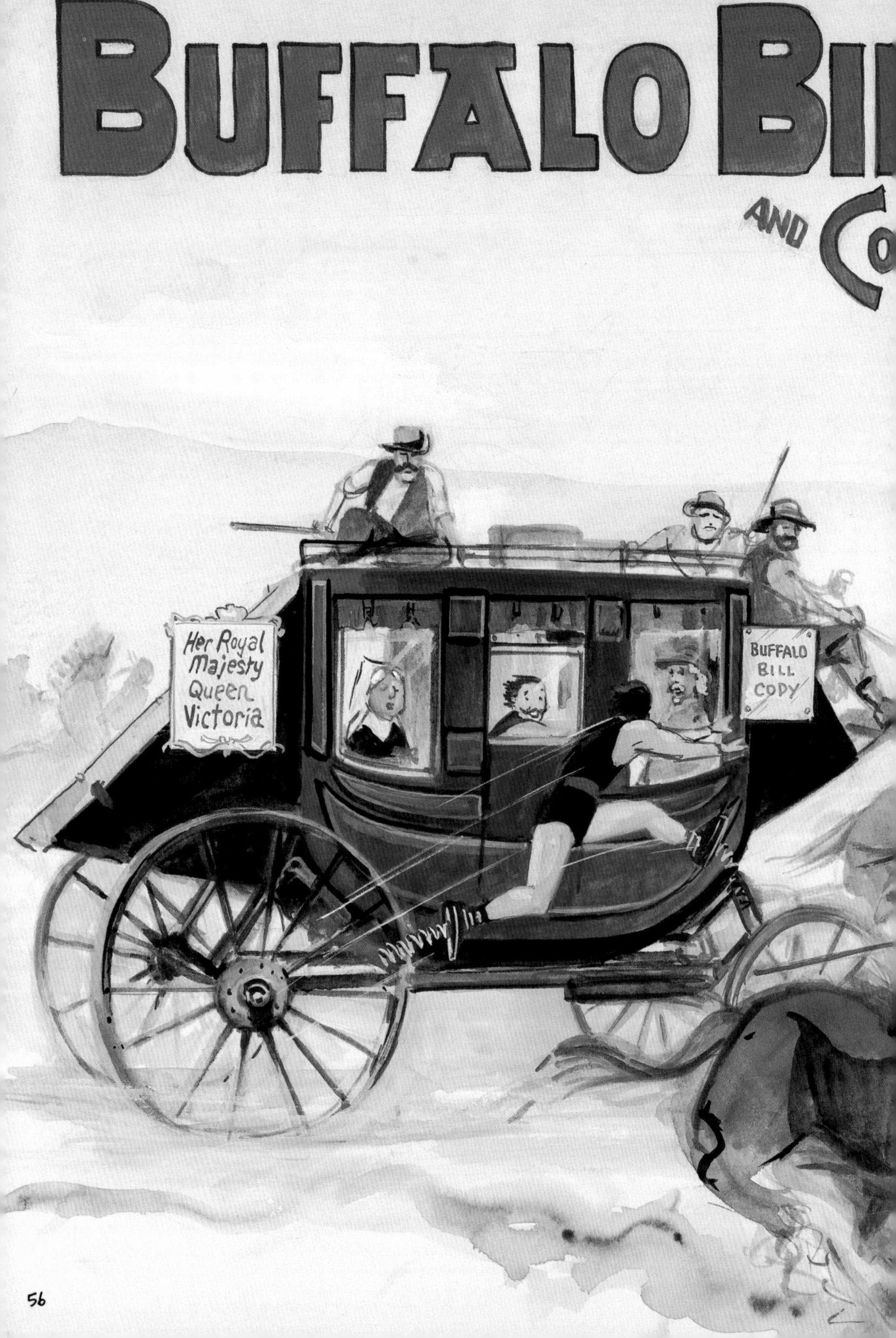
BUFFALO BI
AND CO
Her Royal Majesty Queen Victoria
BUFFALO BILL CODY

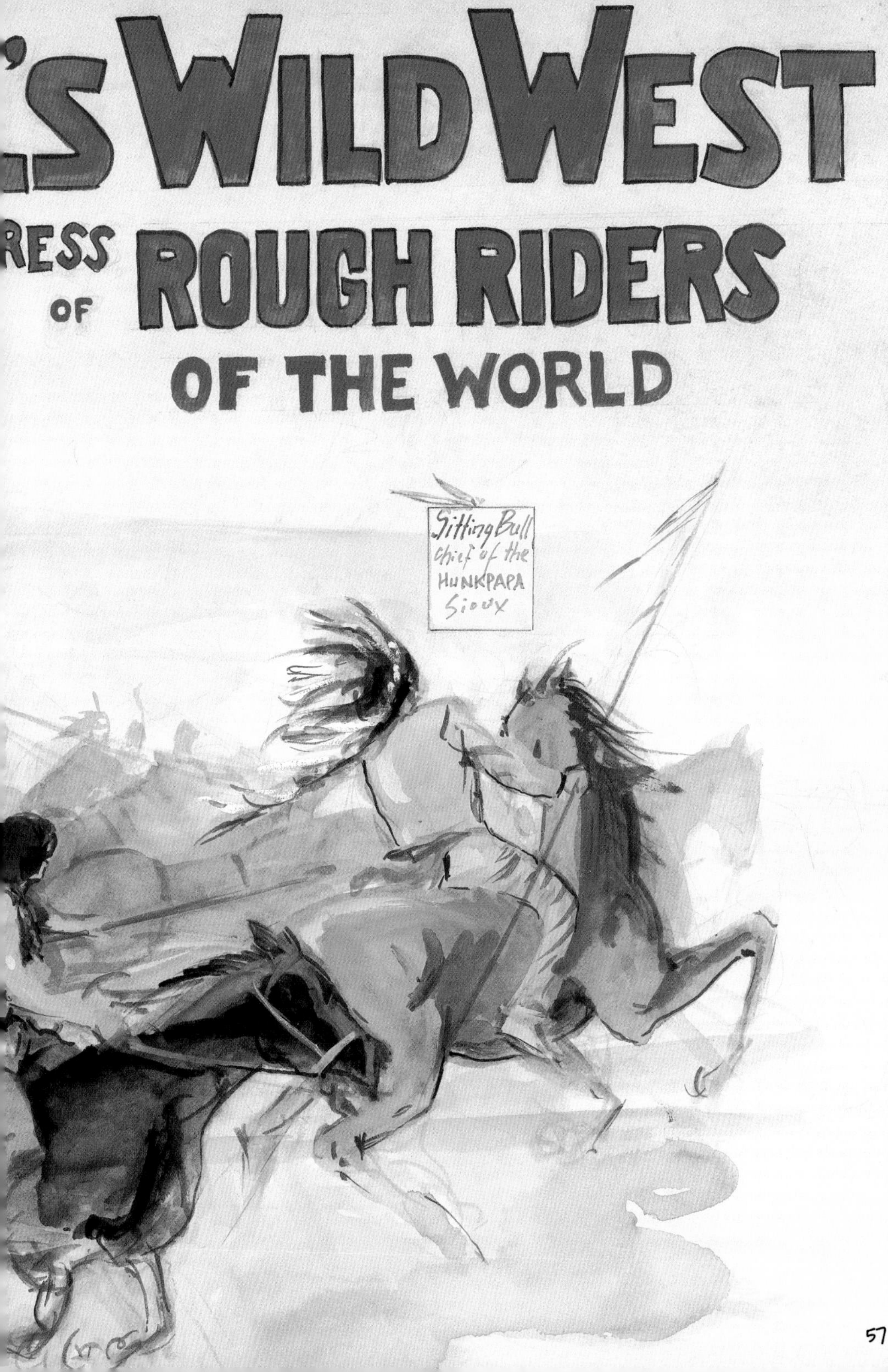
'S WILD WEST
RESS ROUGH RIDERS
OF
OF THE WORLD
Sitting Bull
chief of the
HUNKPAPA
Sioux

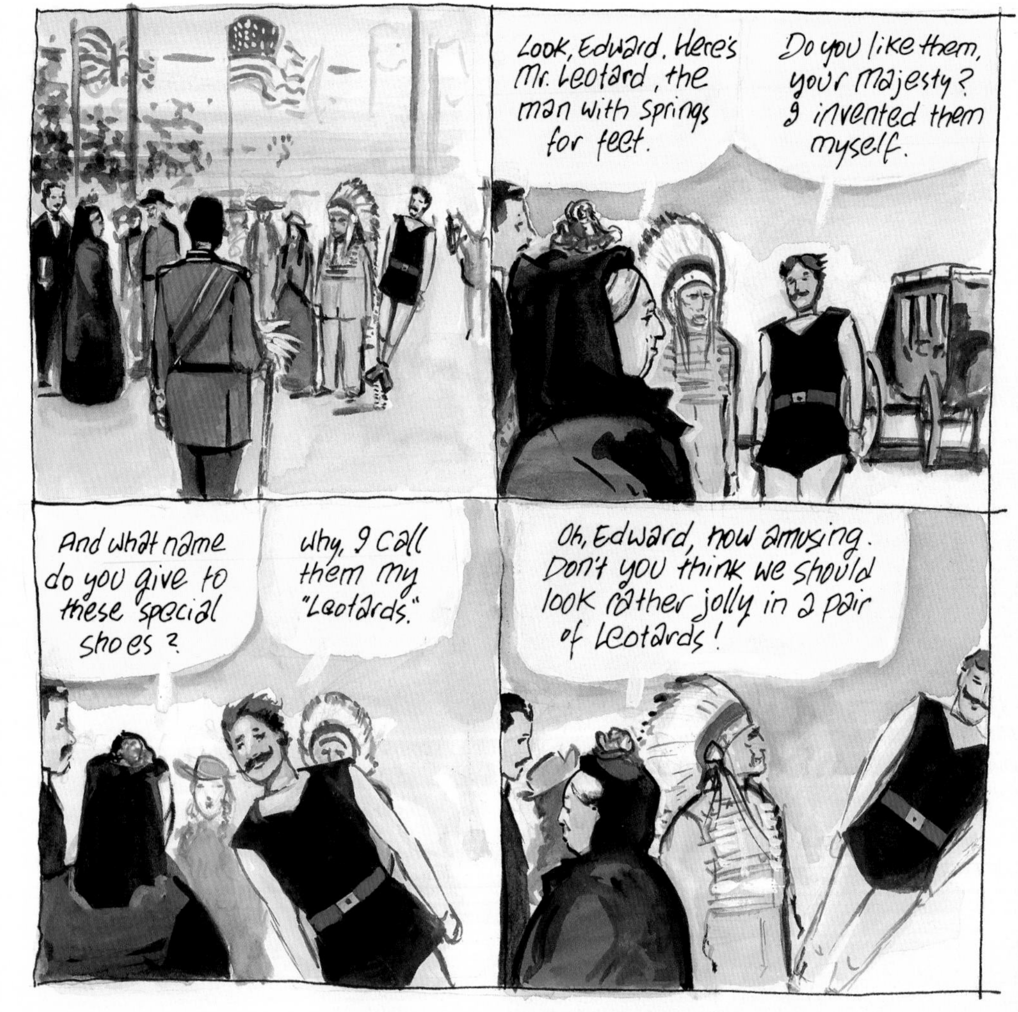
Look, Edward. Here's Mr. Leotard, the man with springs for feet.
Do you like them, your Majesty? I invented them myself.
And what name do you give to these special shoes?
Why, I call them my "Leotards."
Oh, Edward, how amusing. Don't you think we should look rather jolly in a pair of Leotards!

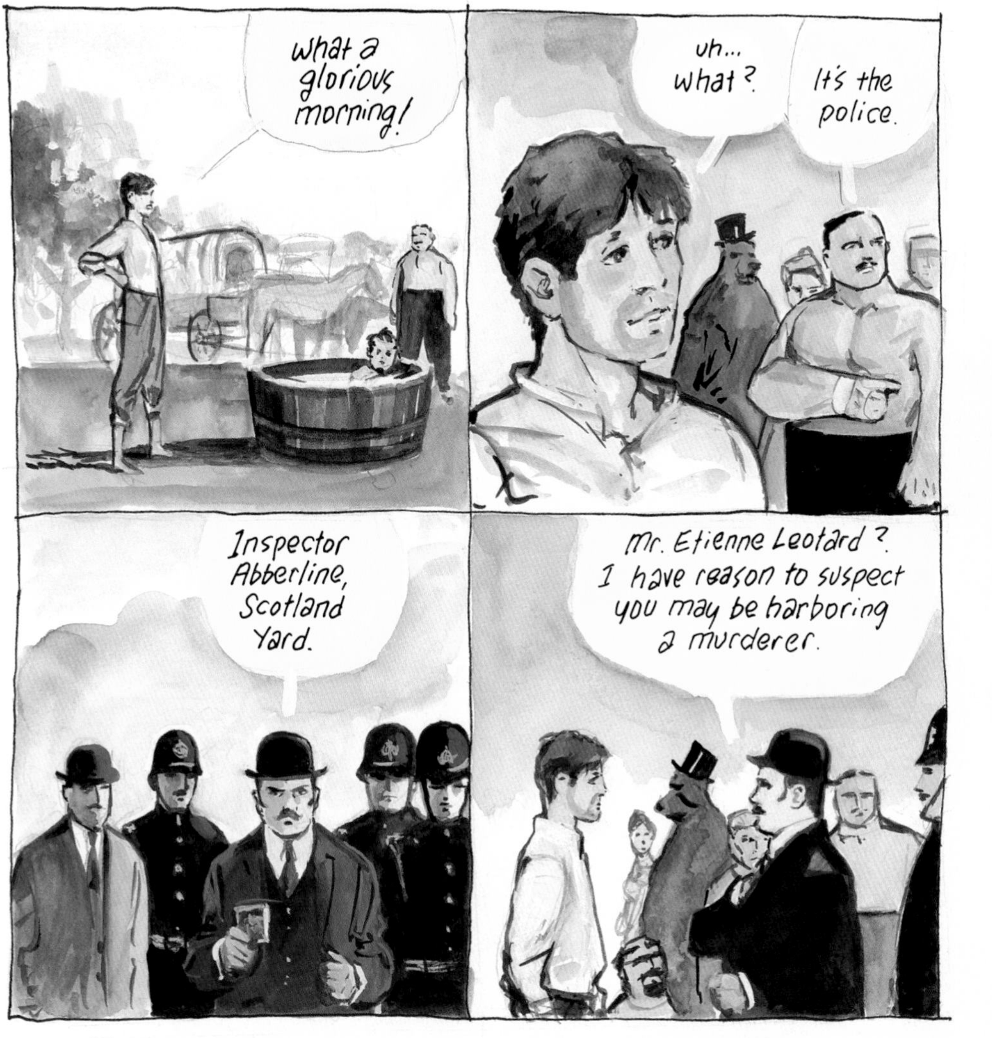
What a glorious morning!
Uh... what?
It's the police.
Inspector Abberline, Scotland Yard.
Mr. Etienne Leotard? I have reason to suspect you may be harboring a murderer.

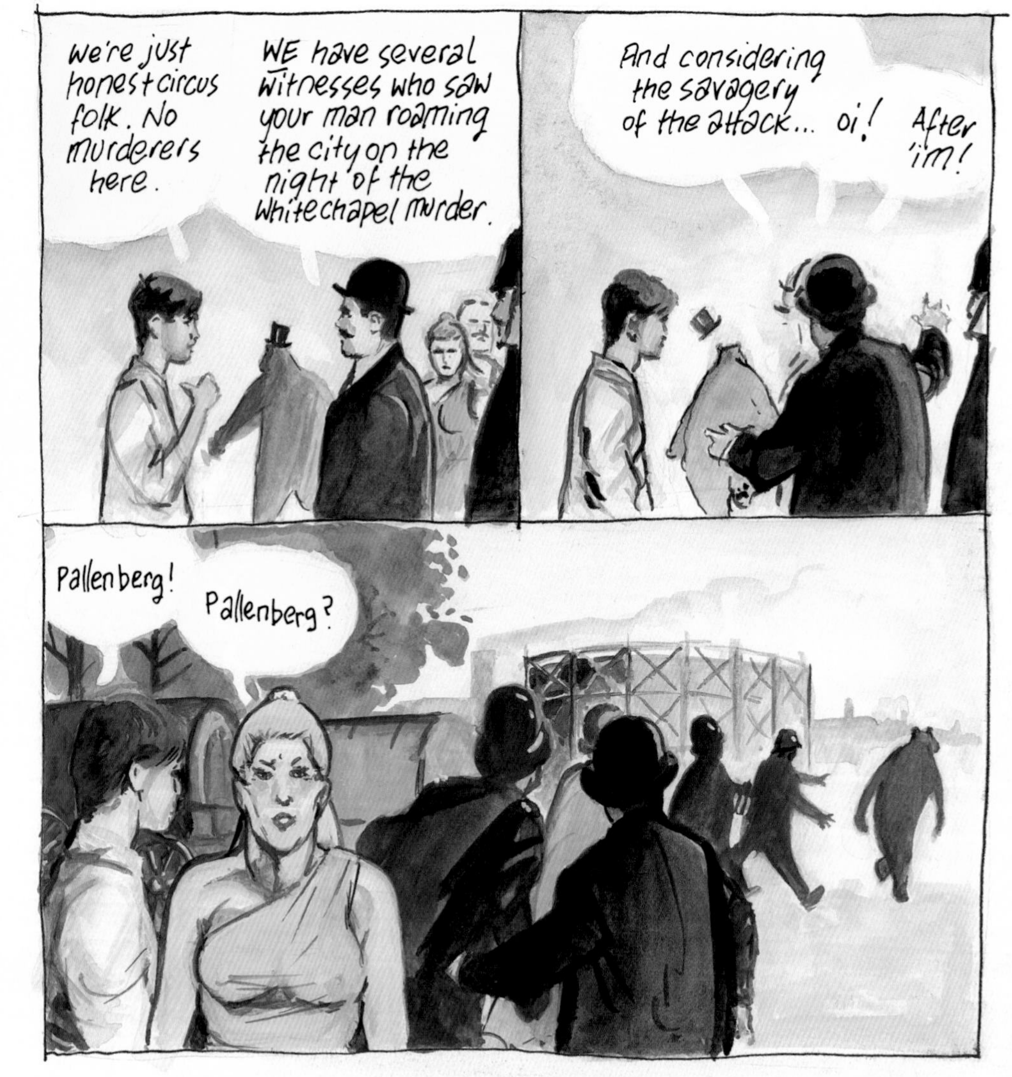
We're just honest circus folk. No murderers here.
WE have several witnesses who saw your man roaming the city on the night of the Whitechapel murder.
And considering the savagery of the attack... oi!
After 'im!
Pallenberg!
Pallenberg?

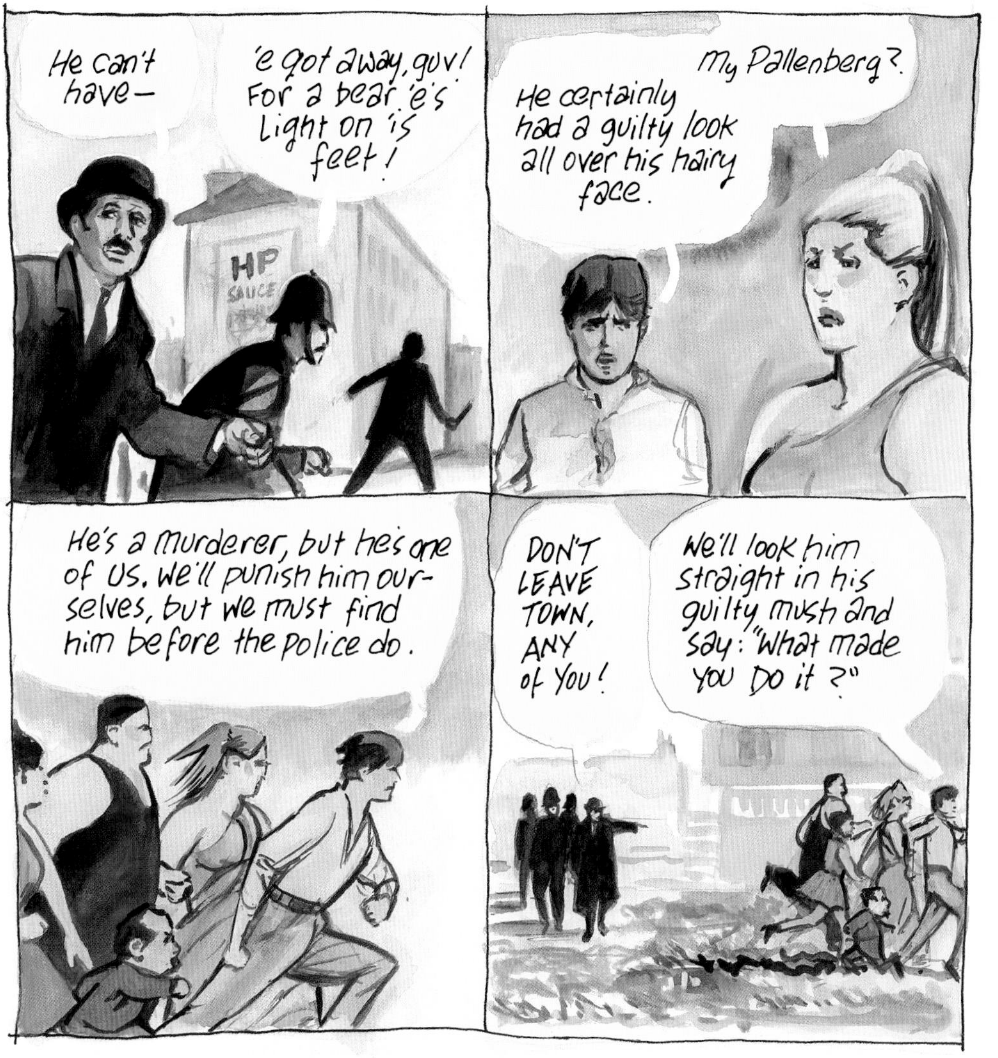
He can't have—
'e got away, guv! For a bear 'e's light on 'is feet!
My Pallenberg?
He certainly had a guilty look all over his hairy face.
He's a murderer, but he's one of us. We'll punish him ourselves, but we must find him before the police do.
DON'T LEAVE TOWN, ANY of YOU!
We'll look him straight in his guilty mush and say: "What made you do it?"

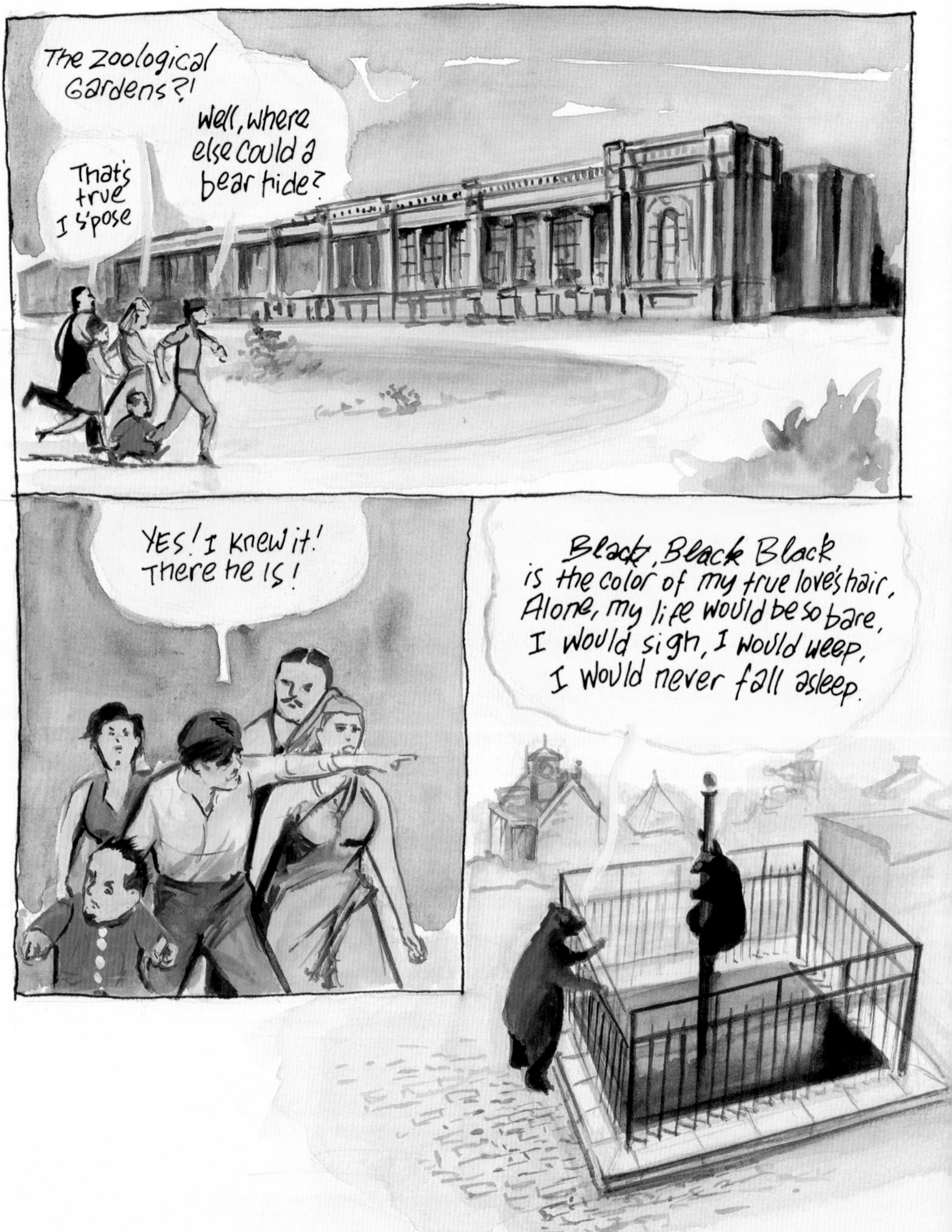
The zoological Gardens?!
That's true I s'pose
Well, where else could a bear hide?
YES! I knew it! There he is!
Black, Black Black
is the color of my true love's hair,
Alone, my life would be so bare,
I would sigh, I would weep,
I would never fall asleep.

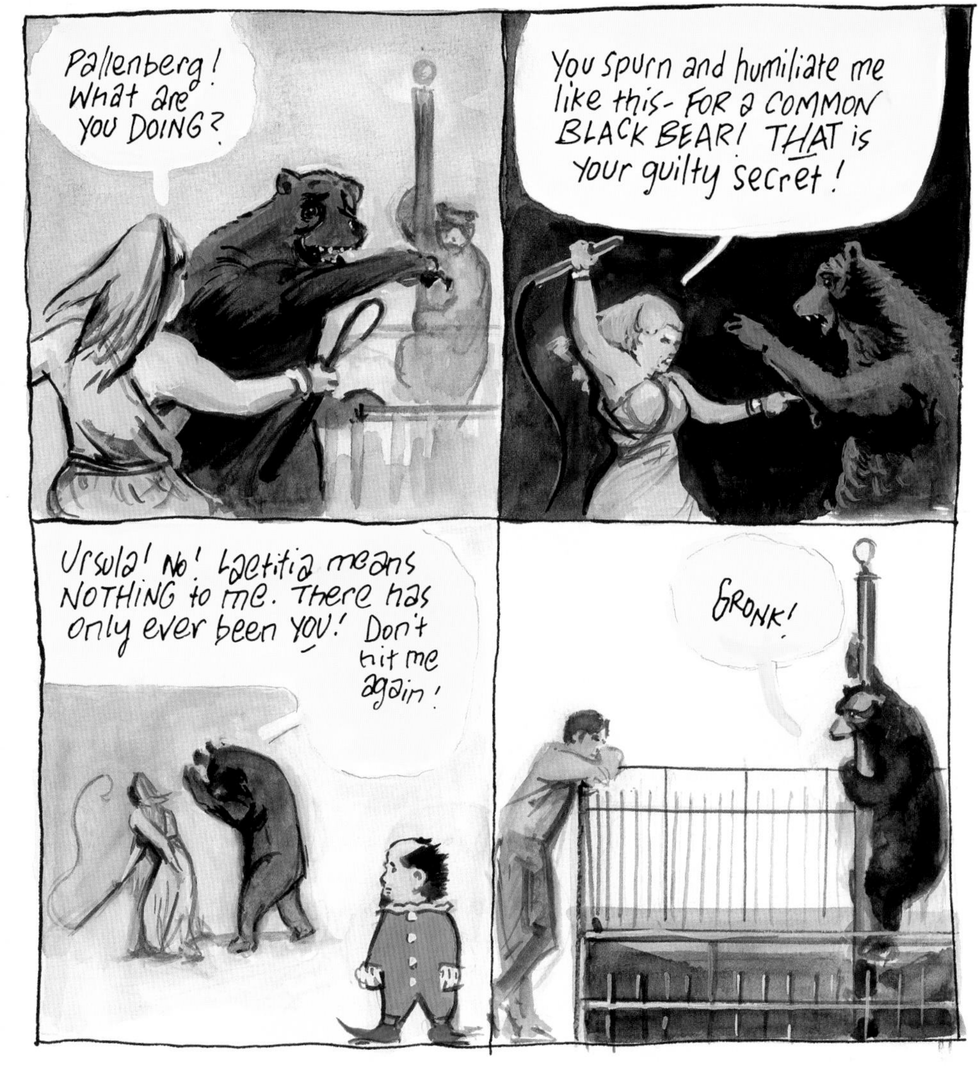
Pallenberg! What are you DOING?
You spurn and humiliate me like this- FOR a COMMON BLACK BEAR! THAT is your guilty secret!
Ursula! No! Laetitia means NOTHING to me. There has only ever been YOU! Don't hit me again!
GRONK!

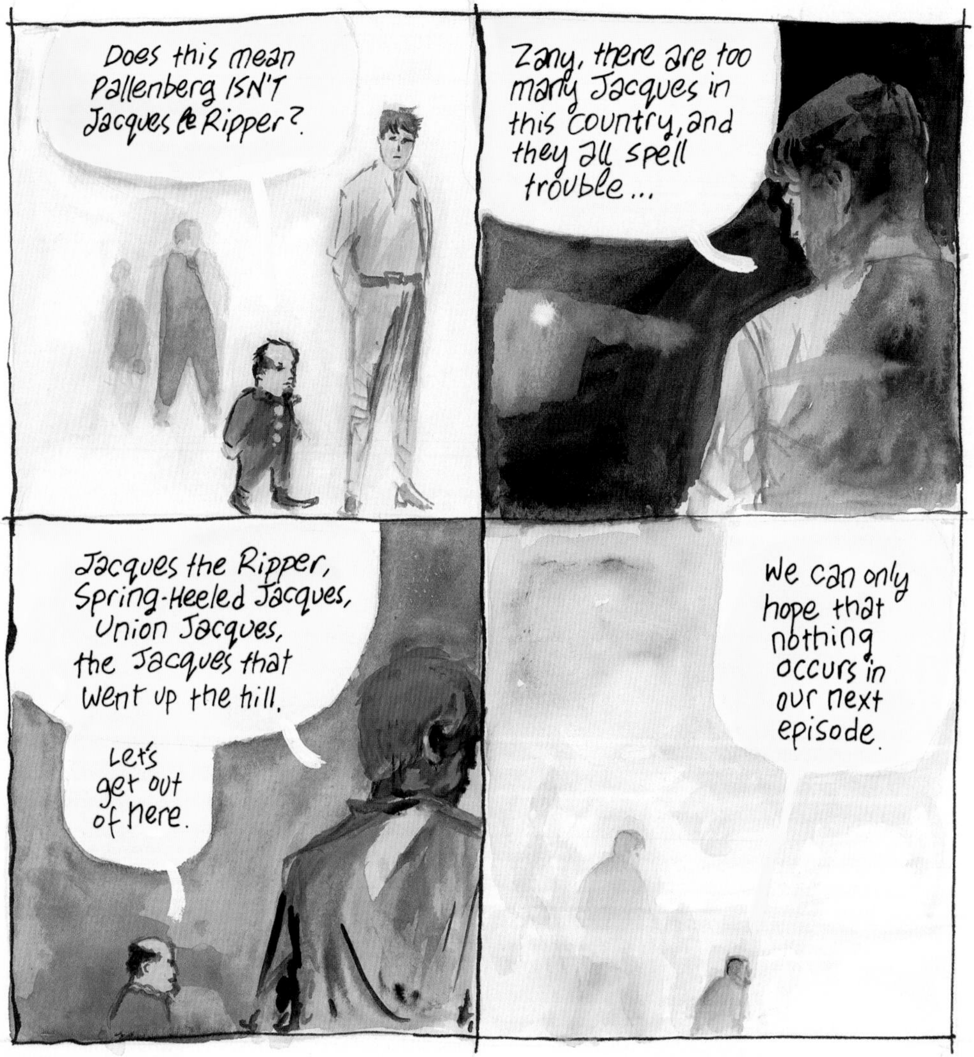
Does this mean Pallenberg ISN'T Jacques le Ripper?
Zany, there are too many Jacques in this country, and they all spell trouble...
Jacques the Ripper, Spring-Heeled Jacques, Union Jacques, the Jacques that went up the hill.
Let's get out of here.
We can only hope that nothing occurs in our next episode.

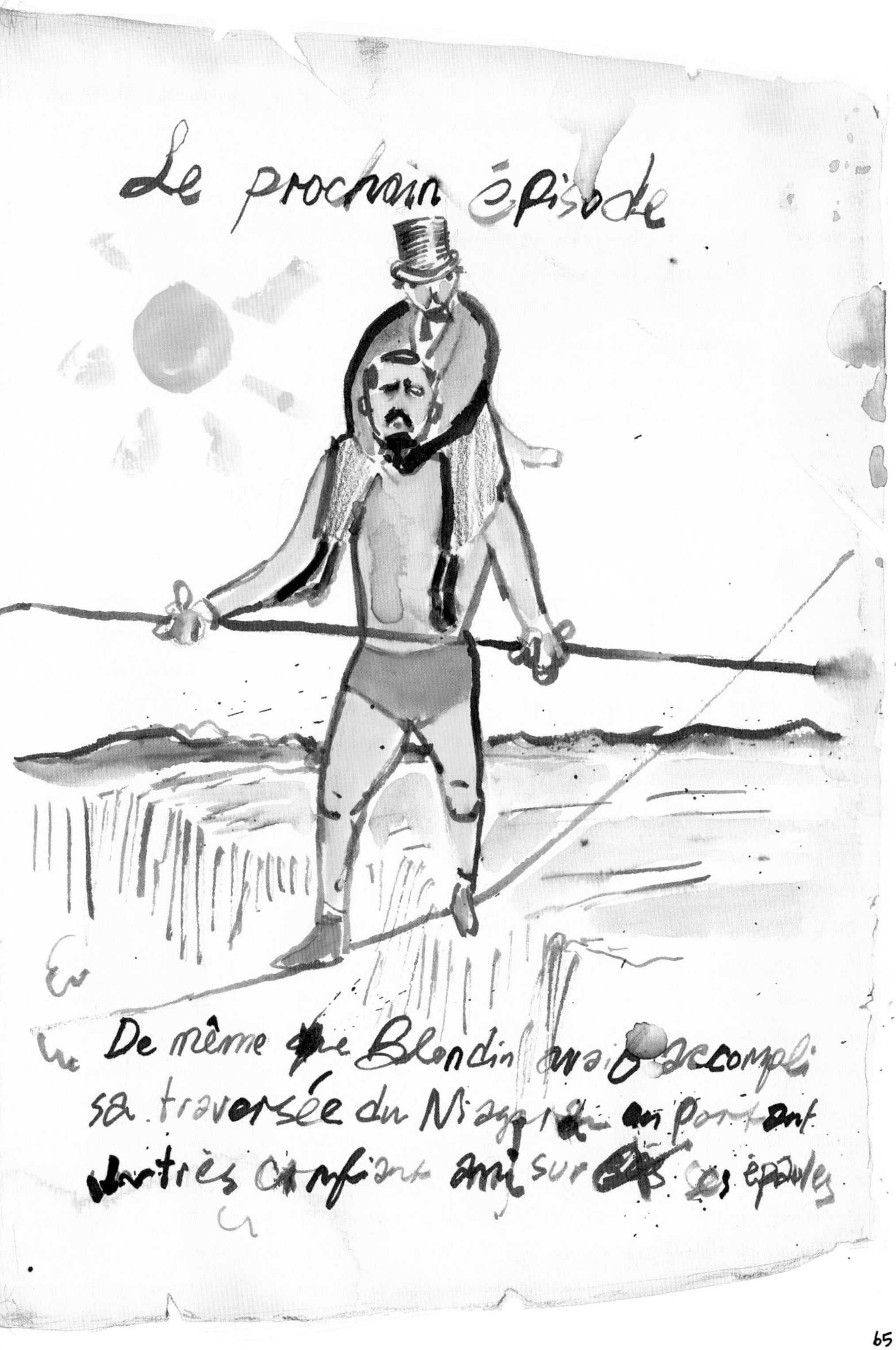
Le prochain épisode
De même que Blondin avait accompli
sa traversée du Niagara en portant
un très confiant ami sur ses épaules

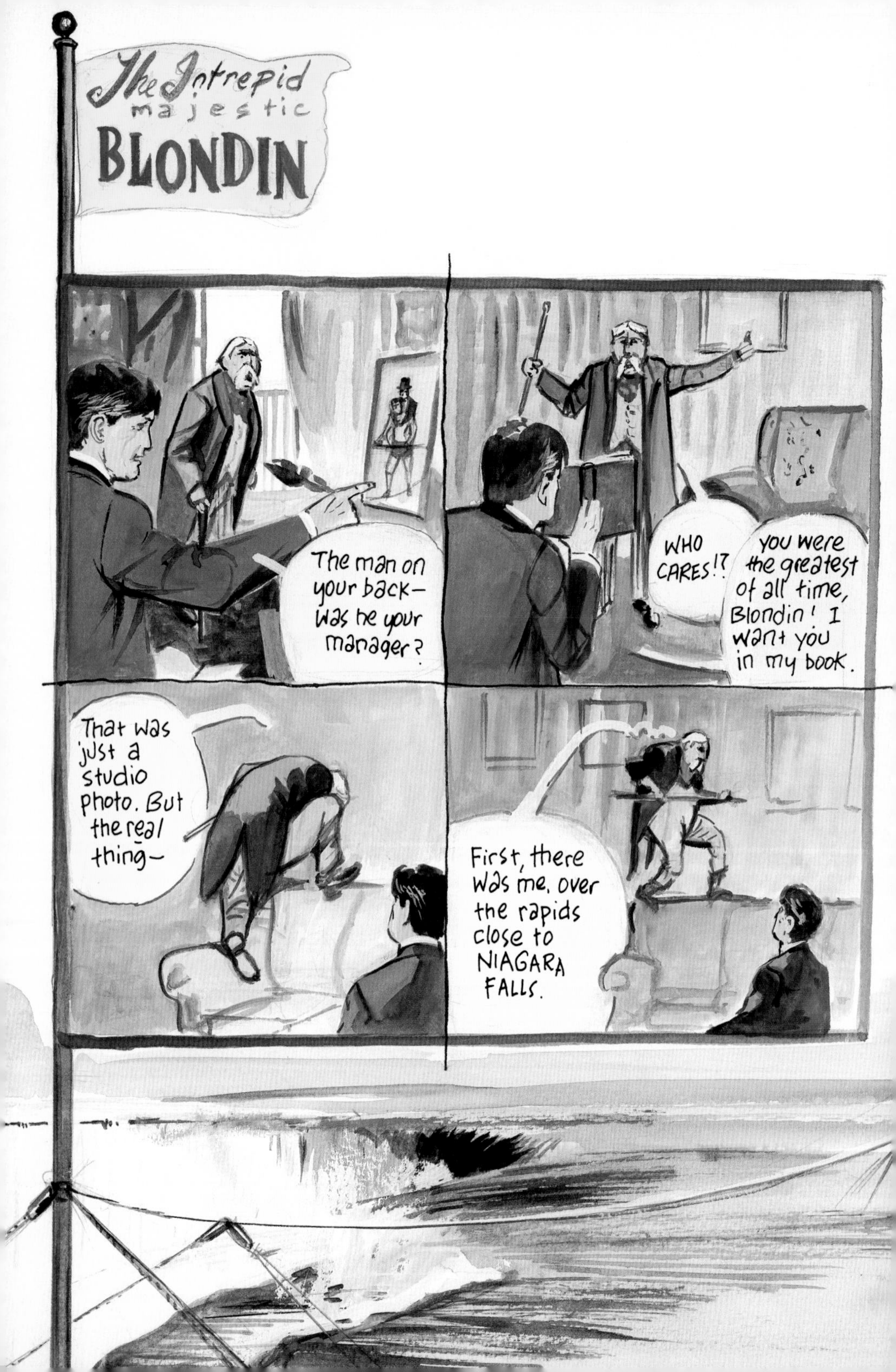
The Intrepid majestic BLONDIN
The man on your back— was he your manager?
WHO CARES!?
You were the greatest of all time, Blondin! I want you in my book.
That was just a studio photo. But the real thing—
First, there was me, over the rapids close to NIAGARA FALLS.

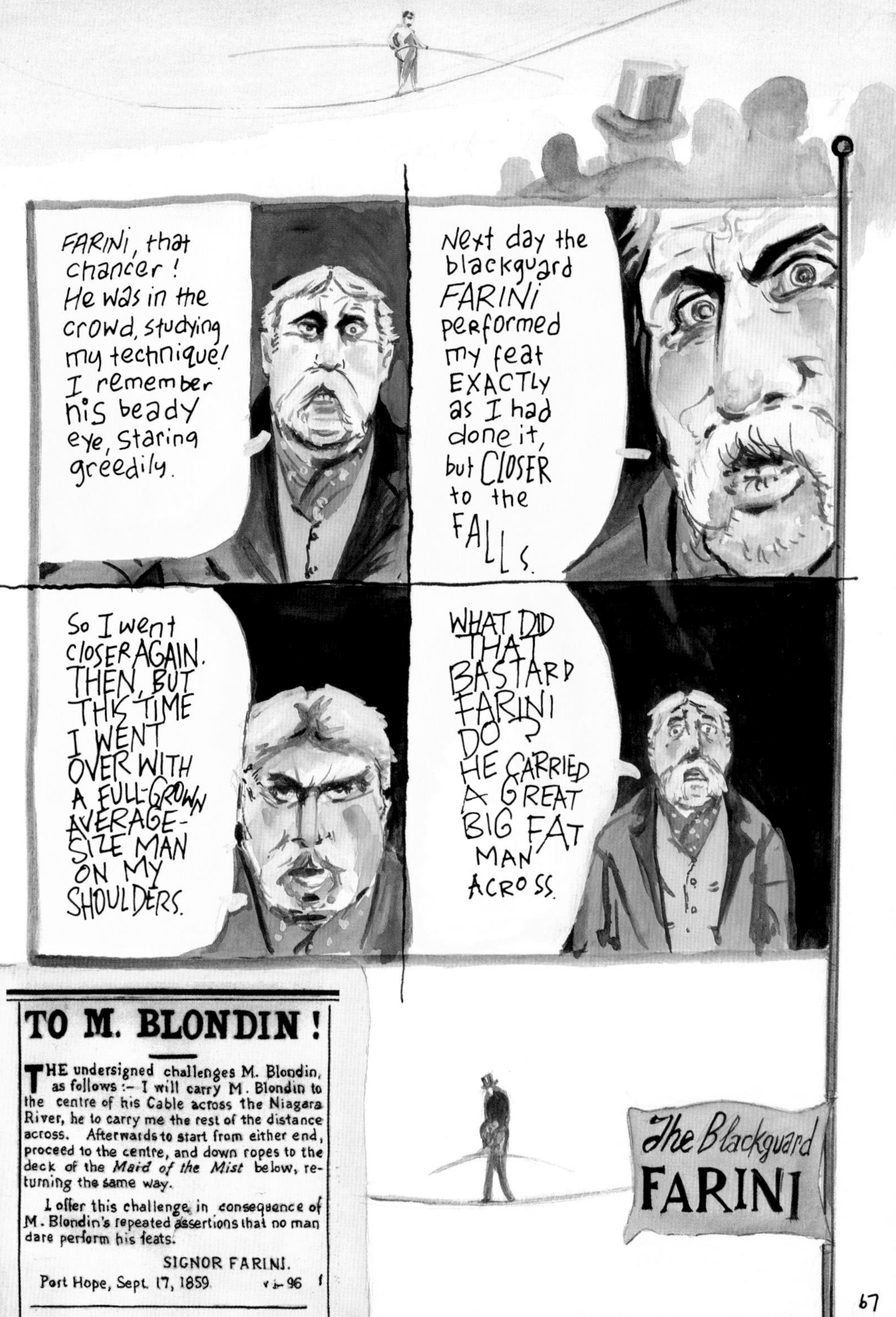
FARINI, that chancer! He was in the crowd, studying my technique! I remember his beady eye, staring greedily.
Next day the blackguard FARINI performed my feat EXACTLY as I had done it, but CLOSER to the FALLS.
So I went CLOSER AGAIN. THEN, BUT THIS TIME I WENT OVER WITH A FULL-GROWN AVERAGE-SIZE MAN ON MY SHOULDERS.
WHAT DID THAT BASTARD FARINI DO? HE CARRIED A GREAT BIG FAT MAN ACROSS.
TO M. BLONDIN!
THE undersigned challenges M. Blondin, as follows:— I will carry M. Blondin to the centre of his Cable across the Niagara River, he to carry me the rest of the distance across. Afterwards to start from either end, proceed to the centre, and down ropes to the deck of the *Maid of the Mist* below, returning the same way.
I offer this challenge in consequence of M. Blondin's repeated assertions that no man dare perform his feats.
SIGNOR FARINI.
Port Hope, Sept. 17, 1859.
The Blackguard FARINI

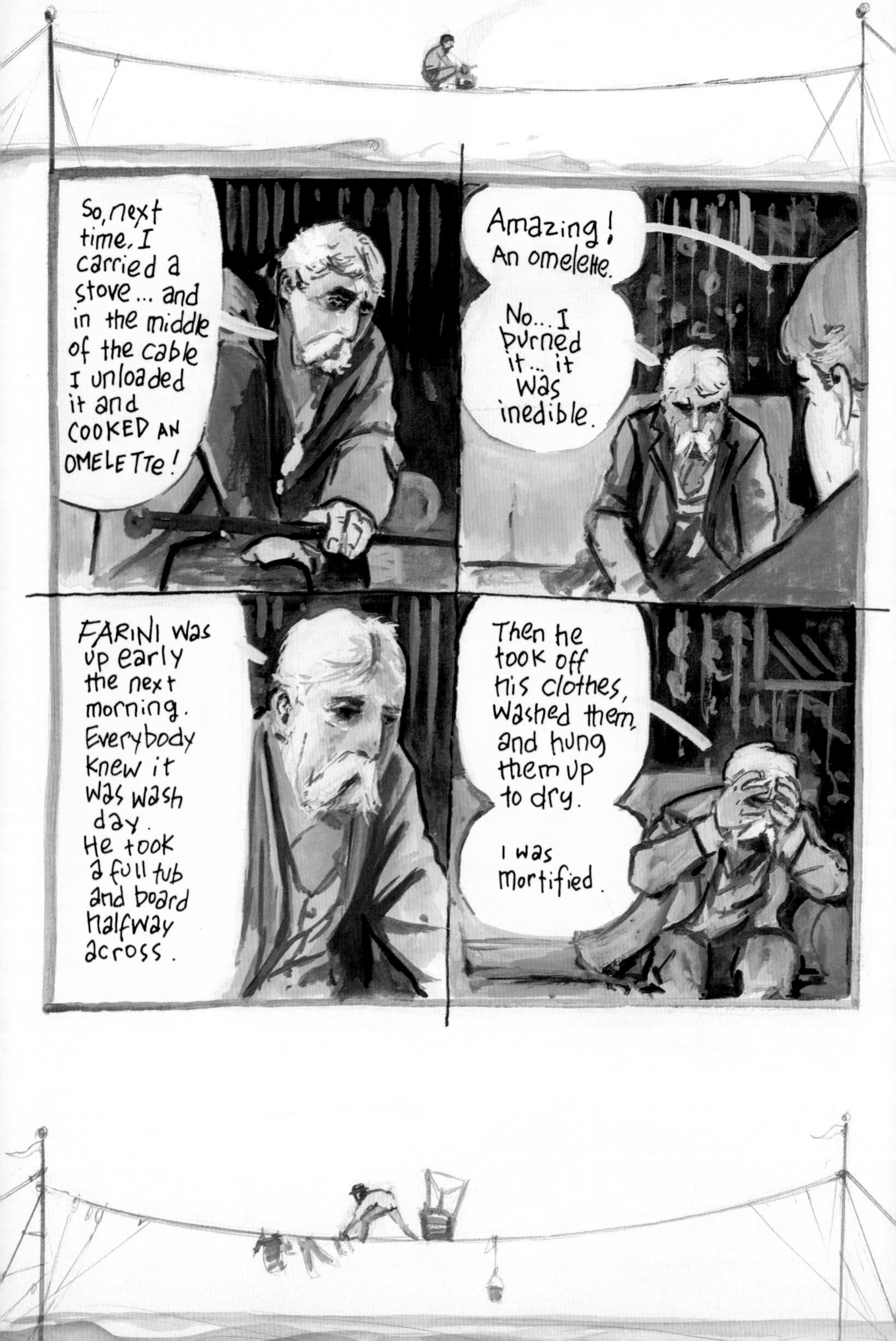
So, next time, I carried a stove ... and in the middle of the cable I unloaded it and COOKED AN OMELETTE!
Amazing! An omelette.
No... I burned it... it was inedible.
FARINI was up early the next morning. Everybody knew it was wash day. He took a full tub and board halfway across.
Then he took off his clothes, washed them, and hung them up to dry.
I was mortified.

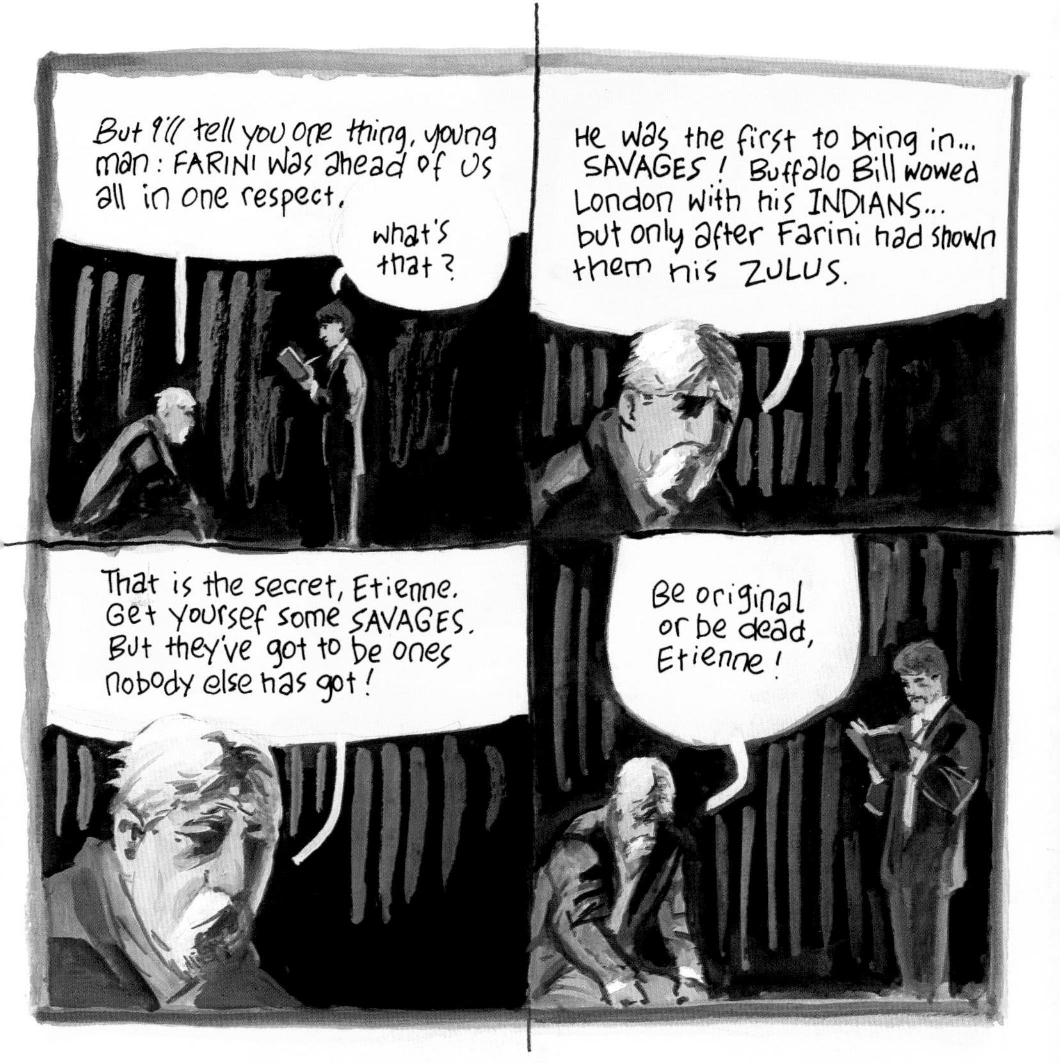
But I'll tell you one thing, young man: FARINI was ahead of us all in one respect.
what's that?
He was the first to bring in... SAVAGES! Buffalo Bill wowed London with his INDIANS... but only after Farini had shown them his ZULUS.
That is the secret, Etienne. Get yoursef some SAVAGES. But they've got to be ones nobody else has got!
Be original or be dead, Etienne!

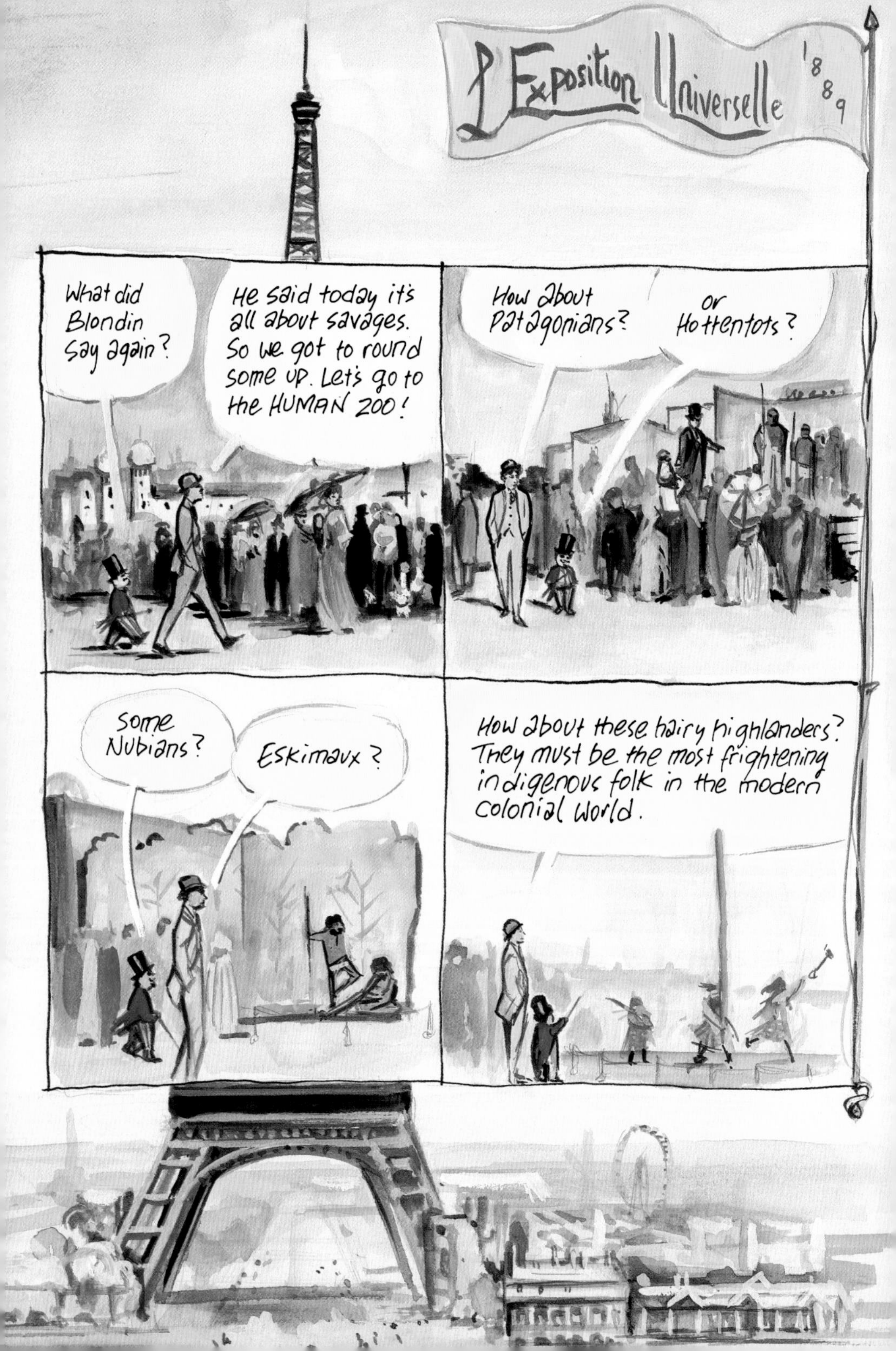
L'Exposition Universelle 1889
What did Blondin say again?
He said today it's all about savages. So we got to round some up. Let's go to the HUMAN ZOO!
How about Patagonians?
or Hottentots?
Some Nubians?
Eskimaux?
How about these hairy highlanders? They must be the most frightening indigenous folk in the modern colonial world.

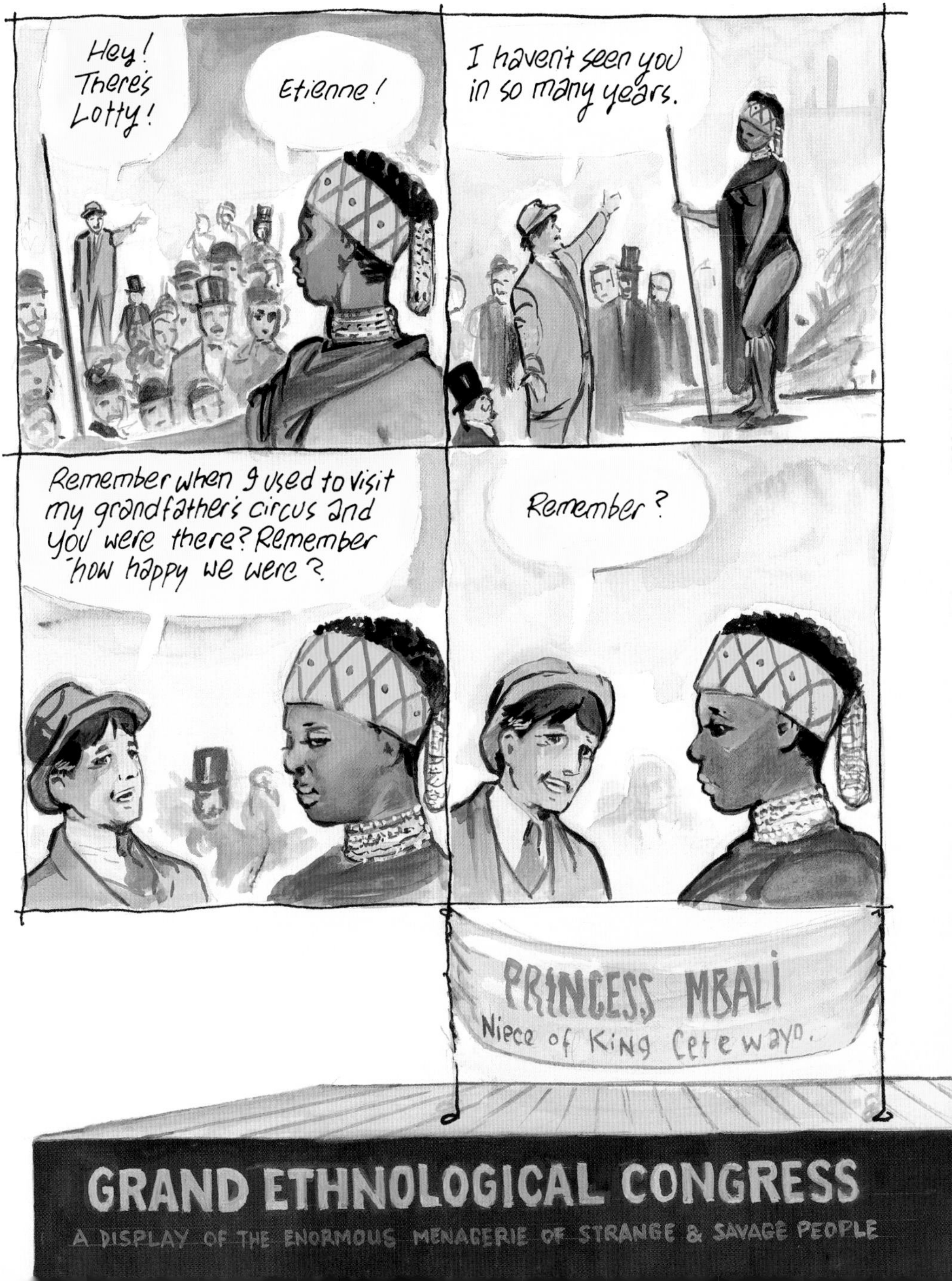
Hey! There's Lotty!
Etienne!
I haven't seen you in so many years.
Remember when I used to visit my grandfather's circus and you were there? Remember how happy we were?
Remember?
PRINCESS MBALI
Niece of King Cetewayo.
GRAND ETHNOLOGICAL CONGRESS
A DISPLAY OF THE ENORMOUS MENAGERIE OF STRANGE & SAVAGE PEOPLE

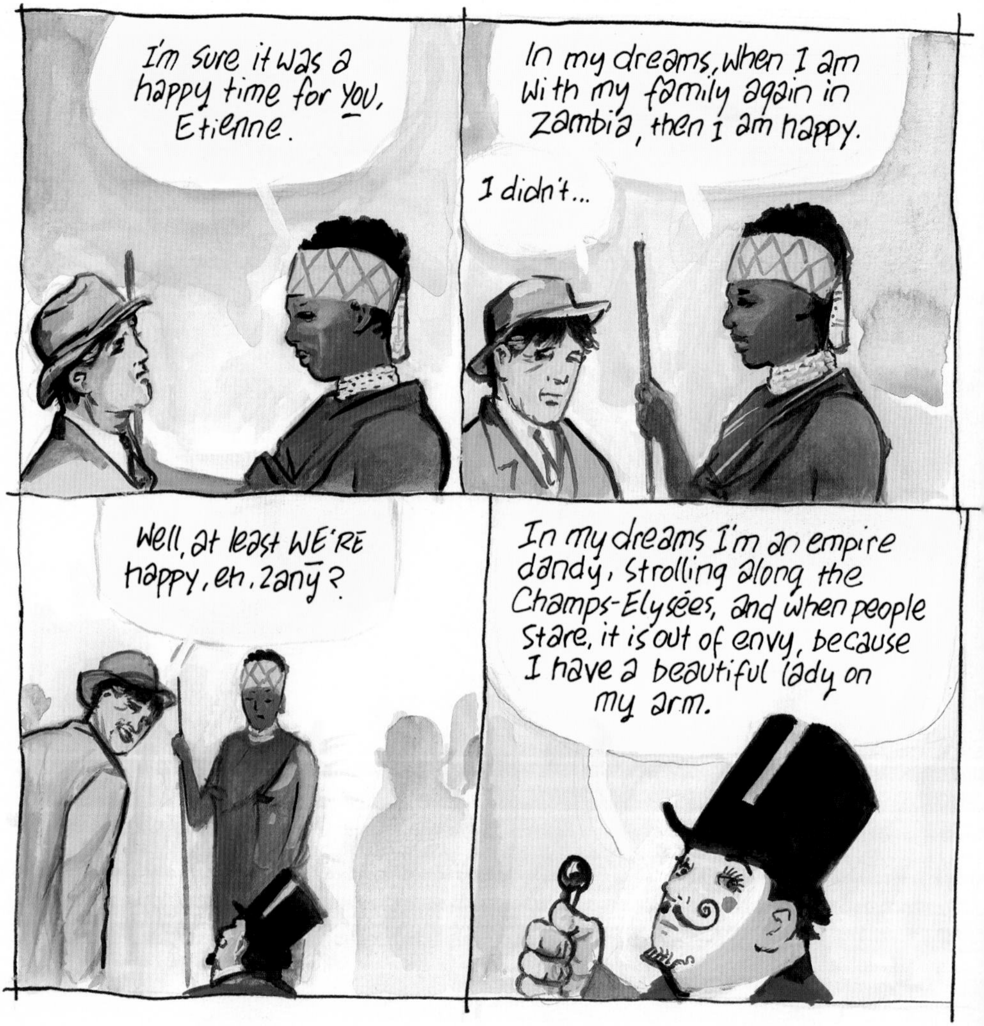
I'm sure it was a happy time for YOU, Etienne.
In my dreams, when I am with my family again in Zambia, then I am happy.
I didn't...
Well, at least WE'RE happy, eh, Zany?
In my dreams I'm an empire dandy, strolling along the Champs-Elysées, and when people stare, it is out of envy, because I have a beautiful lady on my arm.

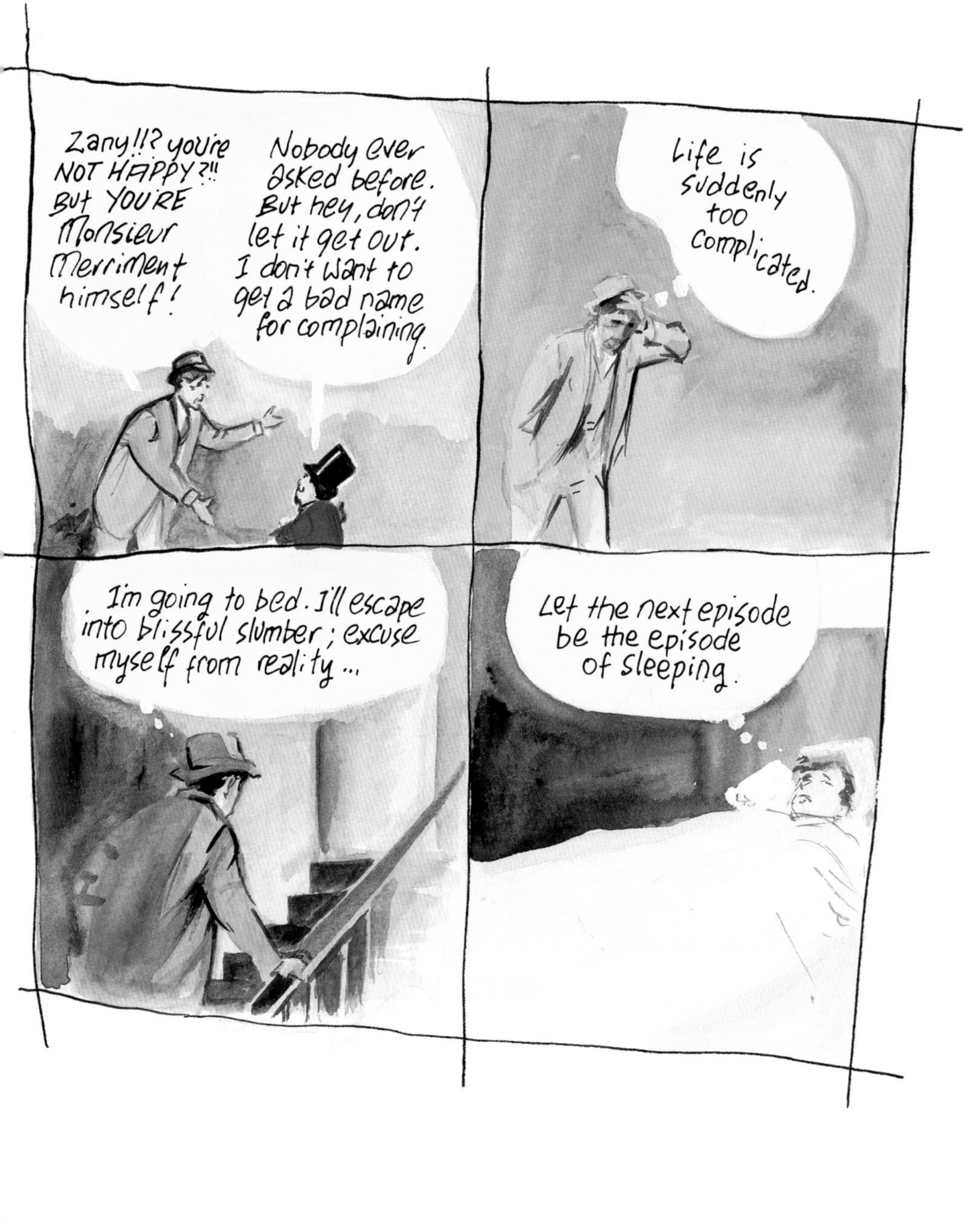
Zany!!? you're NOT HAPPY?!! But YOU'RE Monsieur Merriment himself!
Nobody ever asked before. But hey, don't let it get out. I don't want to get a bad name for complaining.
Life is suddenly too complicated.
I'm going to bed. I'll escape into blissful slumber; excuse myself from reality...
Let the next episode be the episode of sleeping.

The Episode of

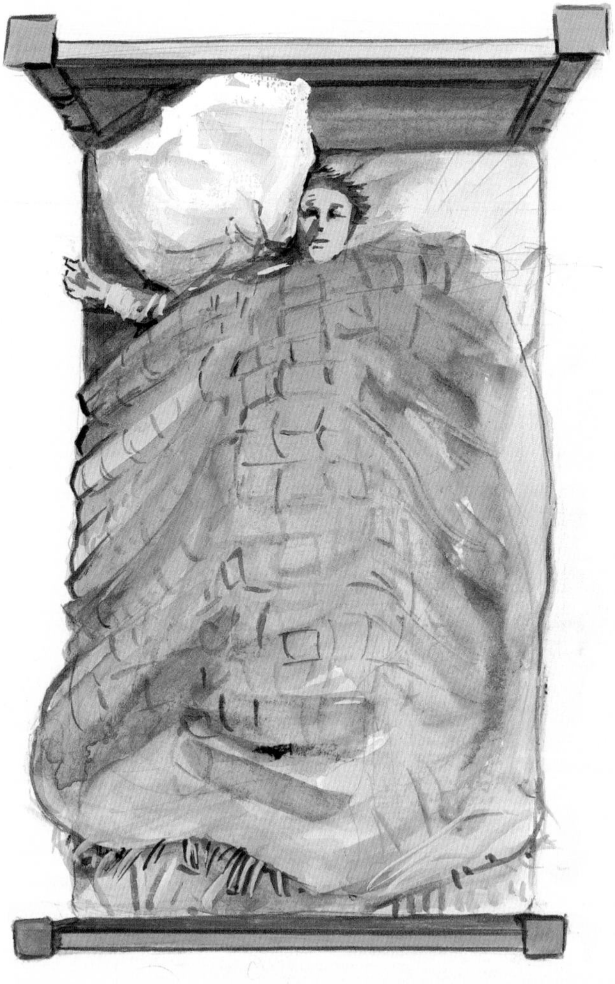

Sleeping

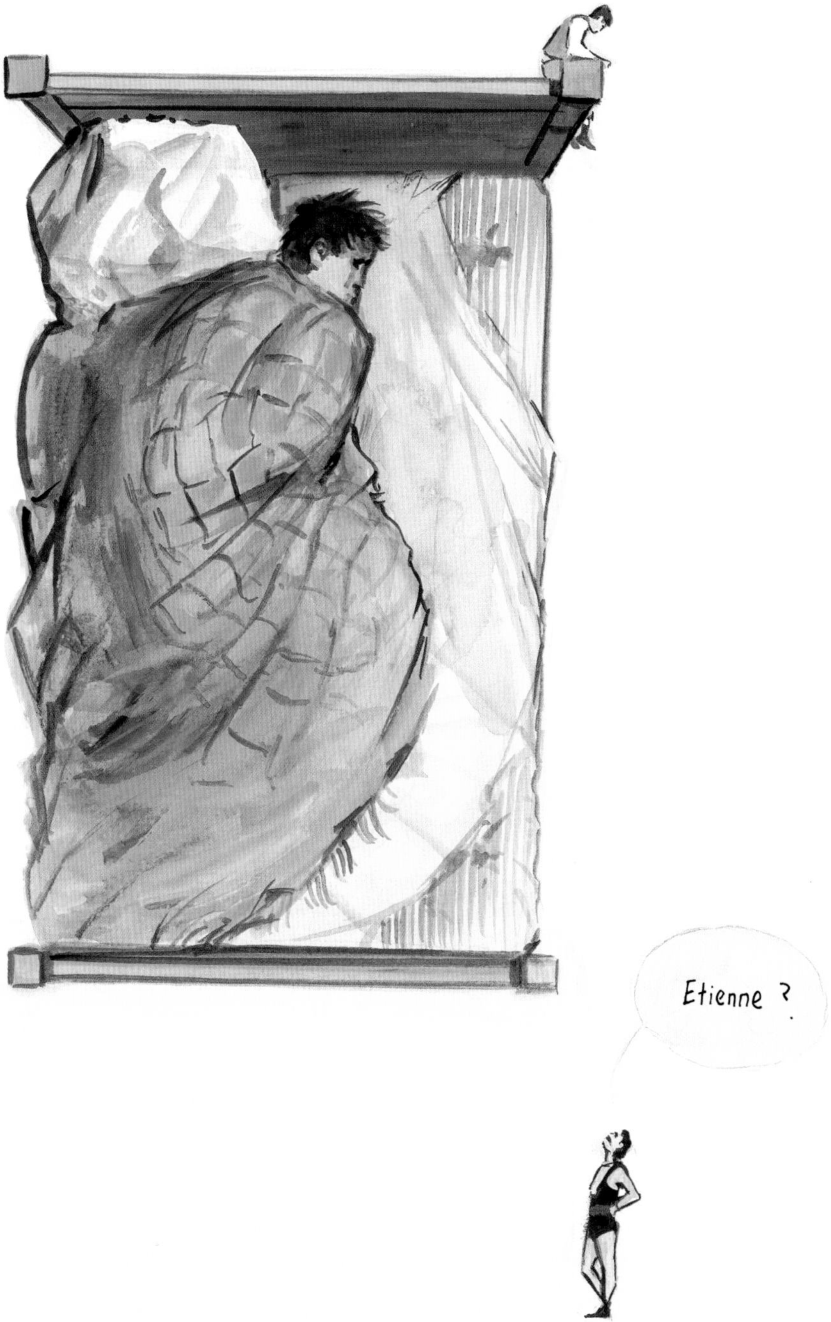
Etienne ?

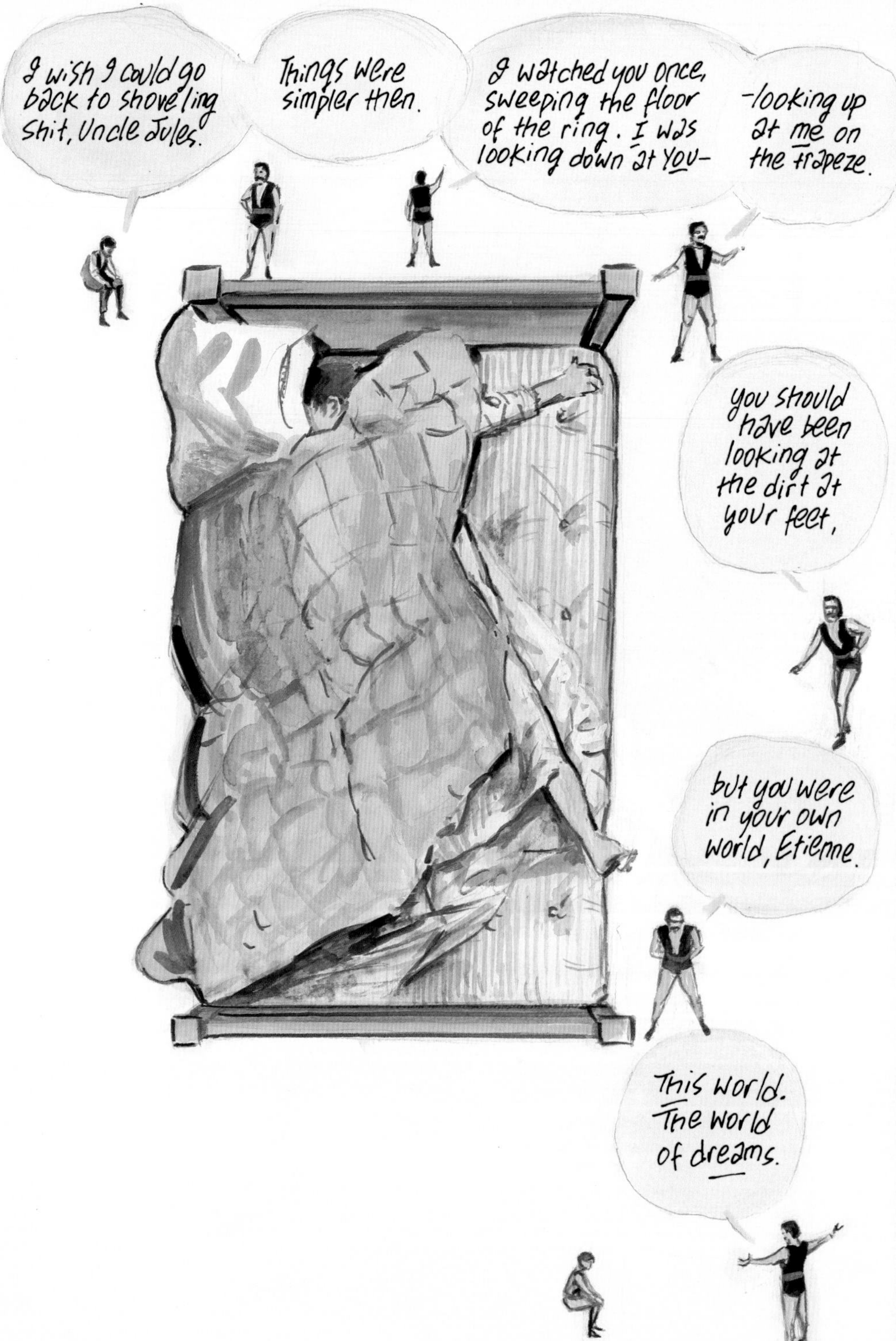
I wish I could go back to shoveling shit, Uncle Jules.
Things were simpler then.
I watched you once, sweeping the floor of the ring. I was looking down at you-
-looking up at me on the trapeze.
you should have been looking at the dirt at your feet,
but you were in your own world, Etienne.
This world. The world of dreams.

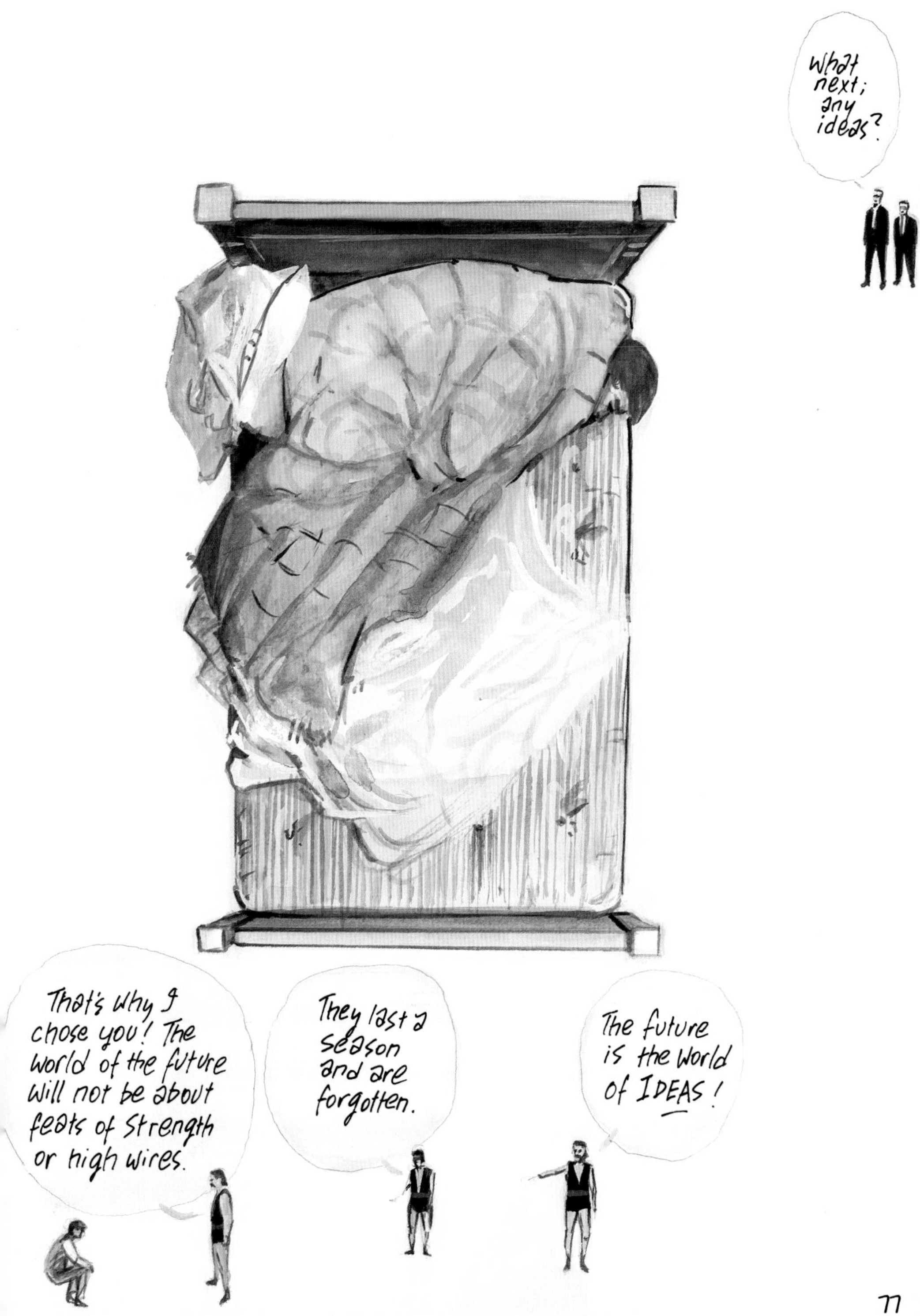
What next; any ideas?
That's why I chose you! The world of the future will not be about feats of strength or high wires.
They last a season and are forgotten.
The future is the world of IDEAS!

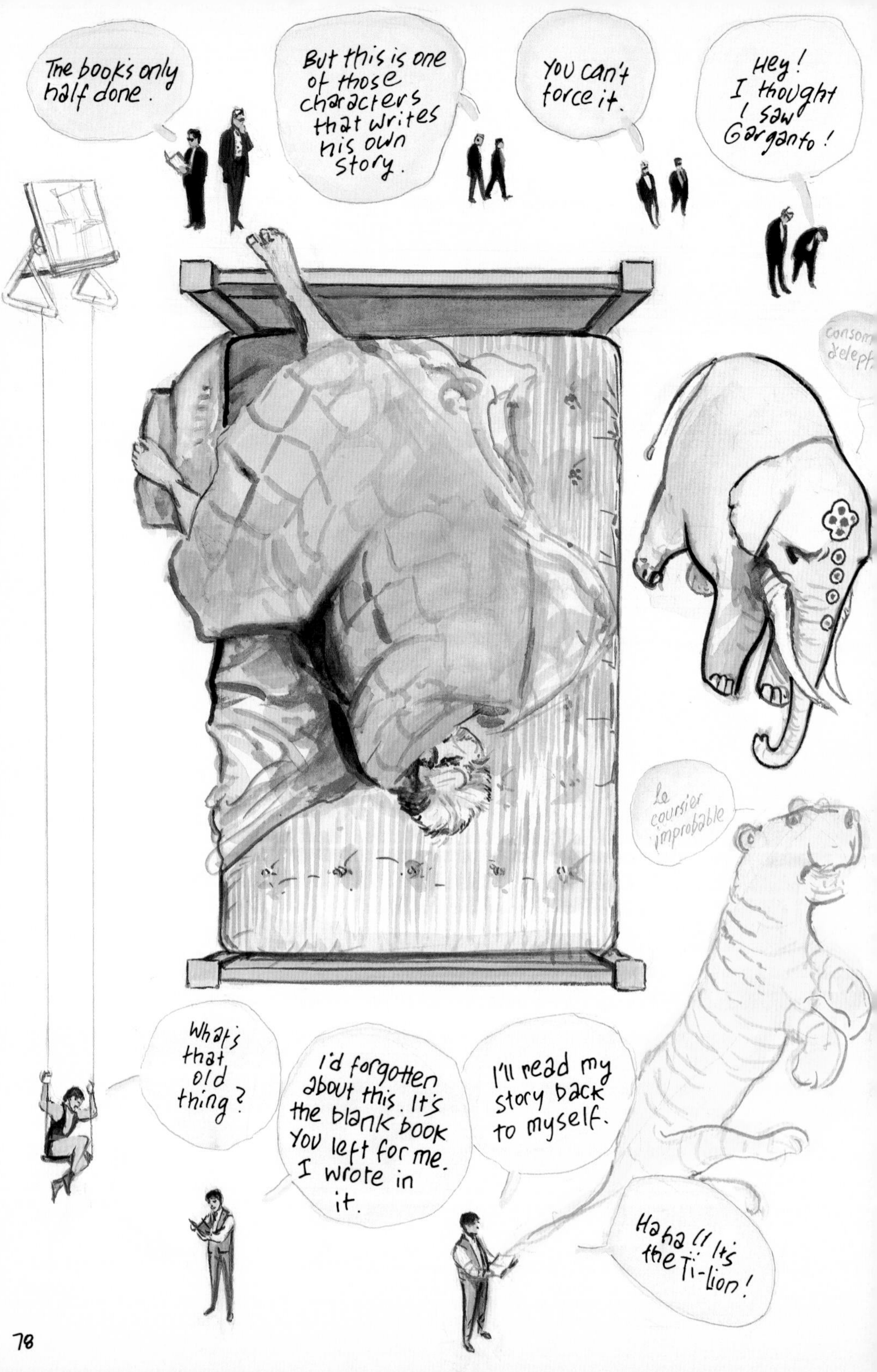
The book's only half done.
But this is one of those characters that writes his own story.
You can't force it.
Hey! I thought I saw Garganto!
consom d'elept.
le coursier improbable
What's that old thing?
I'd forgotten about this. It's the blank book you left for me. I wrote in it.
I'll read my story back to myself.
Haha!! It's the Ti-lion!

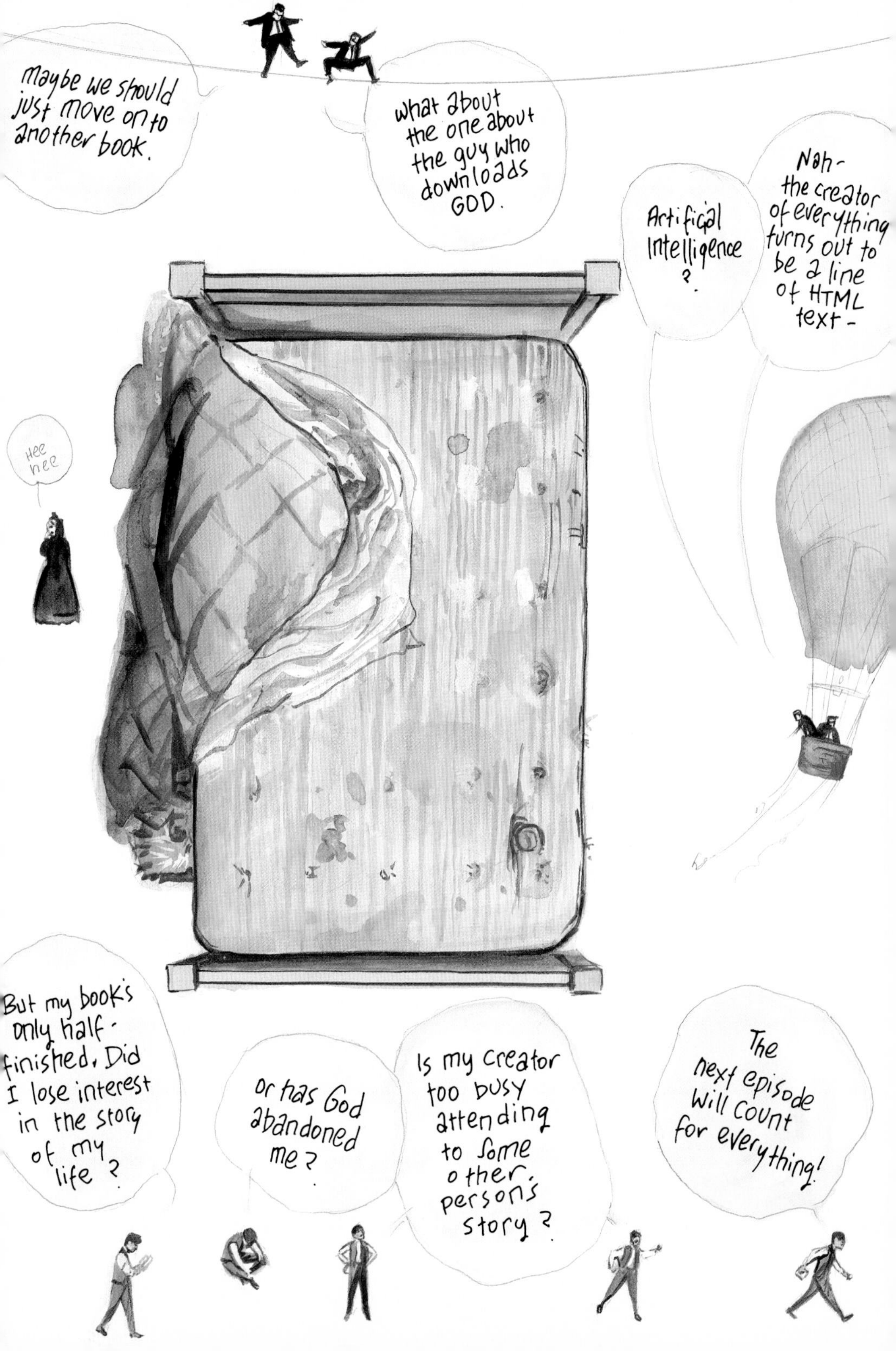
maybe we should just move on to another book.
what about the one about the guy who downloads GOD.
Artifical Intelligence?
Nah- the creator of everything turns out to be a line of HTML text-
Hee hee
But my book's only half-finished. Did I lose interest in the story of my life?
or has God abandoned me?
Is my creator too busy attending to some other person's story?
The next episode will count for everything!

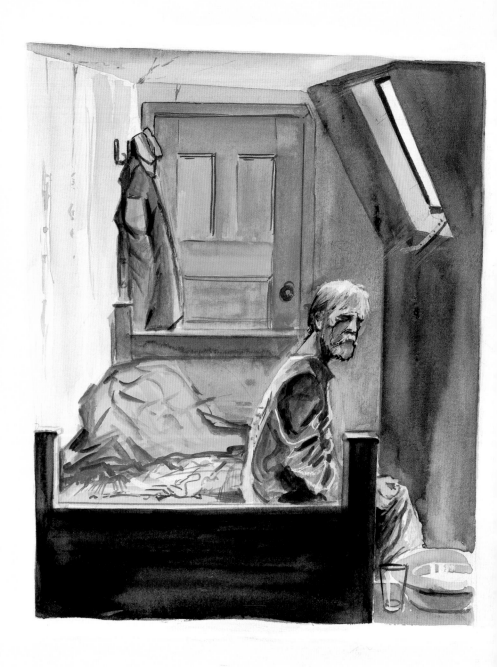

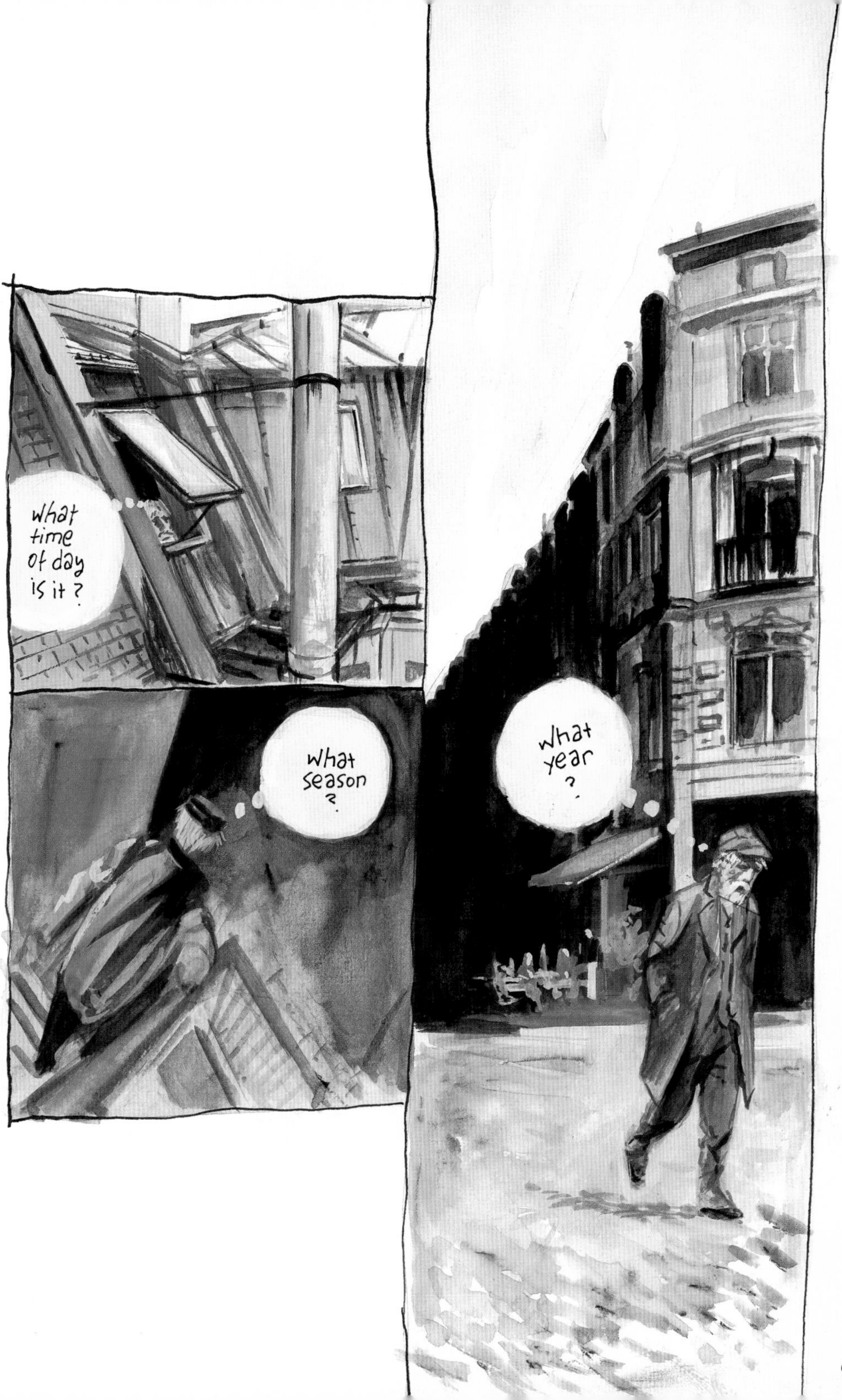
what time of day is it?
what season?
what year?

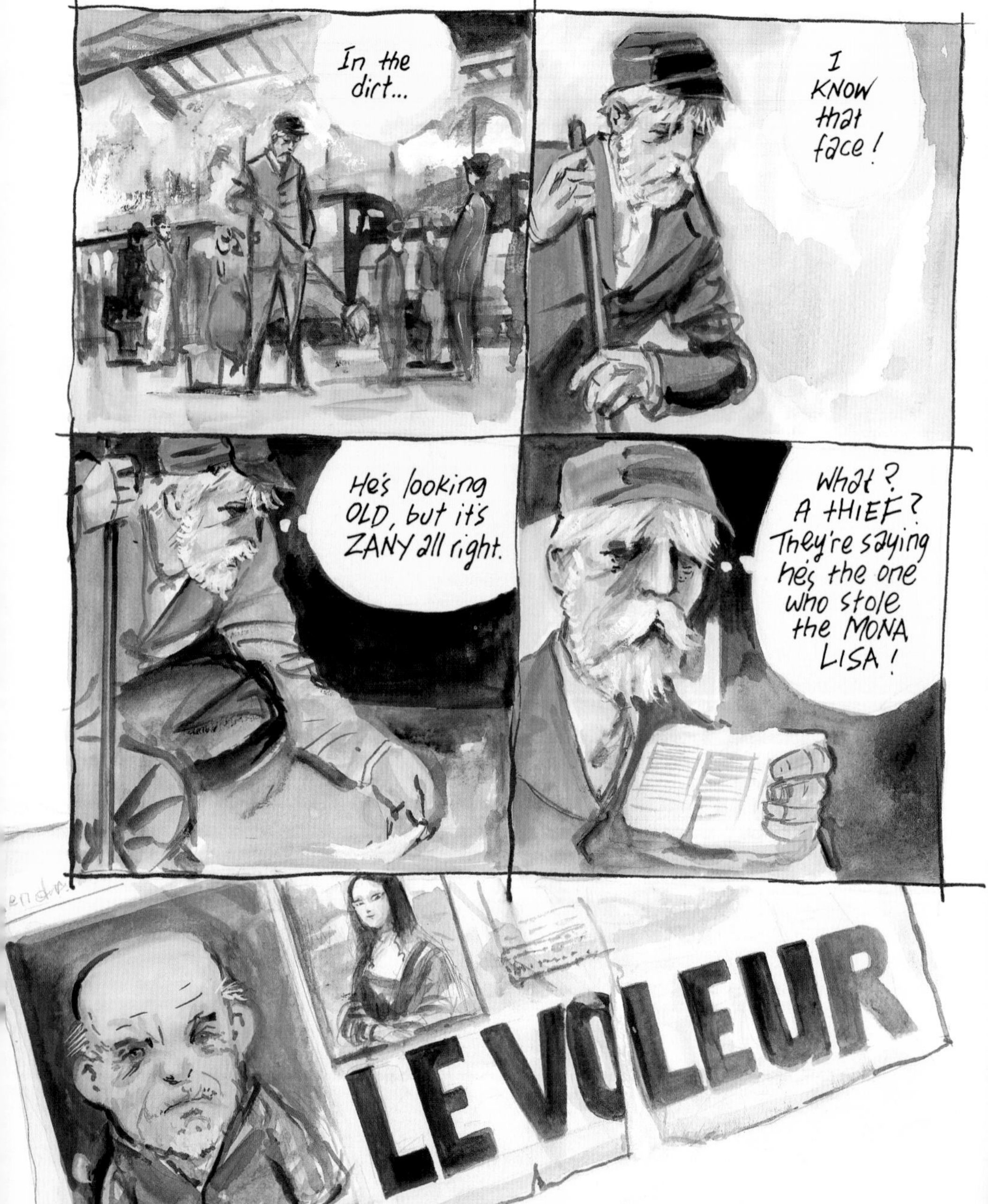
In the dirt...
I KNOW that face!
He's looking OLD, but it's ZANY all right.
What? A THIEF? They're saying he's the one who stole the MONA LISA!
LE VOLEUR

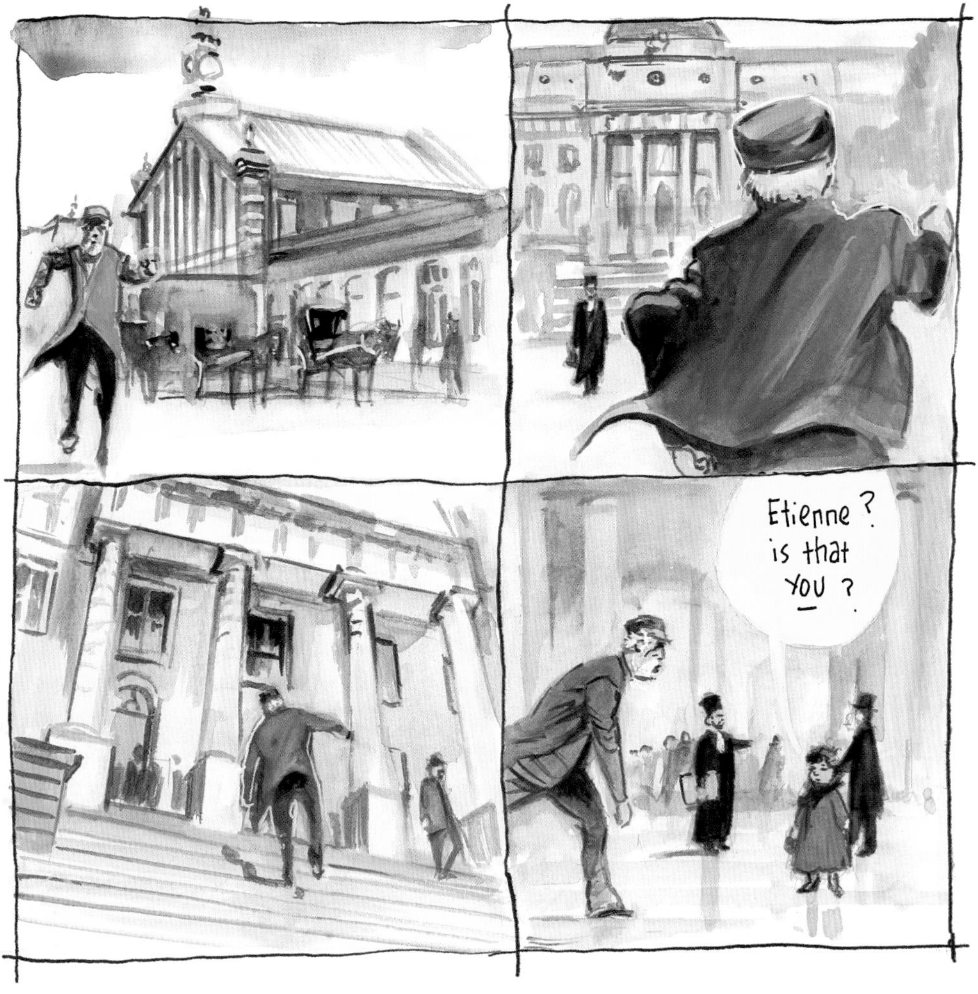
Etienne? is that YOU?

the Imp **TANYA** **ZANY** the Clown

WHO—TANYA? TANYA THE IMP! You were with ZANY under the lion pelt the night we lit up the CIRQUE D'HIVER!

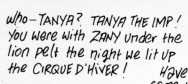

Have you come to show Zany a friendly face in the gallery?

Etienne, It's more than that. I believe I am the cause of his trouble.

Zany and I fell in love all those years ago while practicing our lion act. But we lost touch with each other after I decided not to go to England with all of you.

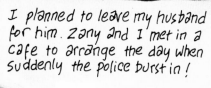

In time I was married to little Pierre Pouce, who left performing and made a lot of money buying and selling Impressionist landscapes. But recently by chance Zany has come back into my life and our love is rekindled.

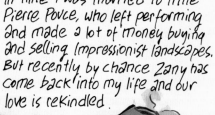

I planned to leave my husband for him. Zany and I met in a cafe to arrange the day when suddenly the police burst in!

Pierre Pouce the **Lilliputian**

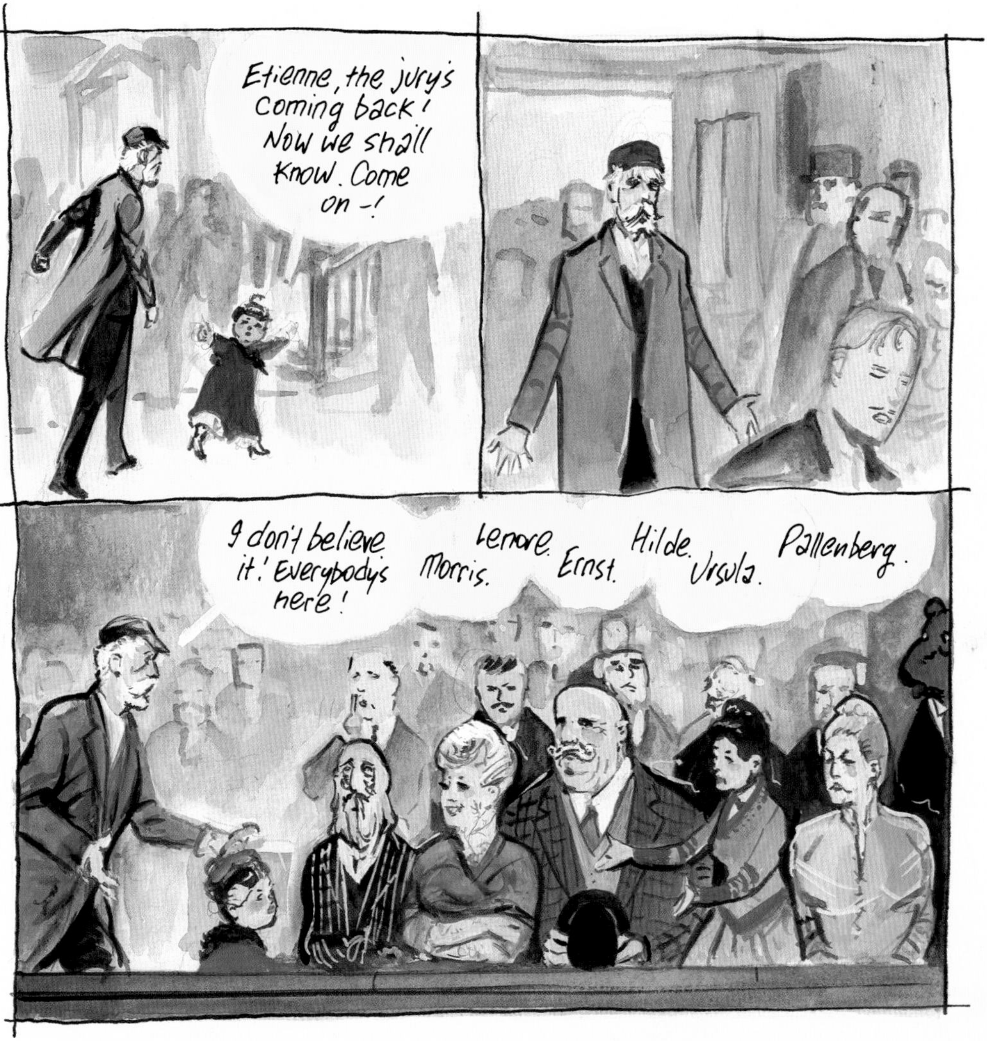
Etienne, the jury's coming back! Now we shall know. Come on -!
I don't believe it! Everybody's here!
Lenore.
Morris.
Ernst.
Hilde.
Ursula.
Pallenberg.

The former circus performer known as Zany the Clown has been presented to the court d' assises, on a single count, that on or about the 21st of August 1911 he feloniously did steal, take and carry away the famous painting by Leonardo, the *Mona Lisa*, from the Musée du Louvre.

Gentlemen of the jury, you have heard how Louis Béroud entered the museum with permission to photograph the *Mona Lisa* and of how he found it to be missing, the only physical evidence of its theft being the remaining precious wooden frame from which it had been hacked.

You have heard from Monsieur Homolle, director of the Louvre, that Zany the Clown was personally employed by him along with three other qualified Italian tradesmen, to construct glass coverings to protect the museum's most precious works of art against vandalism. The accused himself has demonstrated that he has an extensive understanding of the floor plans of the premises. It is not far-fetched to presume therefore that he concealed himself therein on the night prior to the theft. Furthermore, he is unable to otherwise account for himself.

Most importantly, you have heard testimony from fingerprint expert Alphonse Bertillon, who has identified a single set of prints on the frame found by the police. They are the prints of the accused.

Lastly, there is the testimony of witnesses as to the monetary position of the accused and his struggle to accommodate the lavish lifestyle of his illicit lover, a fellow circus performer who once went by the name of Tanya the Imp. There you have the motive.

Gentlemen, this man is an enemy of France. He refuses to identify the location of the painting, guaranteeing the success of his fellow conspirators. He had opportunity, he had motive, and most of all the only piece of physical evidence points to him as the perpetrator.

I call for a finding of guilt.

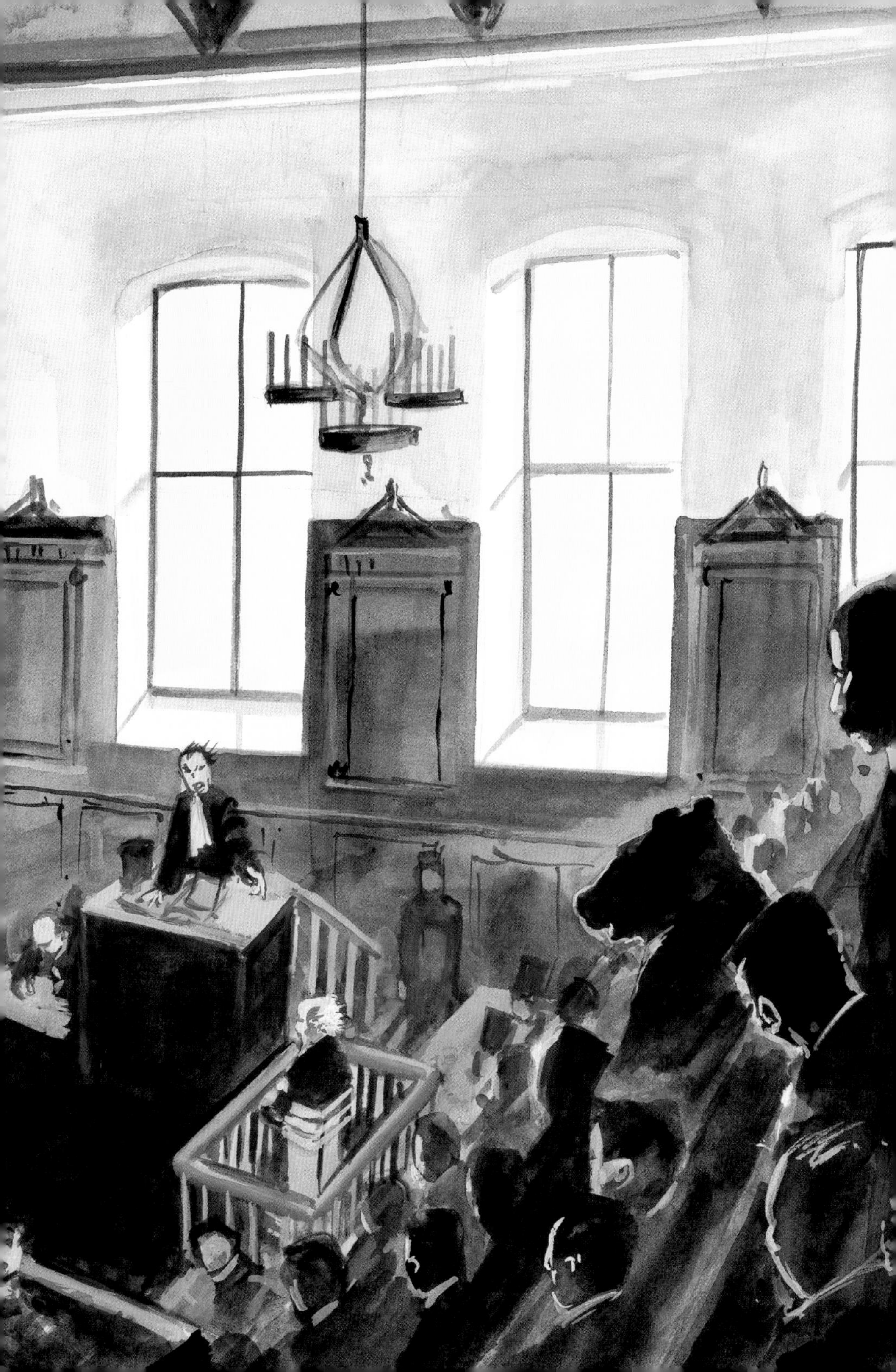

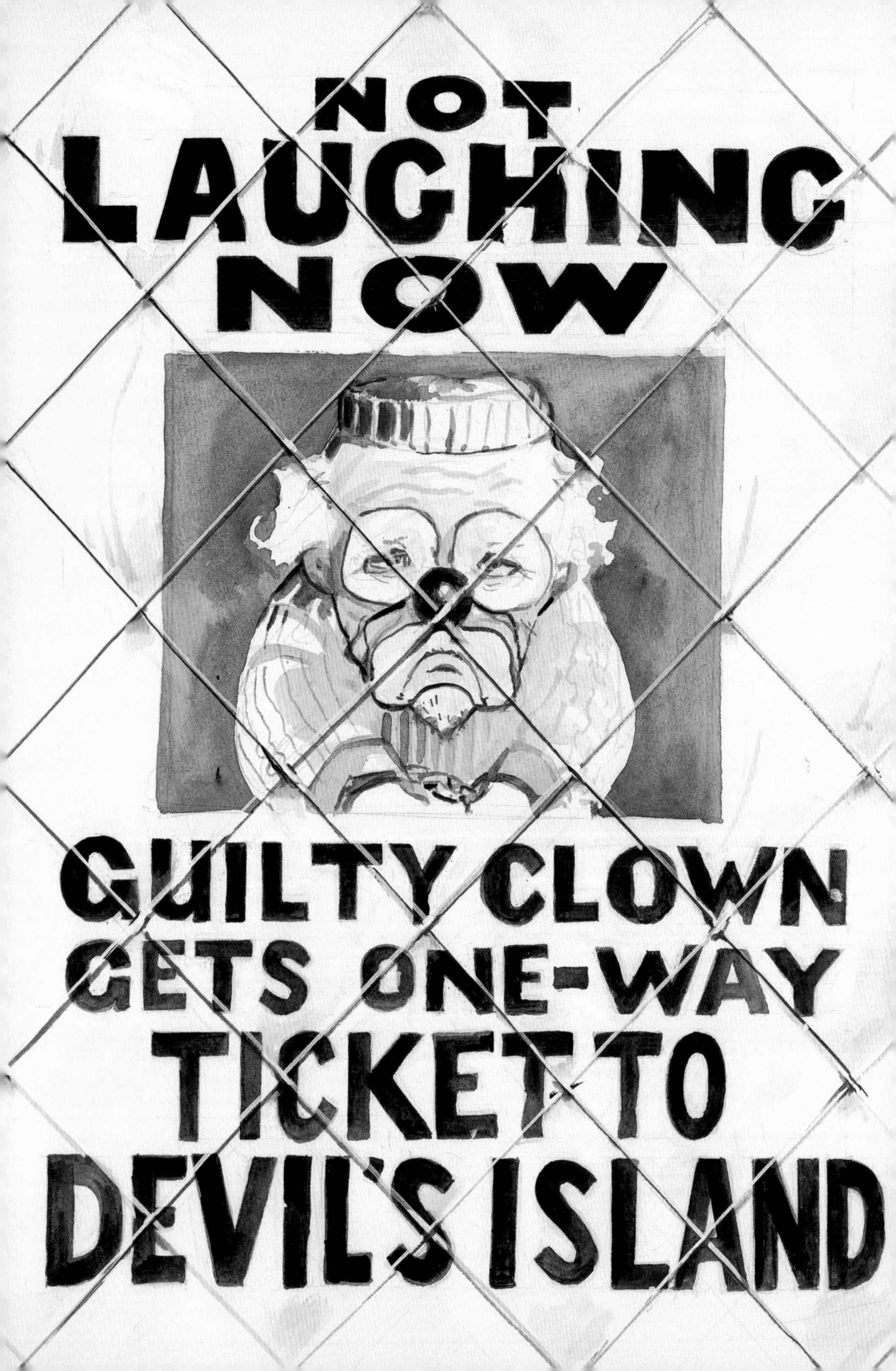
NOT
LAUGHING
NOW
GUILTY CLOWN
GETS ONE-WAY
TICKET TO
DEVIL'S ISLAND

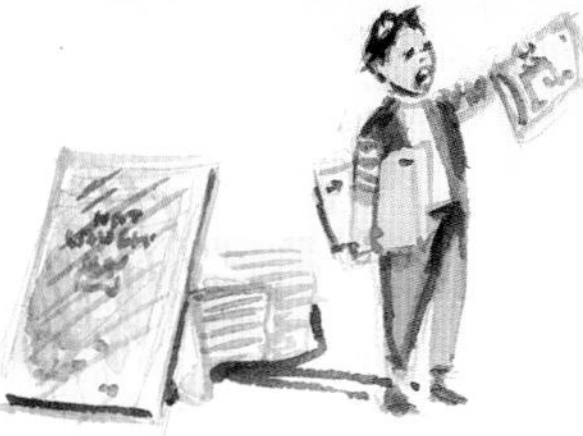

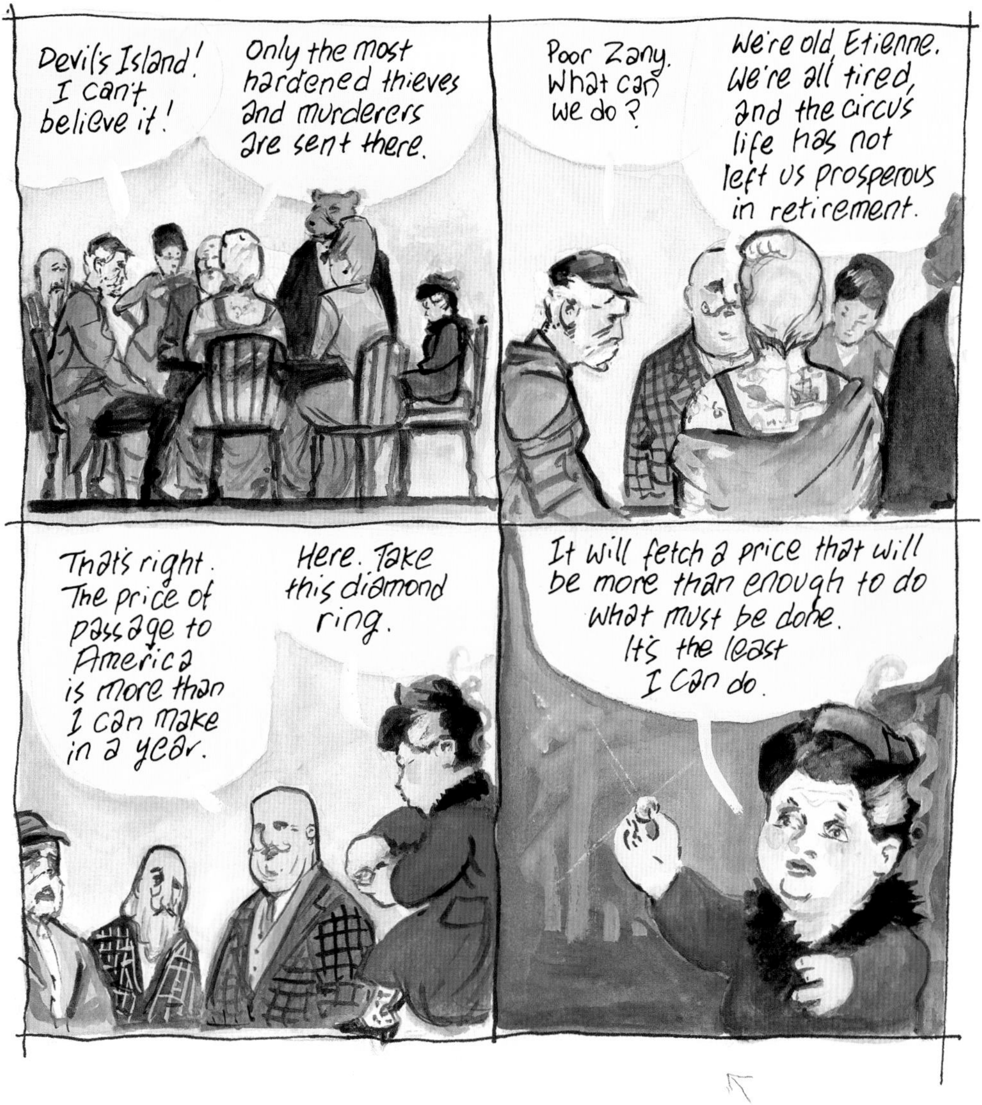

Devil's Island! I can't believe it!
Only the most hardened thieves and murderers are sent there.
Poor Zany. What can we do?
We're old, Etienne. We're all tired, and the circus life has not left us prosperous in retirement.
That's right. The price of passage to America is more than I can make in a year.
Here. Take this diamond ring.
It will fetch a price that will be more than enough to do what must be done. It's the least I can do.

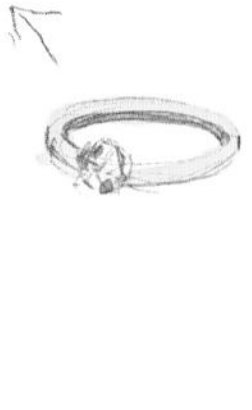

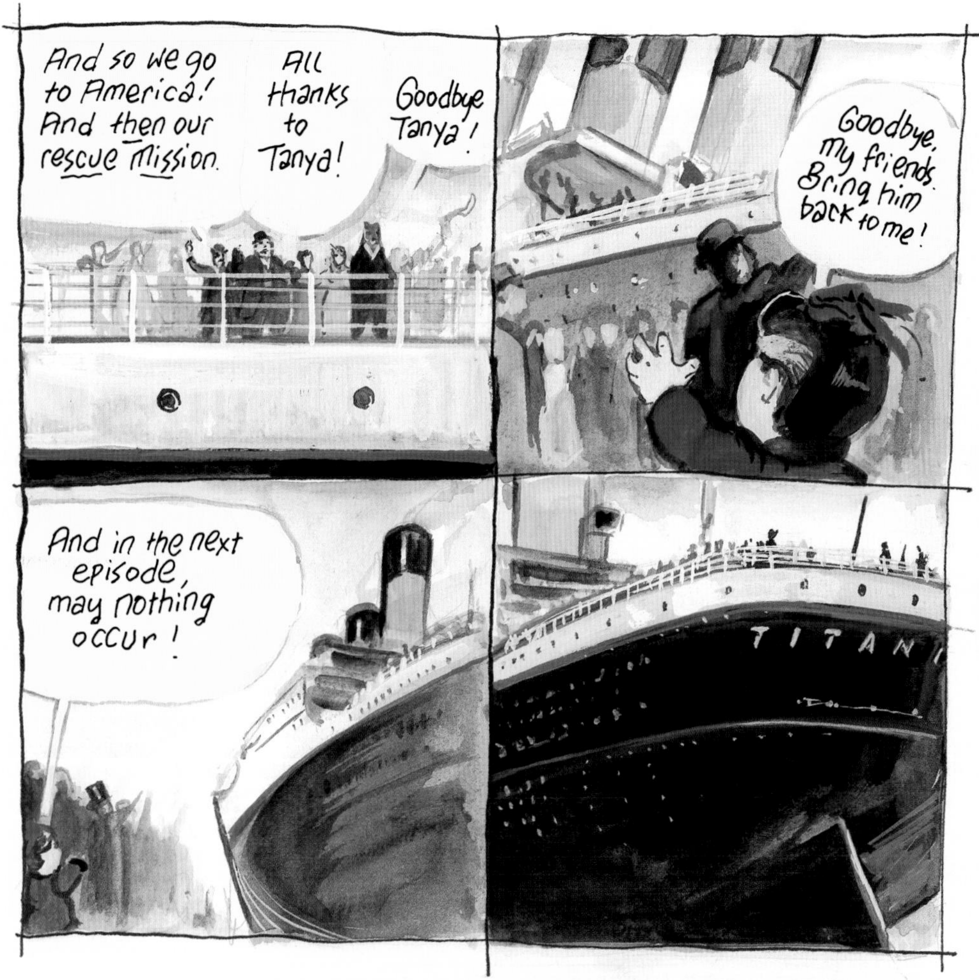
And so we go to America! And then our rescue mission.
All thanks to Tanya!
Goodbye Tanya!
Goodbye, my friends. Bring him back to me!
And in the next episode, may nothing occur!
TITAN

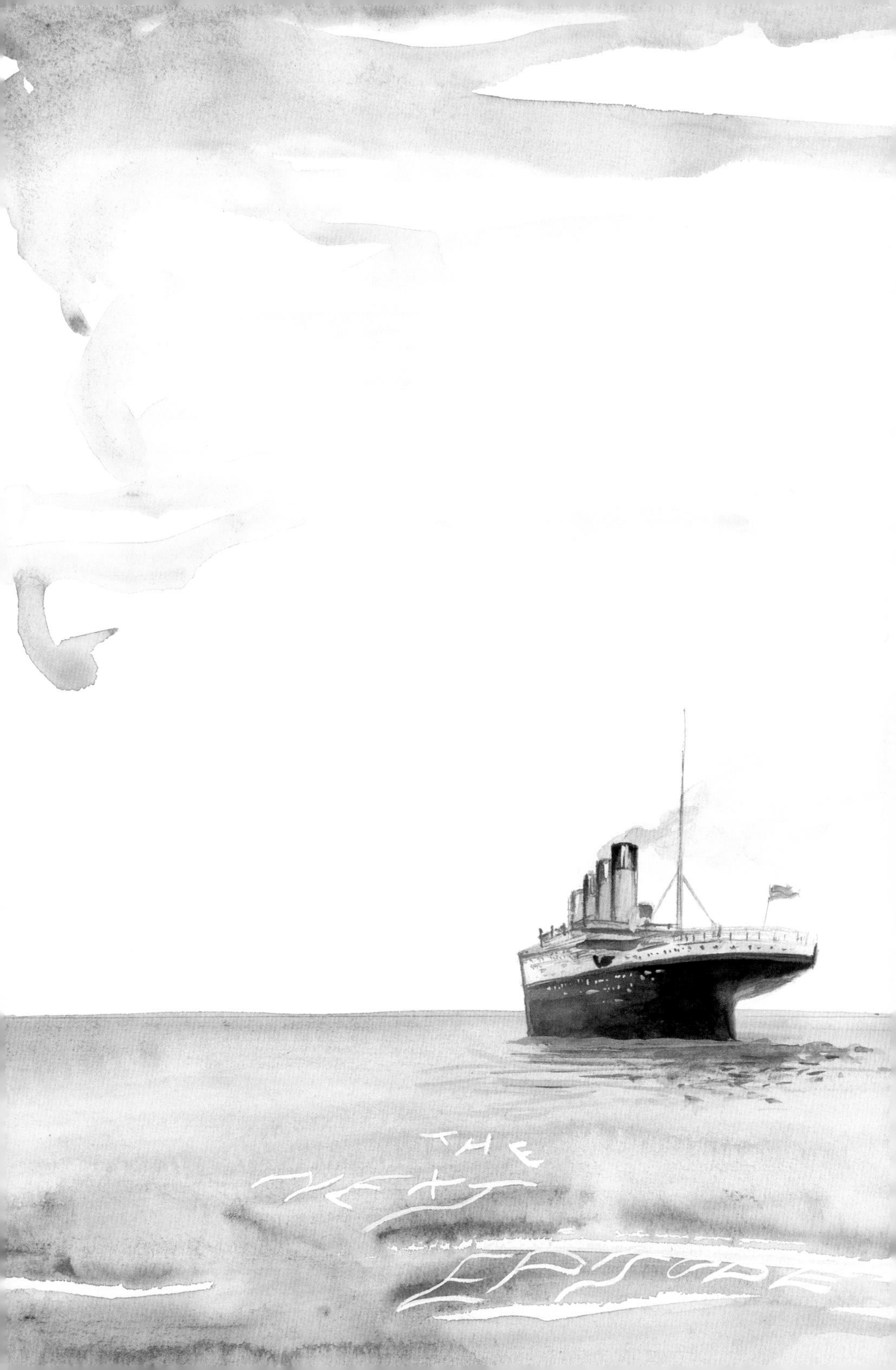
THE
NEXT
EPISODE

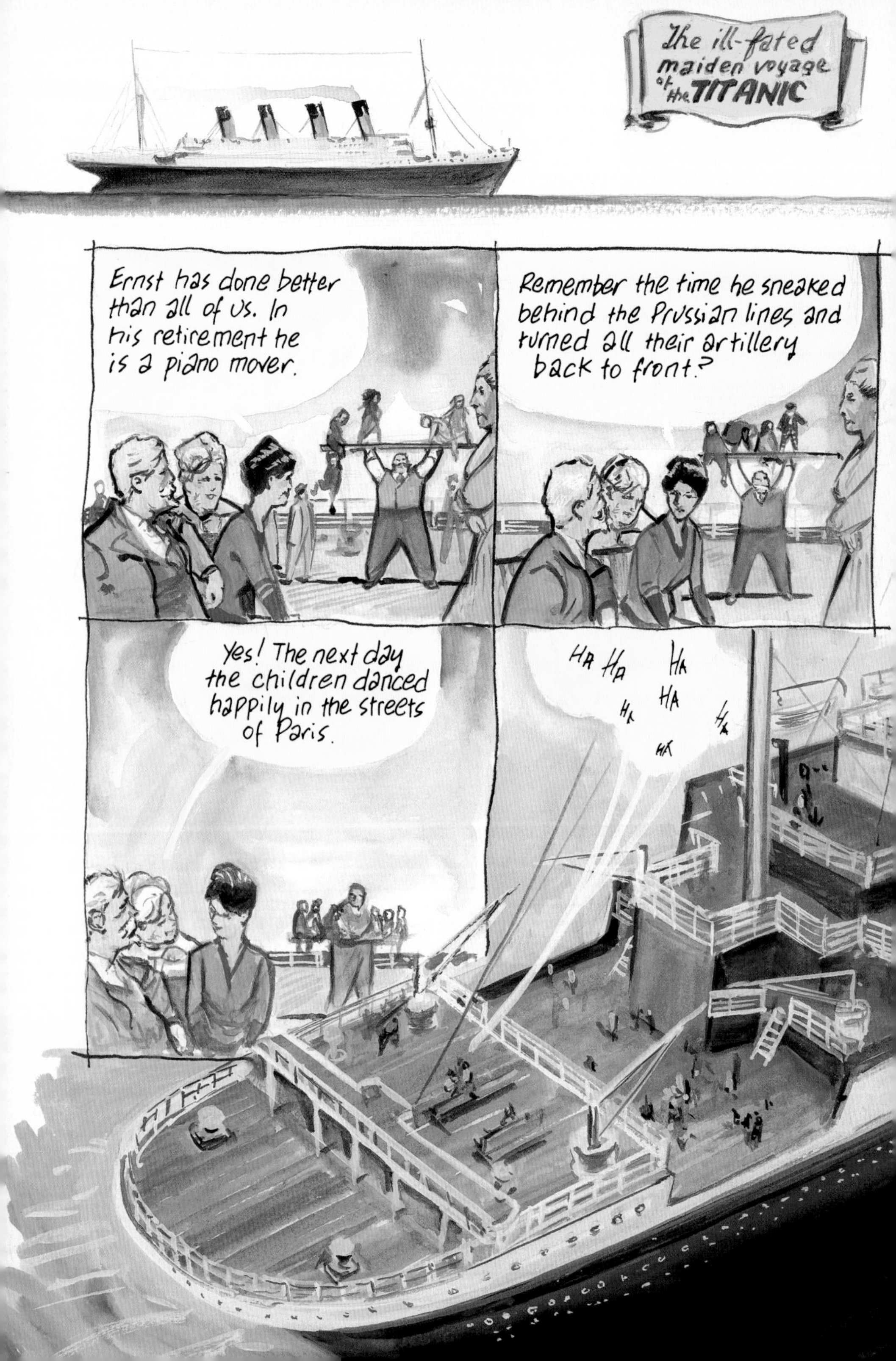
The ill-fated maiden voyage of the TITANIC
Ernst has done better than all of us. In his retirement he is a piano mover.
Remember the time he sneaked behind the Prussian lines and turned all their artillery back to front?
Yes! The next day the children danced happily in the streets of Paris.
HA HA HA HA HA HA HA

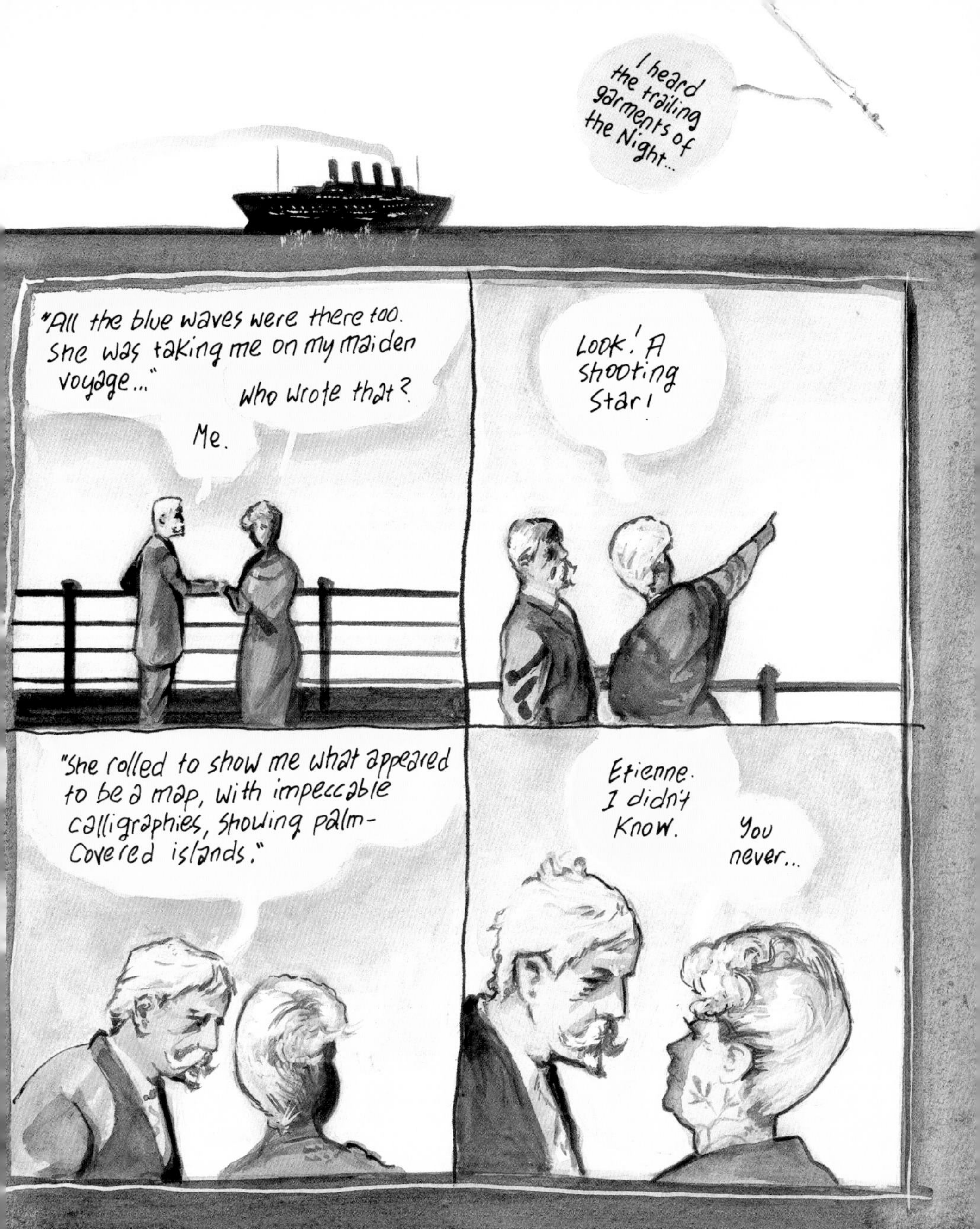
I heard the trailing garments of the Night...
"All the blue waves were there too. She was taking me on my maiden voyage..."
Who wrote that?
Me.
Look! A shooting star!
"She rolled to show me what appeared to be a map, with impeccable calligraphies, showing palm-covered islands."
Etienne. I didn't know.
You never...

I heard the sounds of sorrow and delight,
The manifold, soft chimes,
That fill the haunted chambers of the Night
Like some old poet's rhymes.
— Longfellow

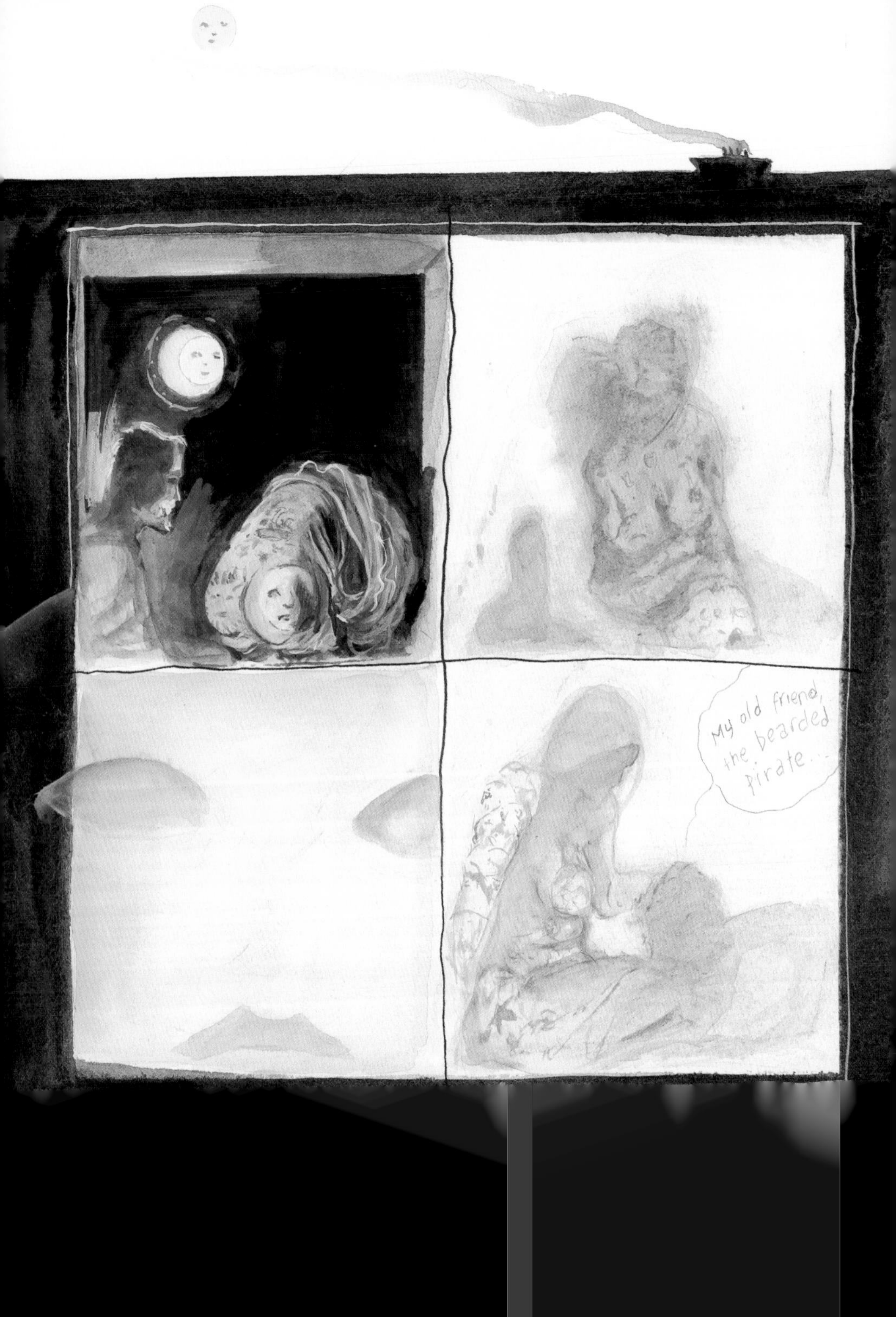
My old friend, the bearded pirate...

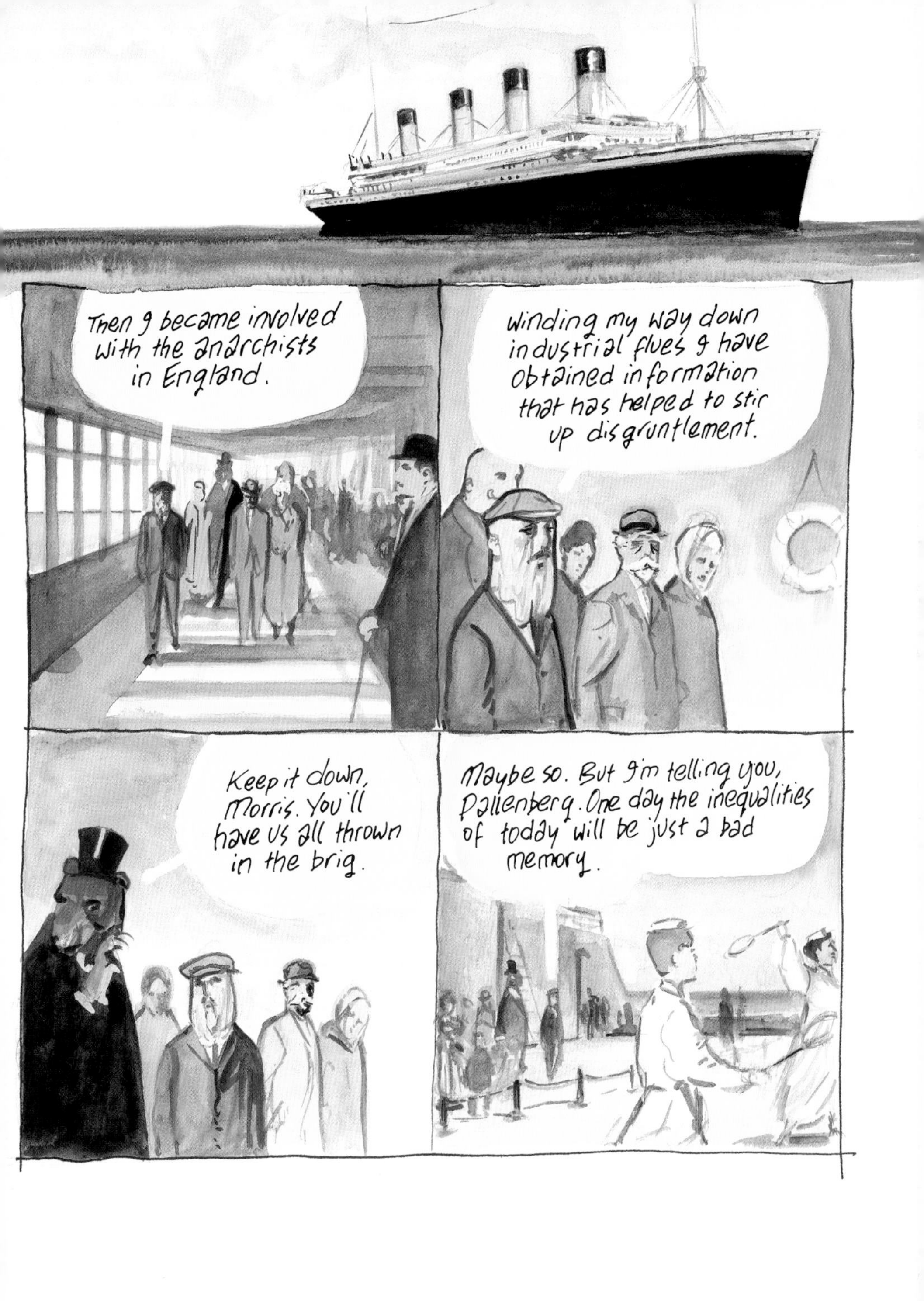
Then I became involved with the anarchists in England.
Winding my way down industrial flues I have obtained information that has helped to stir up disgruntlement.
Keep it down, Morris. You'll have us all thrown in the brig.
Maybe so. But I'm telling you, Pallenberg. One day the inequalities of today will be just a bad memory.

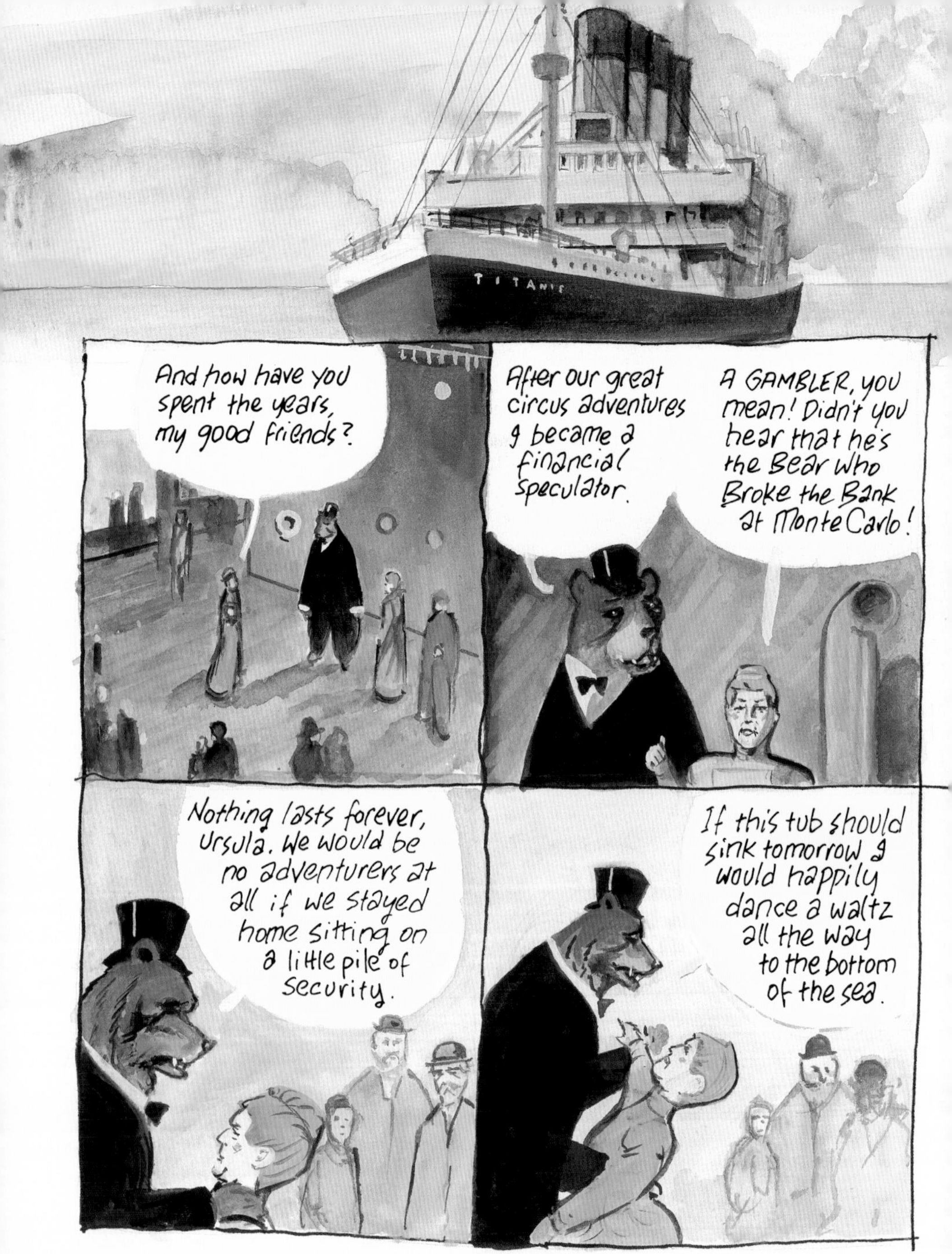
T I T A N I C
And how have you spent the years, my good friends?
After our great circus adventures I became a financial speculator.
A GAMBLER, you mean! Didn't you hear that he's the Bear Who Broke the Bank at Monte Carlo!
Nothing lasts forever, Ursula. We would be no adventurers at all if we stayed home sitting on a little pile of security.
If this tub should sink tomorrow I would happily dance a waltz all the way to the bottom of the sea.

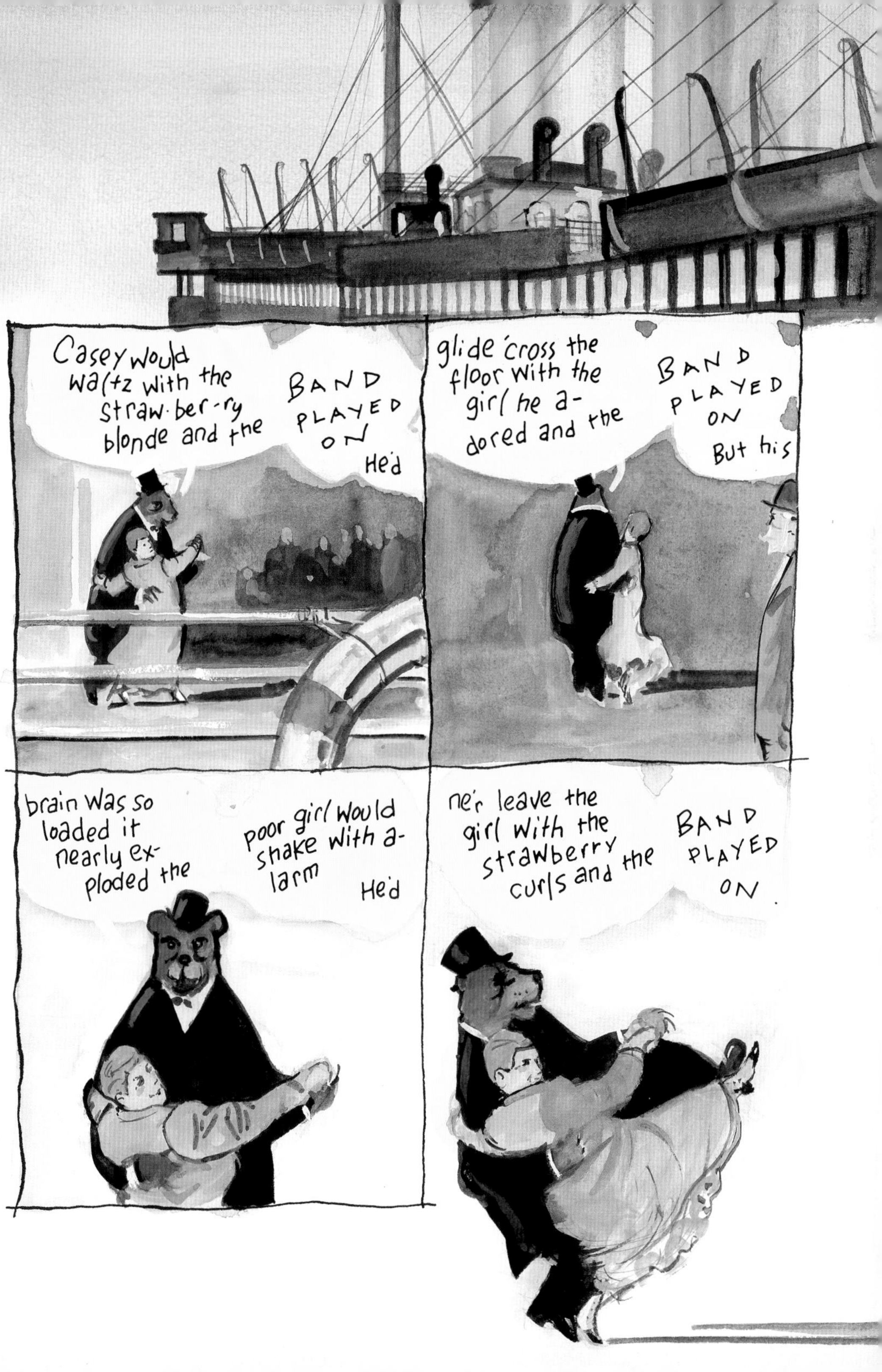

Casey would waltz with the straw-ber-ry blonde and the
BAND PLAYED ON
He'd
glide 'cross the floor with the girl he a-dored and the
BAND PLAYED ON
But his
brain was so loaded it nearly ex-ploded the
poor girl would shake with a-larm
He'd
ne'r leave the girl with the strawberry curls and the
BAND PLAYED ON.

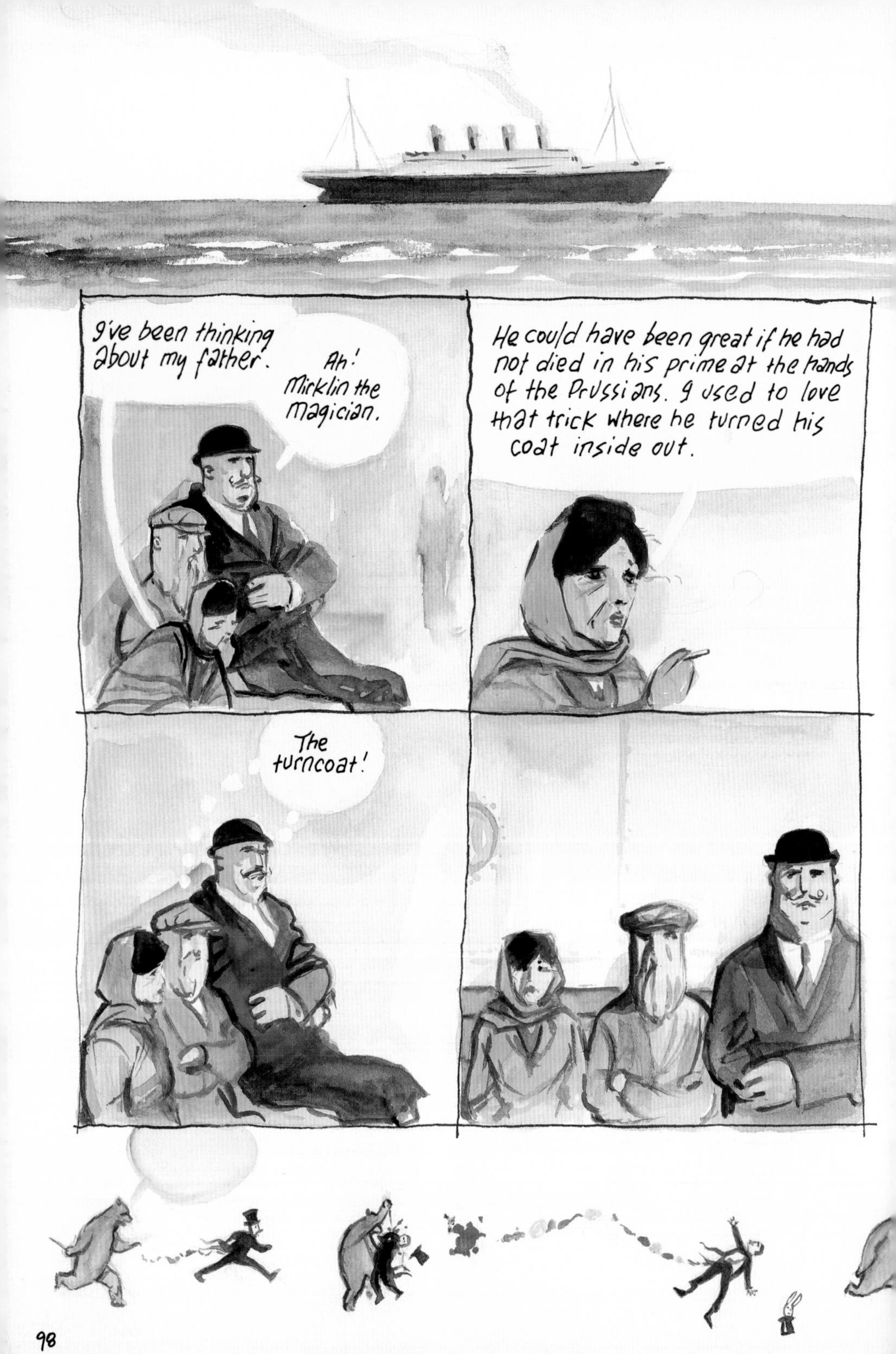
I've been thinking about my father.
Ah! Micklin the Magician.
He could have been great if he had not died in his prime at the hands of the Prussians. I used to love that trick where he turned his coat inside out.
The turncoat!

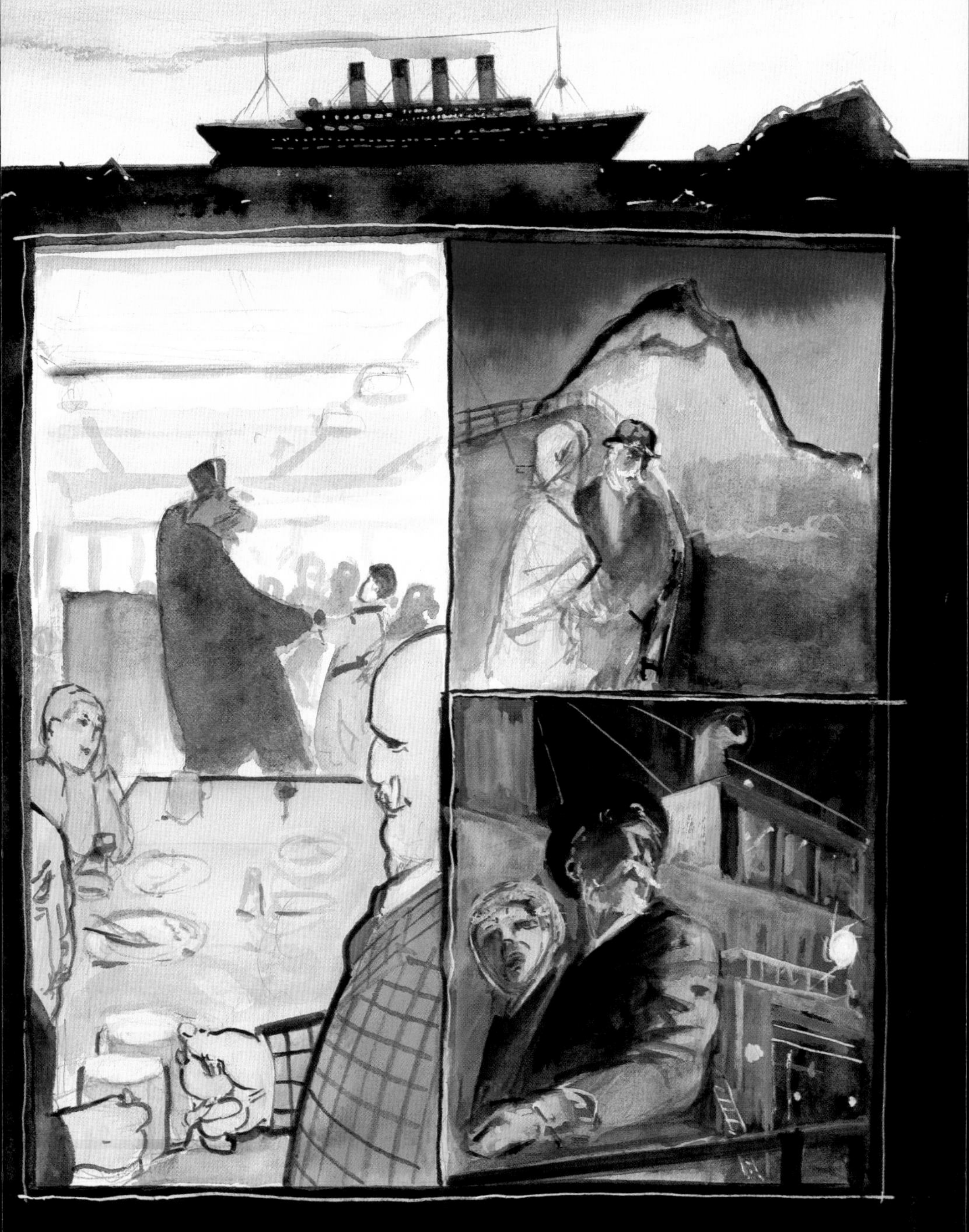

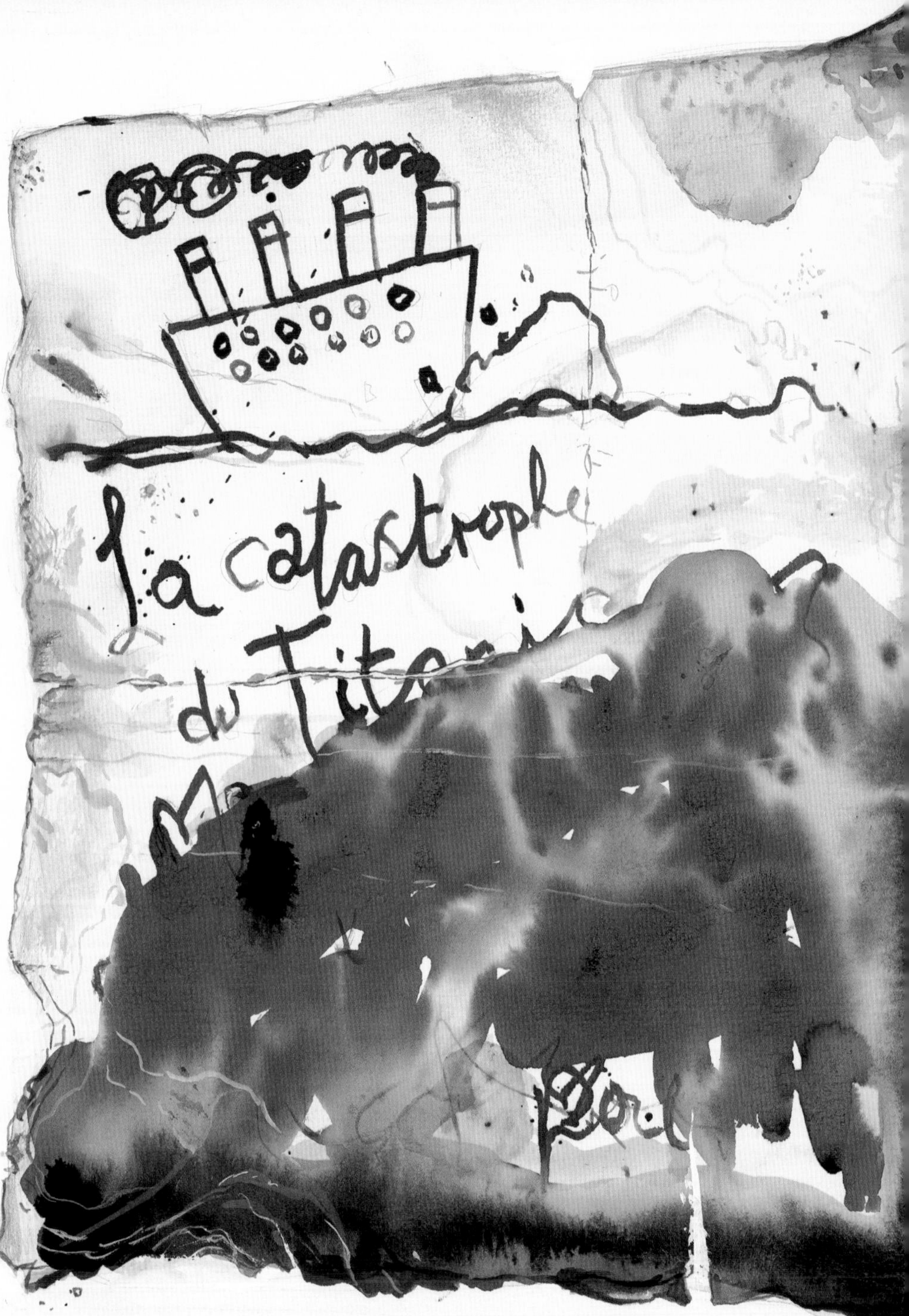
la catastrophe
du Titanic

The severe water damage concentrated at this part of Etienne's diary curiously was not caused during the sinking of the Titanic, but occurred later on Les Iles du Salut.

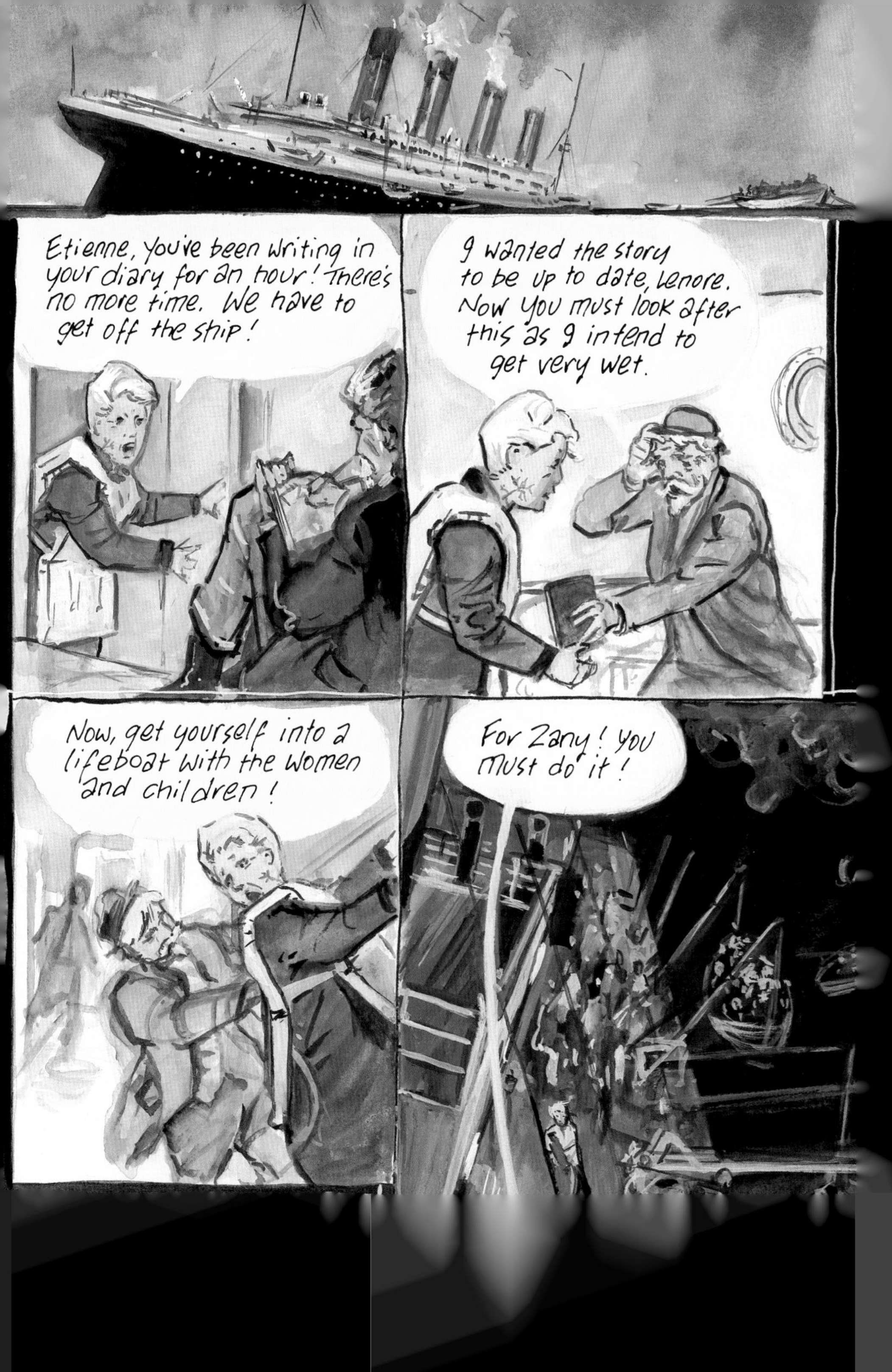
Etienne, you've been writing in your diary for an hour! There's no more time. We have to get off the ship!
I wanted the story to be up to date, Lenore. Now you must look after this as I intend to get very wet.
Now, get yourself into a lifeboat with the women and children!
For Zany! You must do it!

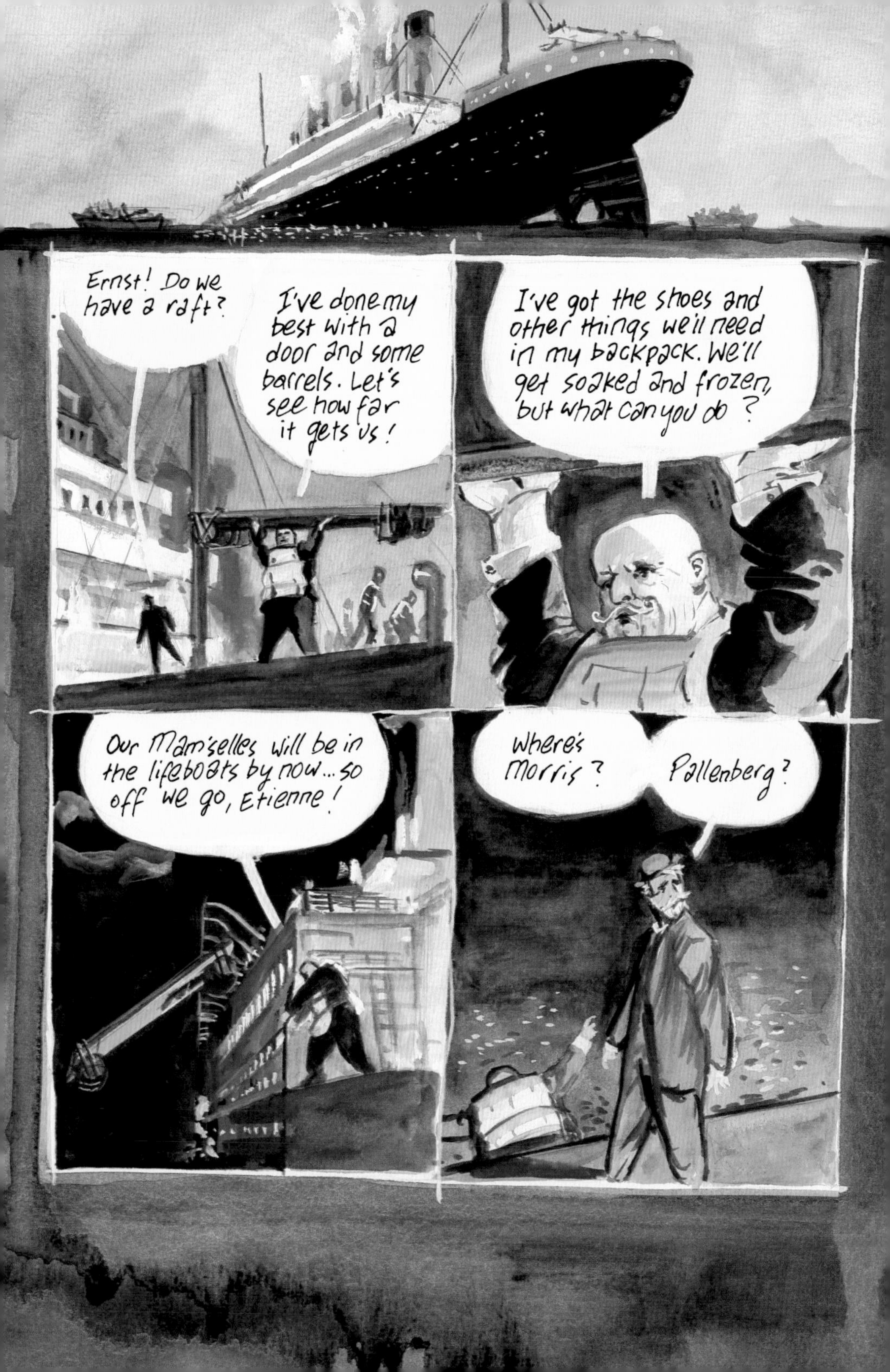
Ernst! Do we have a raft?
I've done my best with a door and some barrels. Let's see how far it gets us!
I've got the shoes and other things we'll need in my backpack. We'll get soaked and frozen, but what can you do?
Our Mam'selles will be in the lifeboats by now... so off we go, Etienne!
Where's Morris?
Pallenberg?

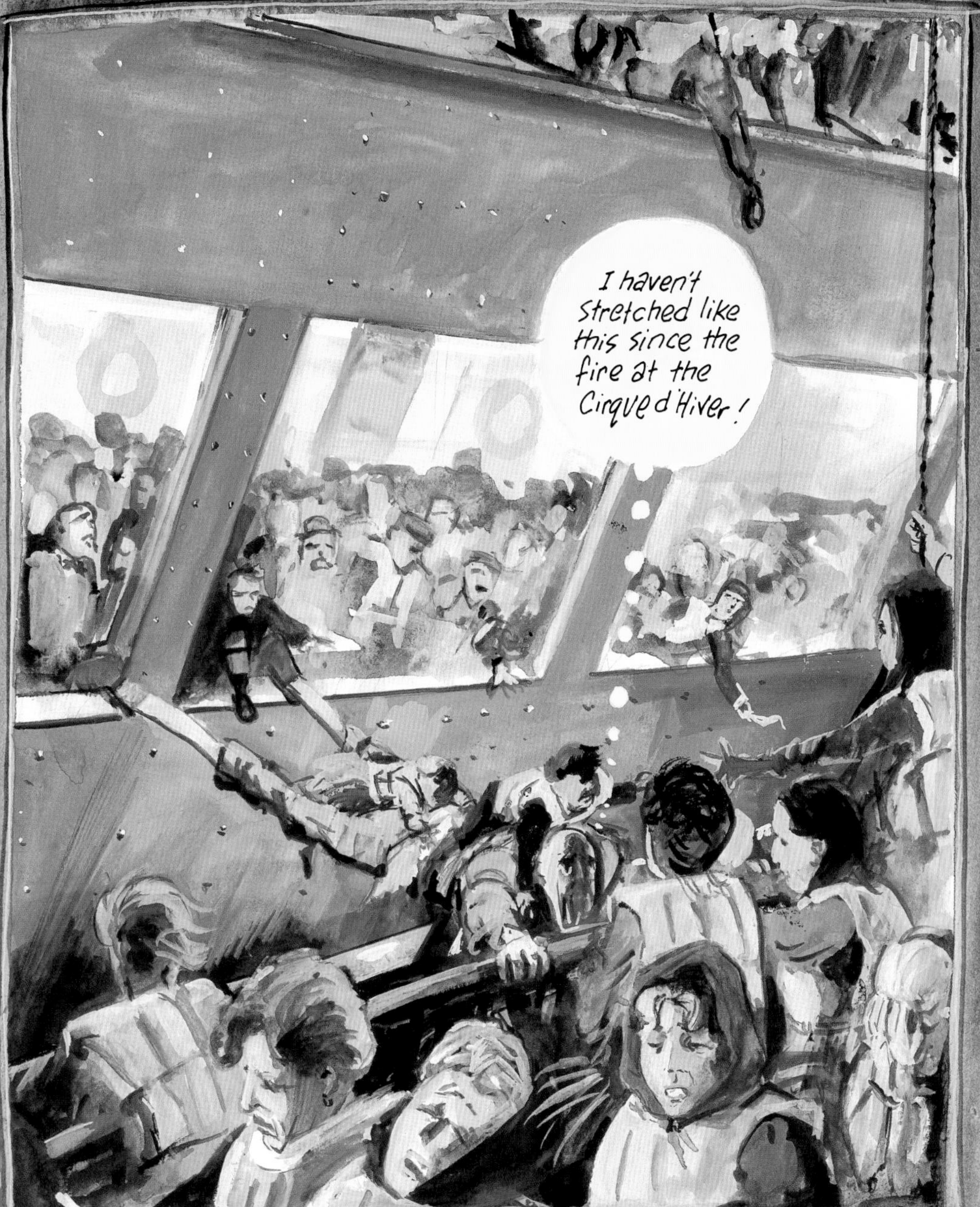
I haven't stretched like this since the fire at the Cirque d'Hiver!

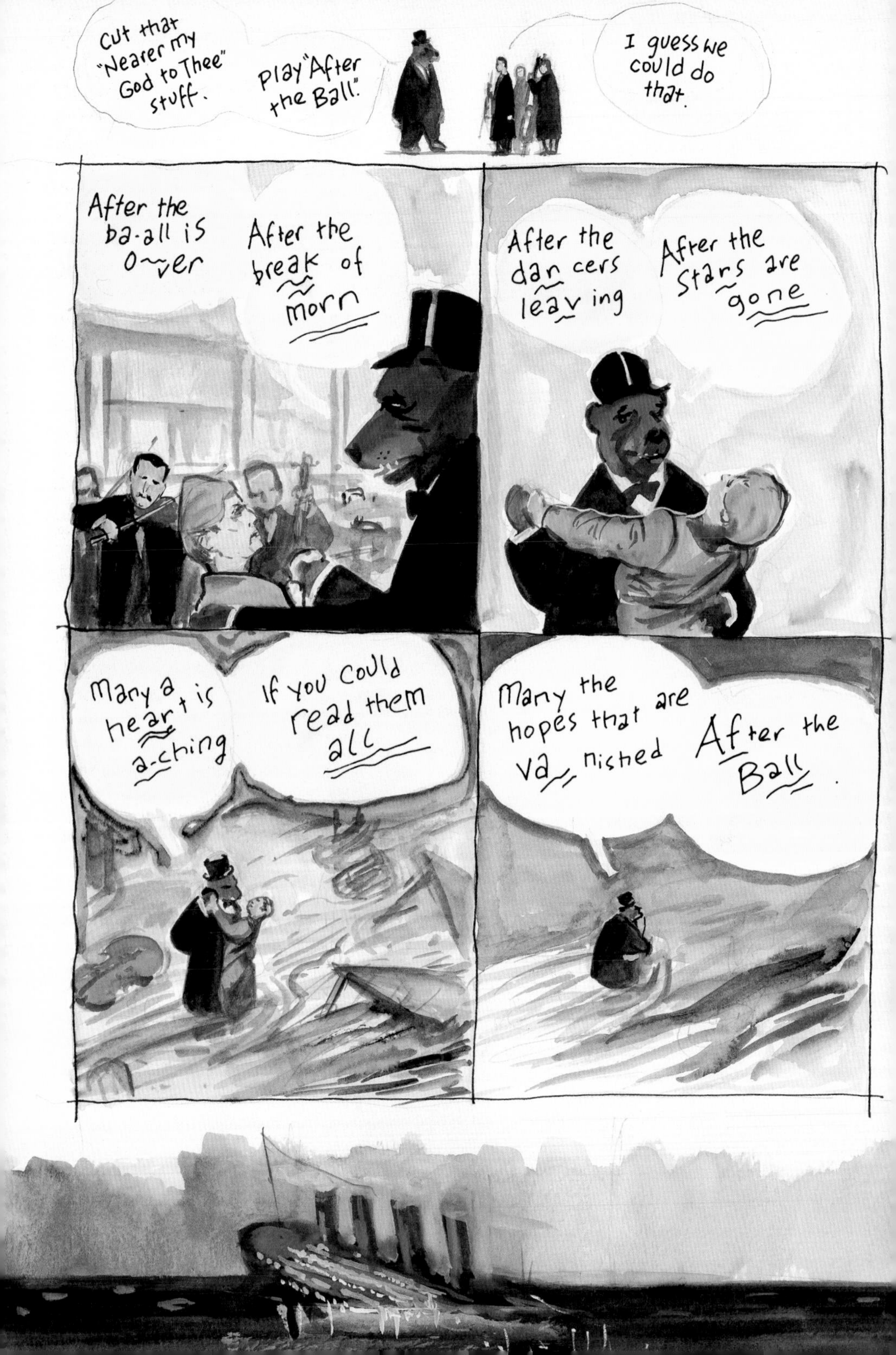
Cut that "Nearer my God to Thee" stuff.
Play "After the Ball."
I guess we could do that.
After the ba-all is o-ver
After the break of morn
After the dan cers leav ing
After the stars are gone
Many a heart is a-ching
If you could read them all
Many the hopes that are va nished After the Ball.

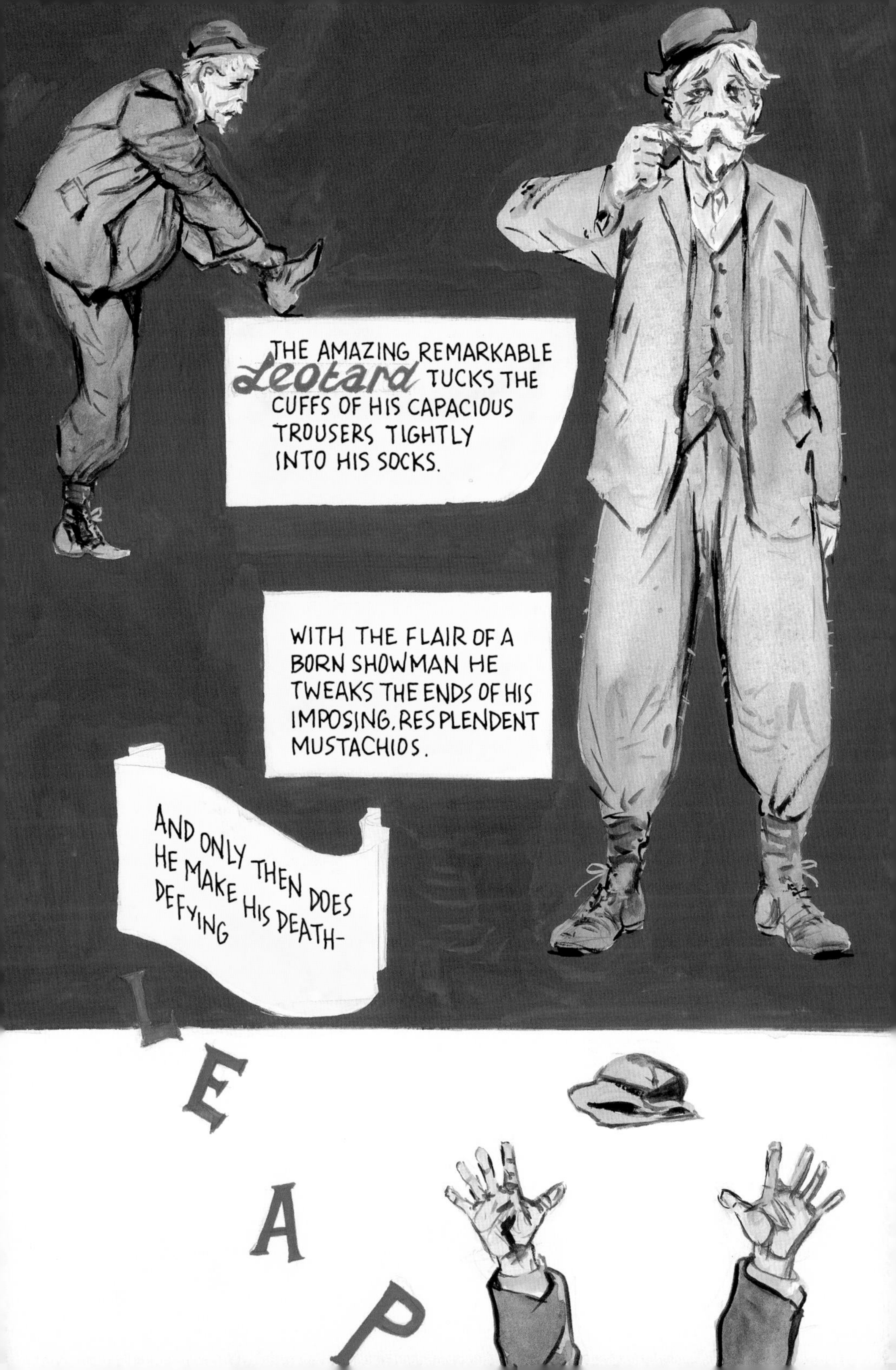
THE AMAZING REMARKABLE Leotard TUCKS THE CUFFS OF HIS CAPACIOUS TROUSERS TIGHTLY INTO HIS SOCKS.
WITH THE FLAIR OF A BORN SHOWMAN HE TWEAKS THE ENDS OF HIS IMPOSING, RESPLENDENT MUSTACHIOS.
AND ONLY THEN DOES HE MAKE HIS DEATH-DEFYING
LEAP

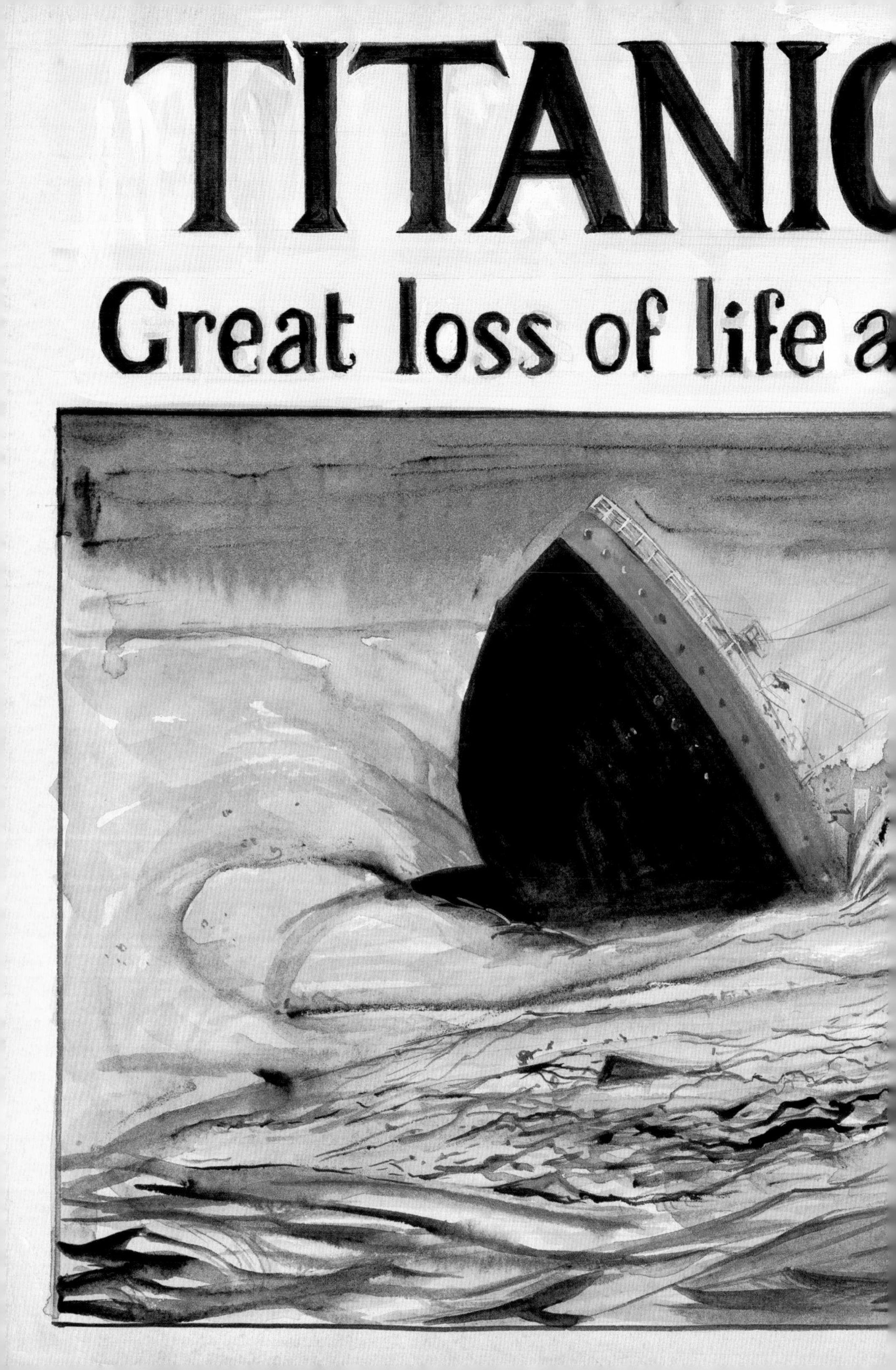
TITANI
Great loss of life a

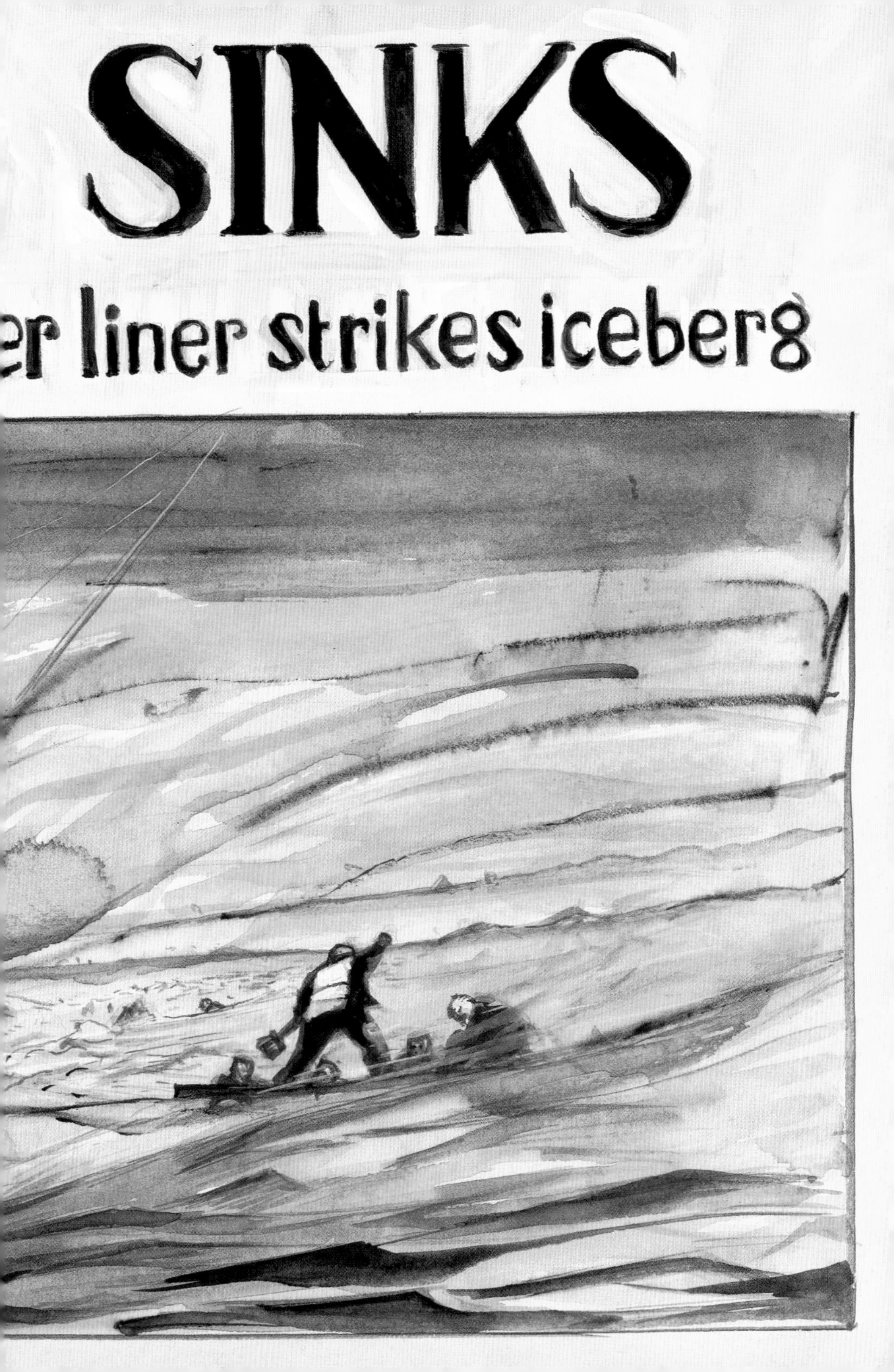
SINKS
er liner strikes iceberg

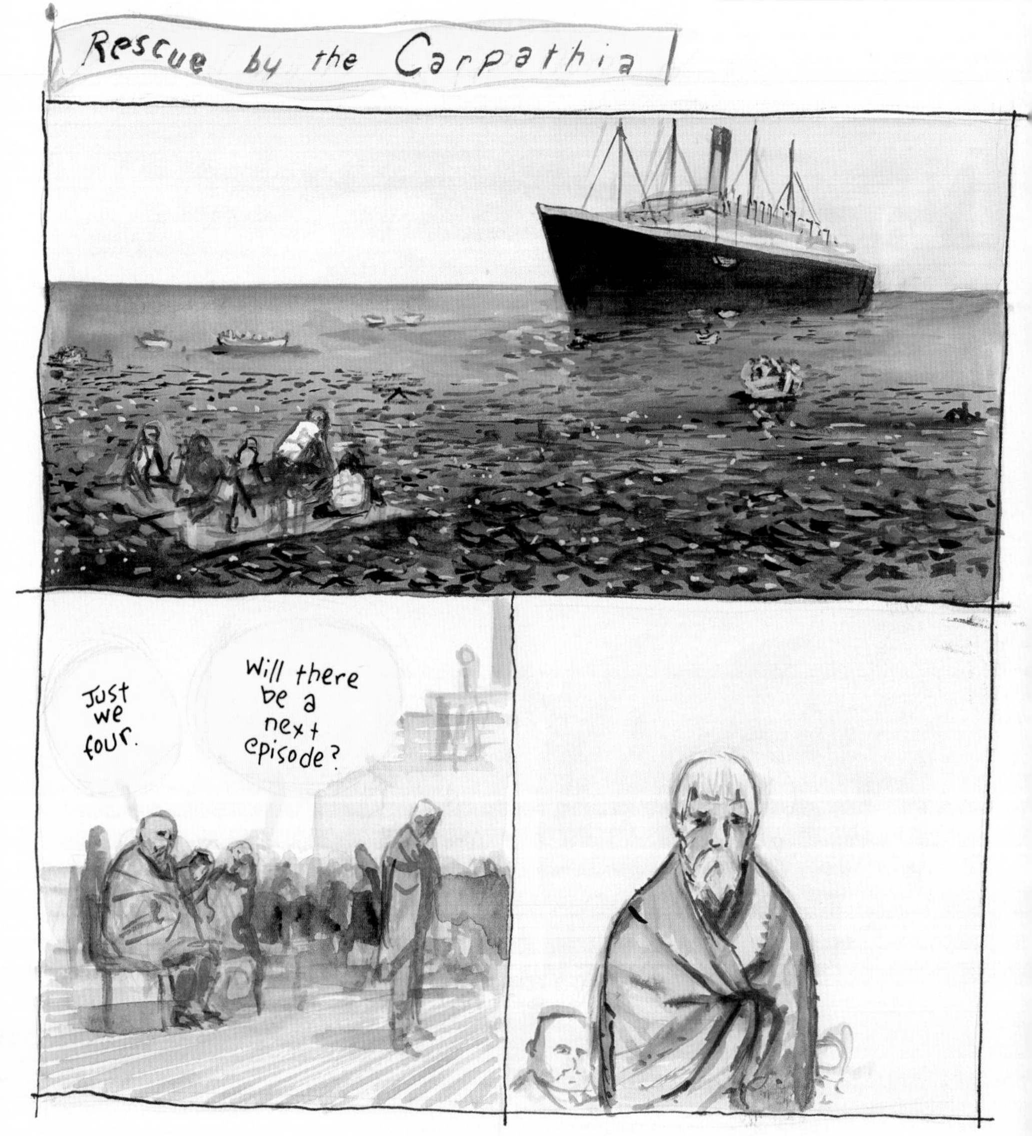
Rescue by the Carpathia
Just we four.
Will there be a next episode?

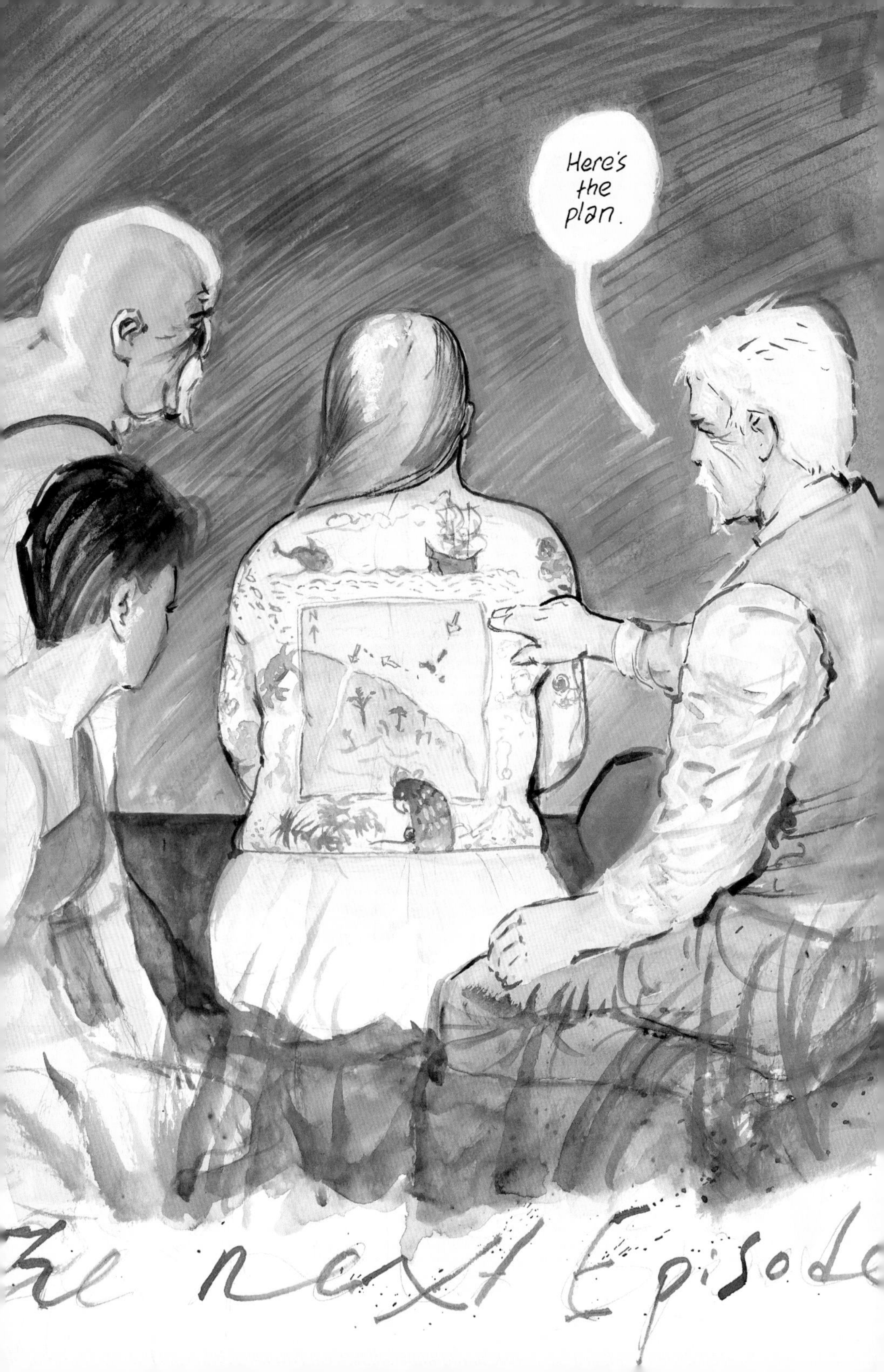
Here's the plan.
next Episode

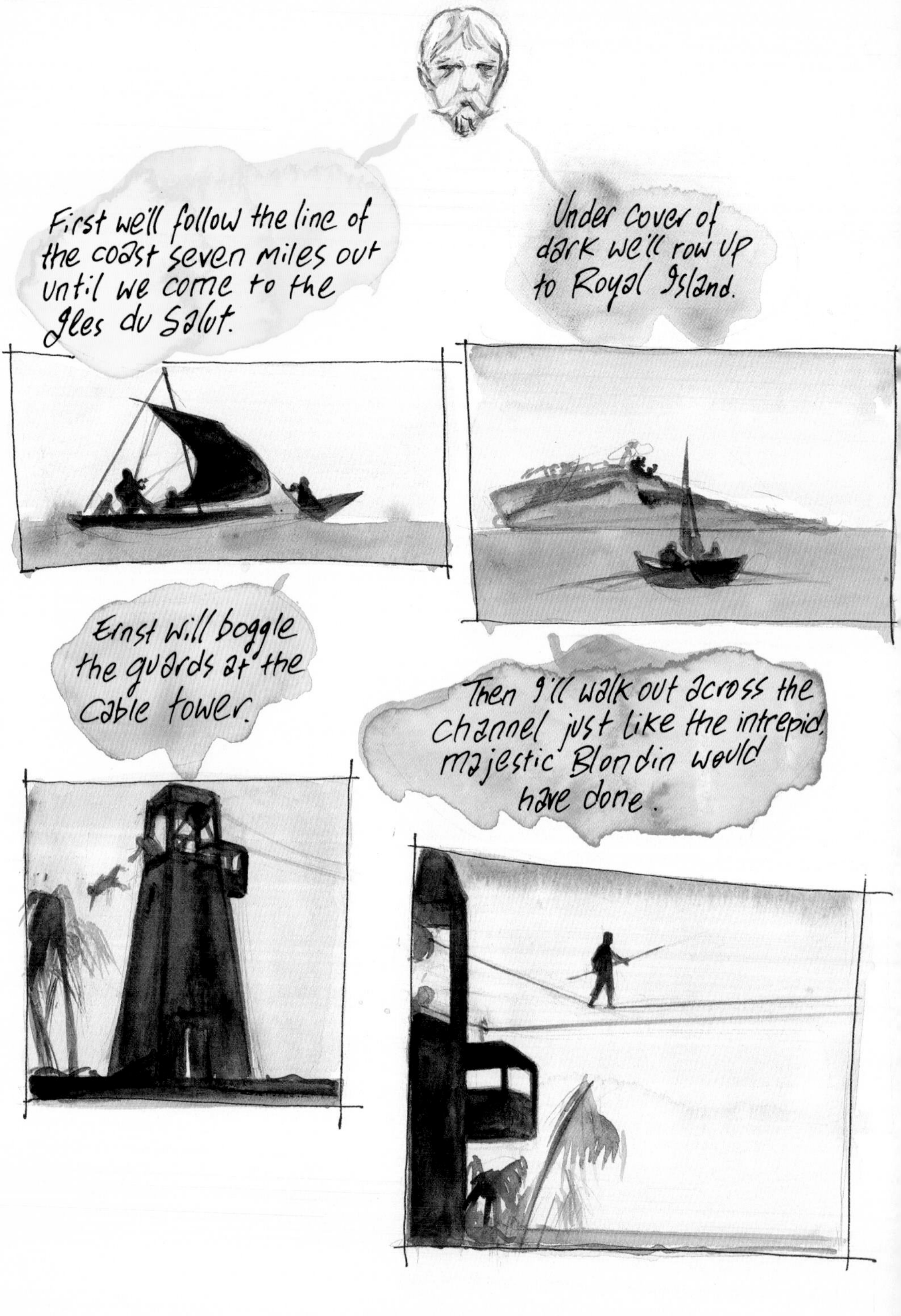
First we'll follow the line of the coast seven miles out until we come to the Iles du Salut.
Under cover of dark we'll row up to Royal Island.
Ernst will boggle the guards at the cable tower.
Then I'll walk out across the channel just like the intrepid, majestic Blondin would have done.

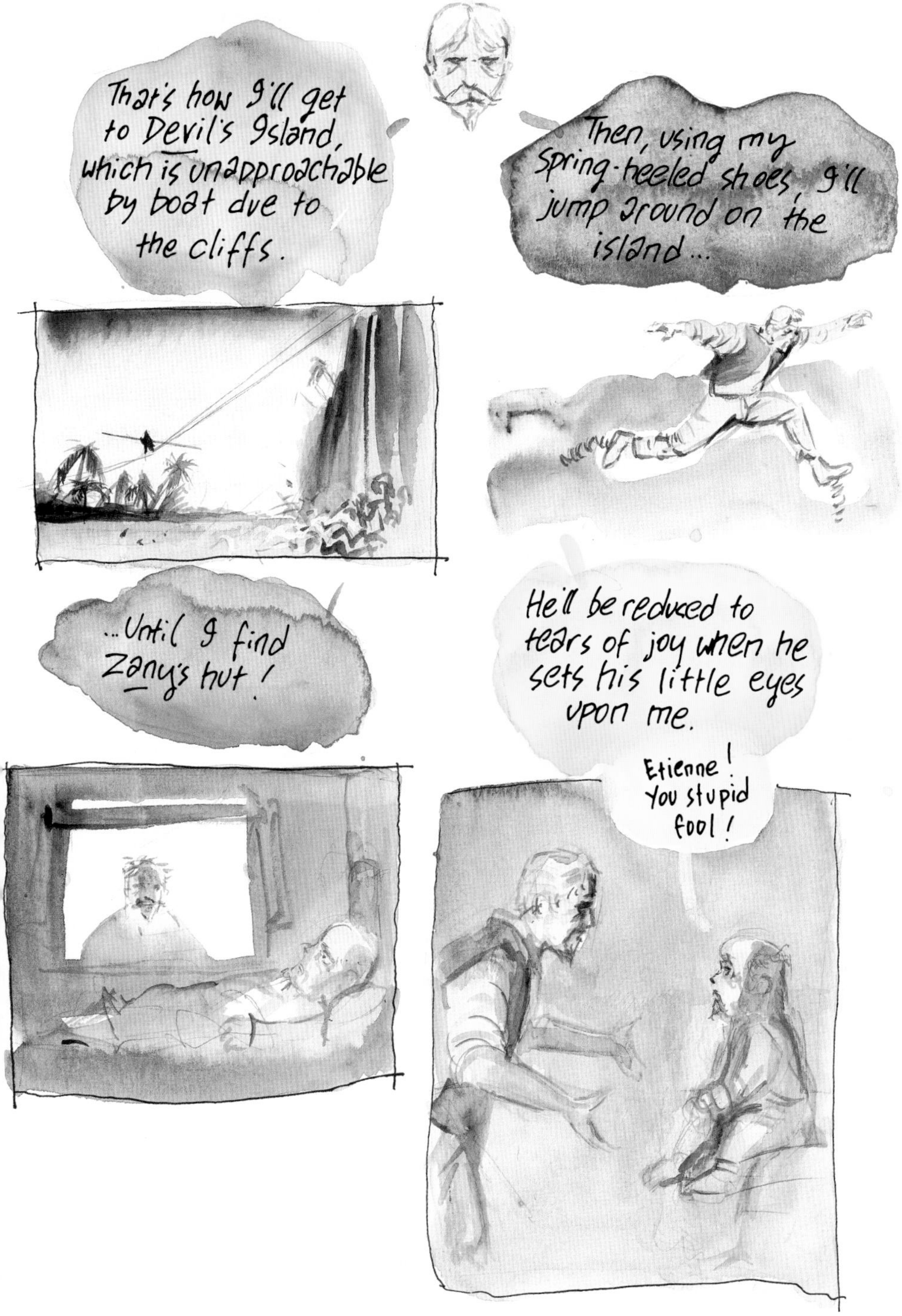
That's how I'll get to Devil's Island, which is unapproachable by boat due to the cliffs.
Then, using my spring-heeled shoes, I'll jump around on the island...
...Until I find Zany's hut!
He'll be reduced to tears of joy when he sets his little eyes upon me.
Etienne! You stupid fool!

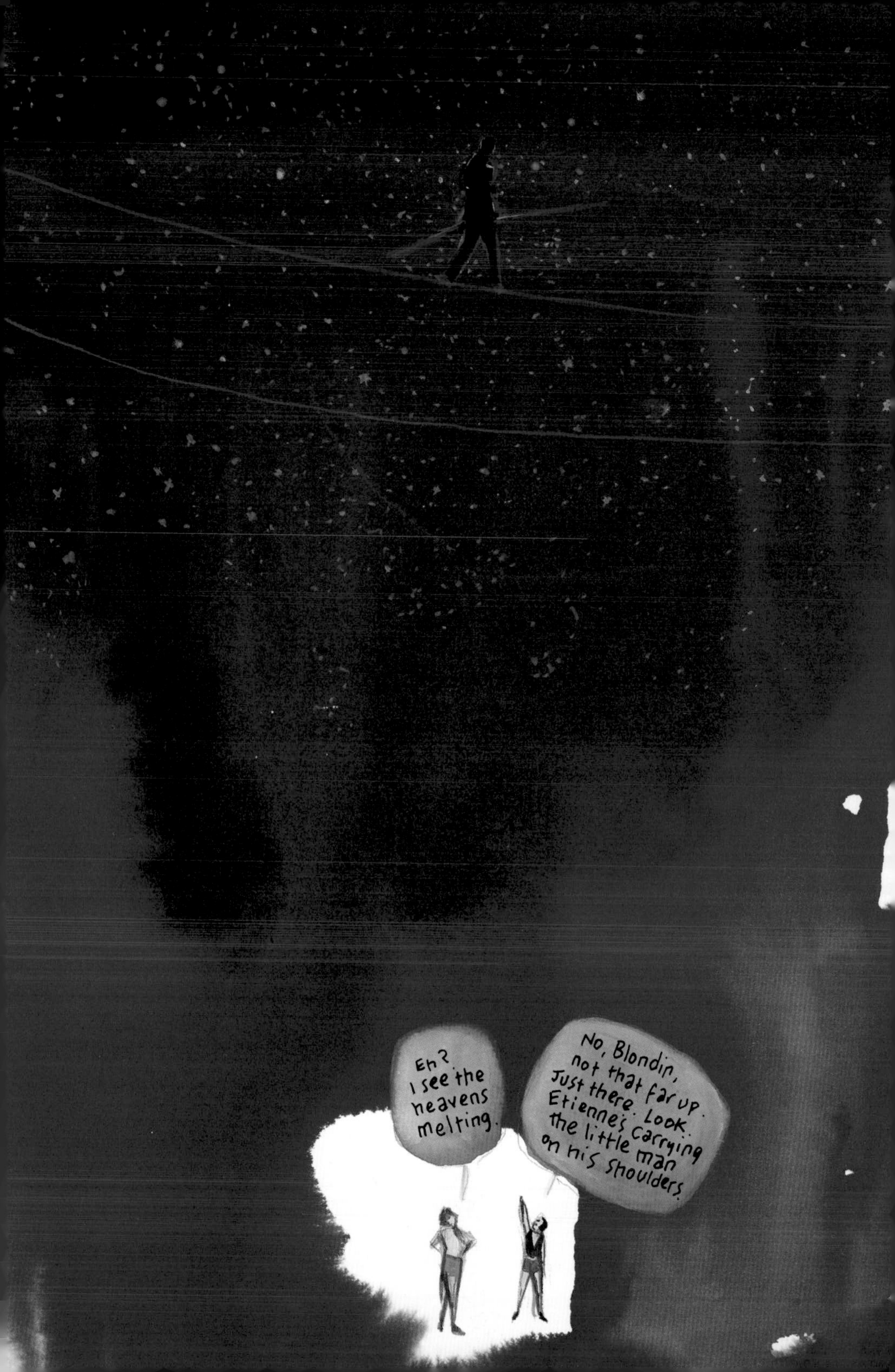
Eh? I see the heavens melting.
No, Blondin, not that far up. Just there. Look. Etienne's carrying the little man on his shoulders.

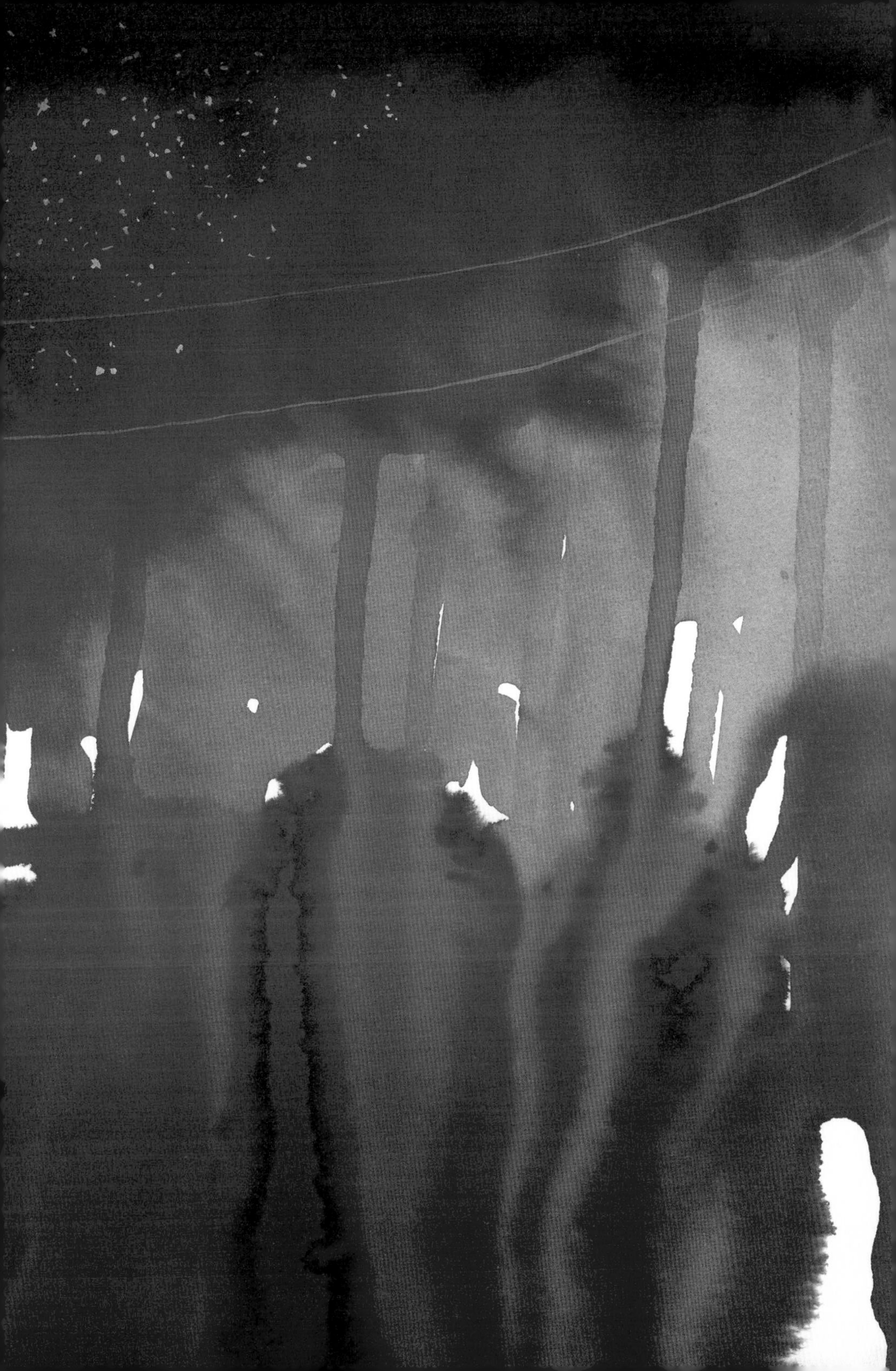

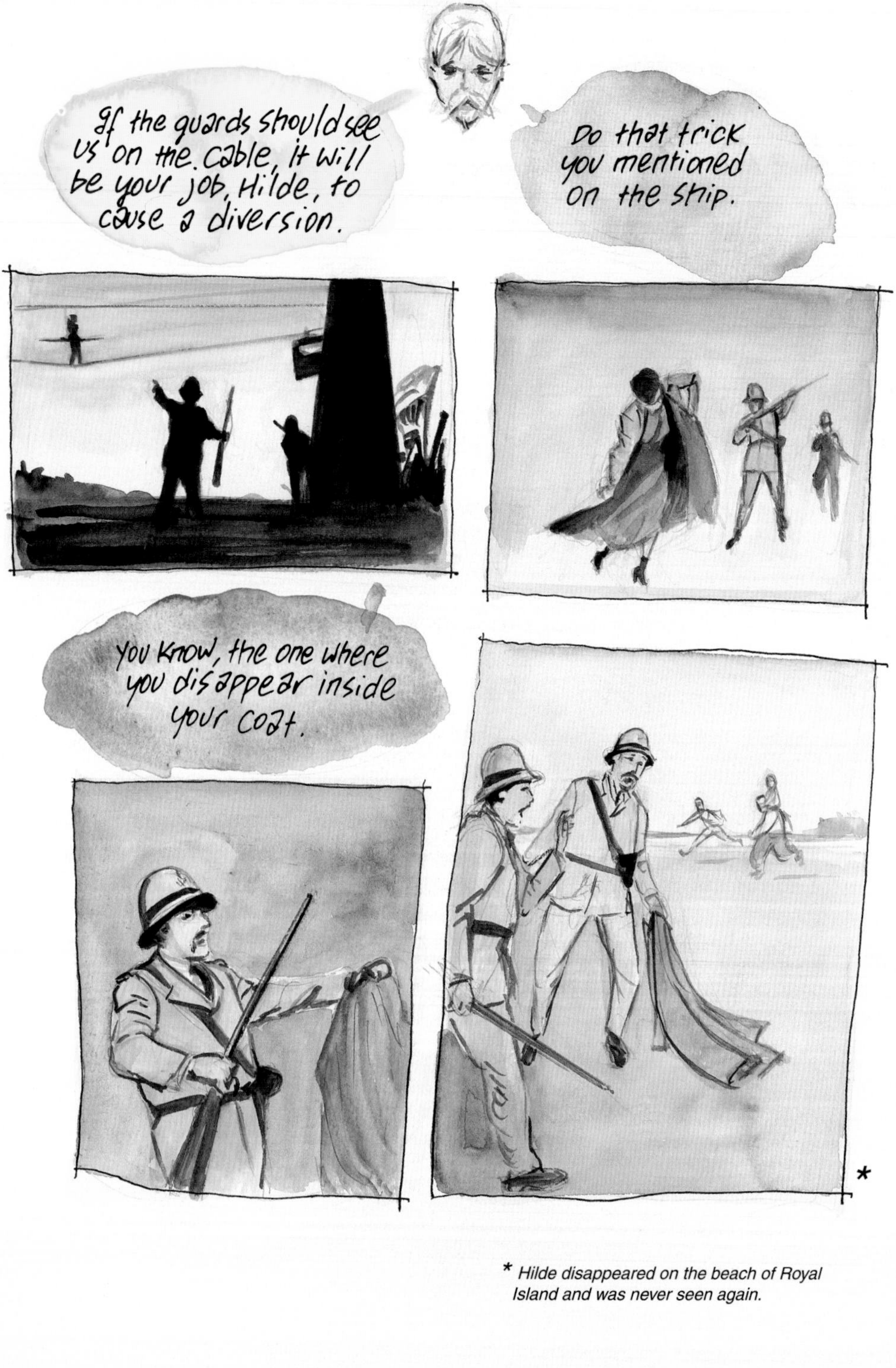
If the guards should see us on the cable, it will be your job, Hilde, to cause a diversion.
Do that trick you mentioned on the ship.
You know, the one where you disappear inside your coat.
*

* Hilde disappeared on the beach of Royal Island and was never seen again.

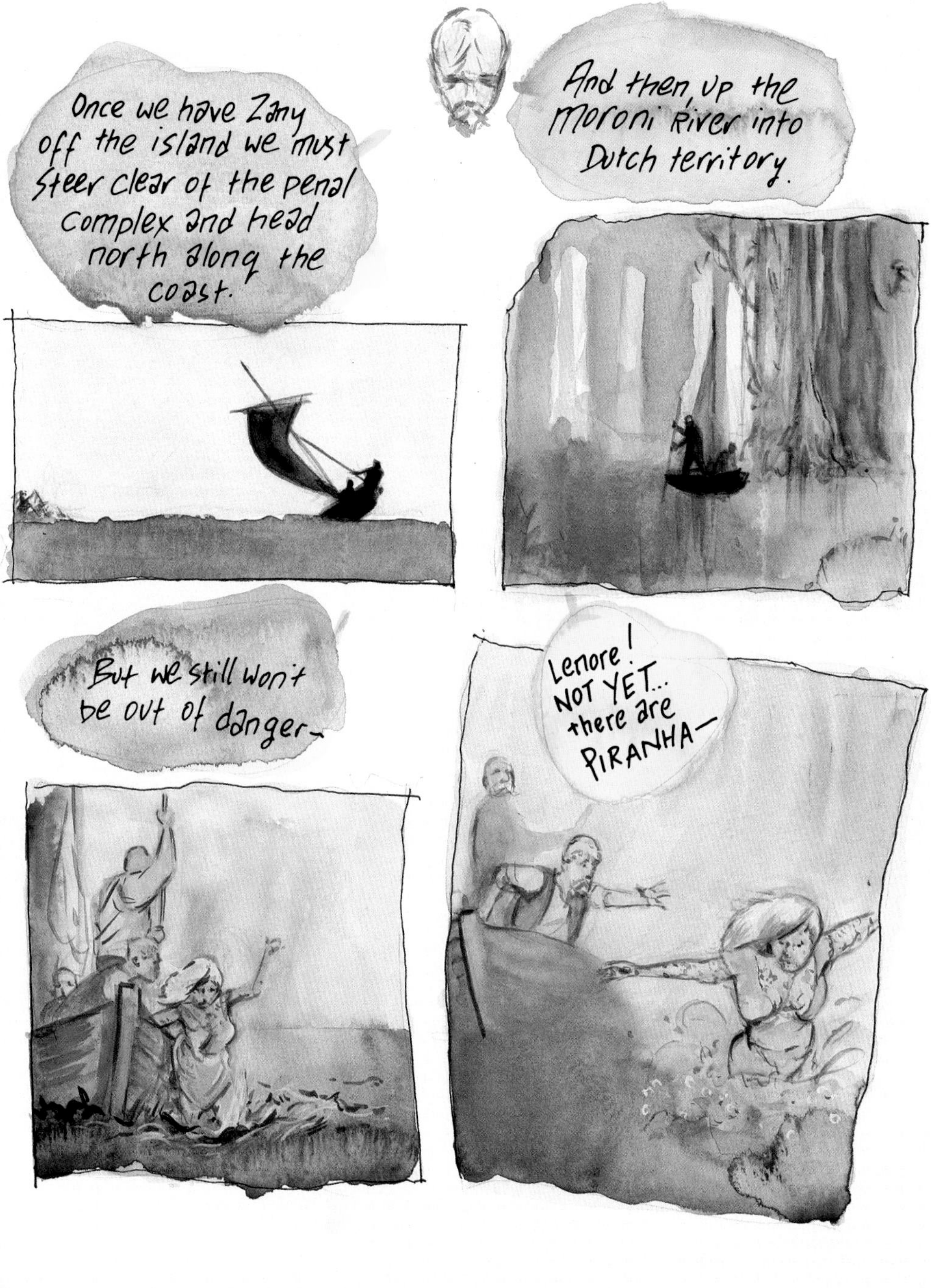
Once we have Zany off the island we must steer clear of the penal complex and head north along the coast.
And then, up the Moroni River into Dutch territory.
But we still won't be out of danger–
Lenore! NOT YET... there are PIRANHA–

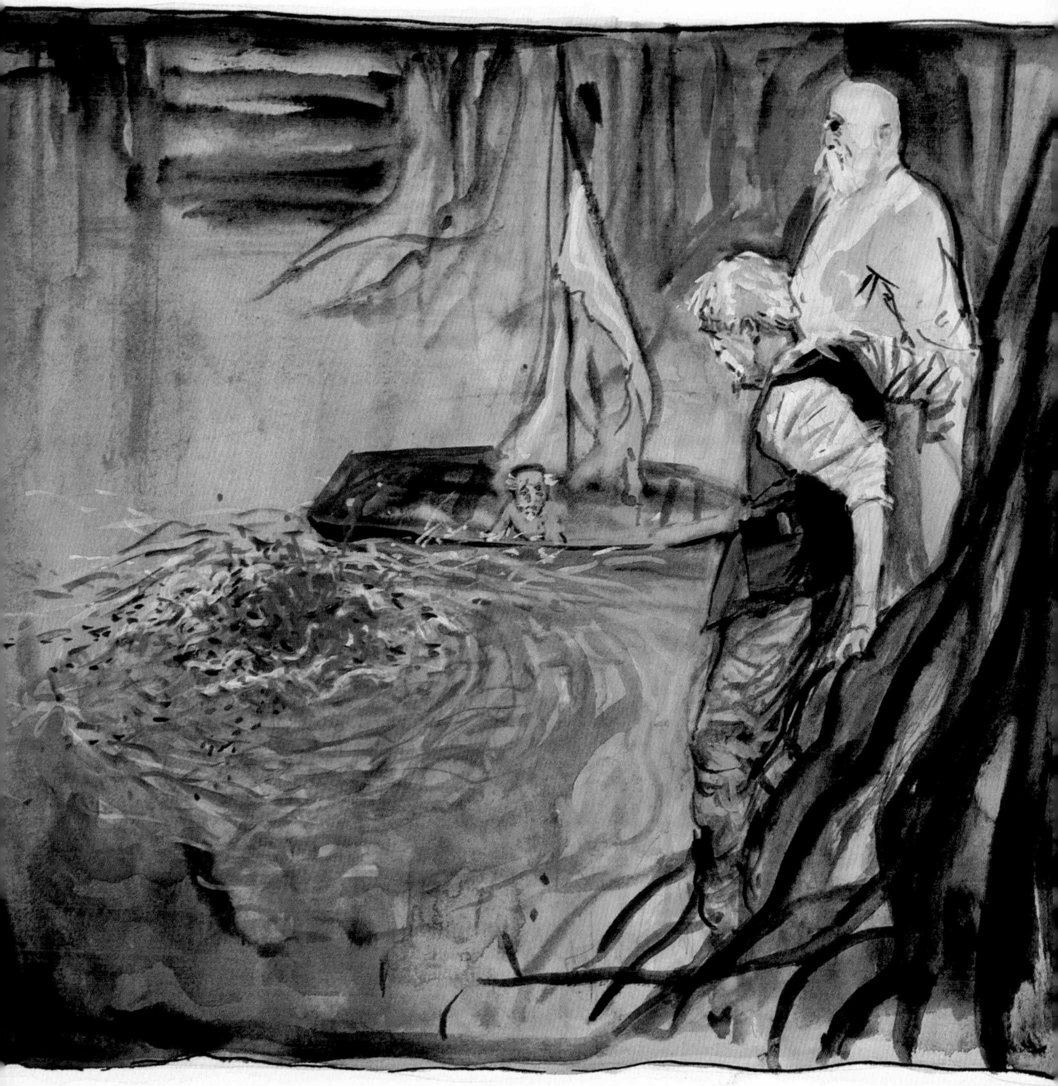

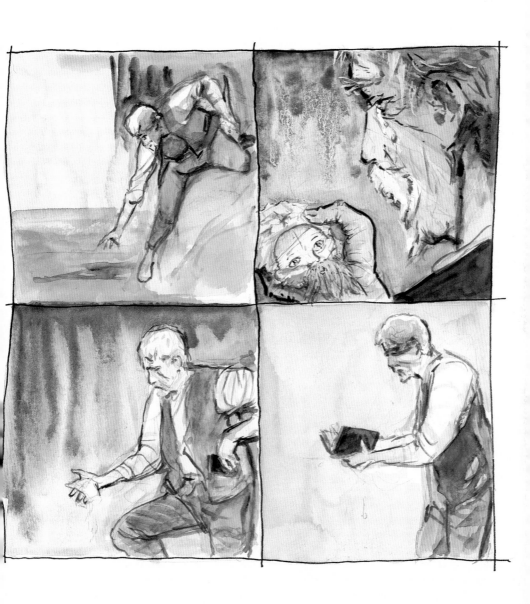

117

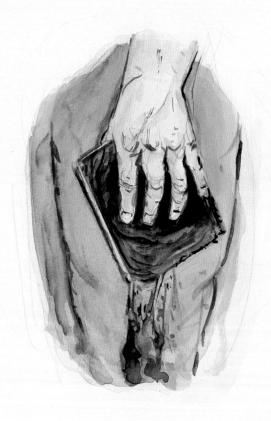

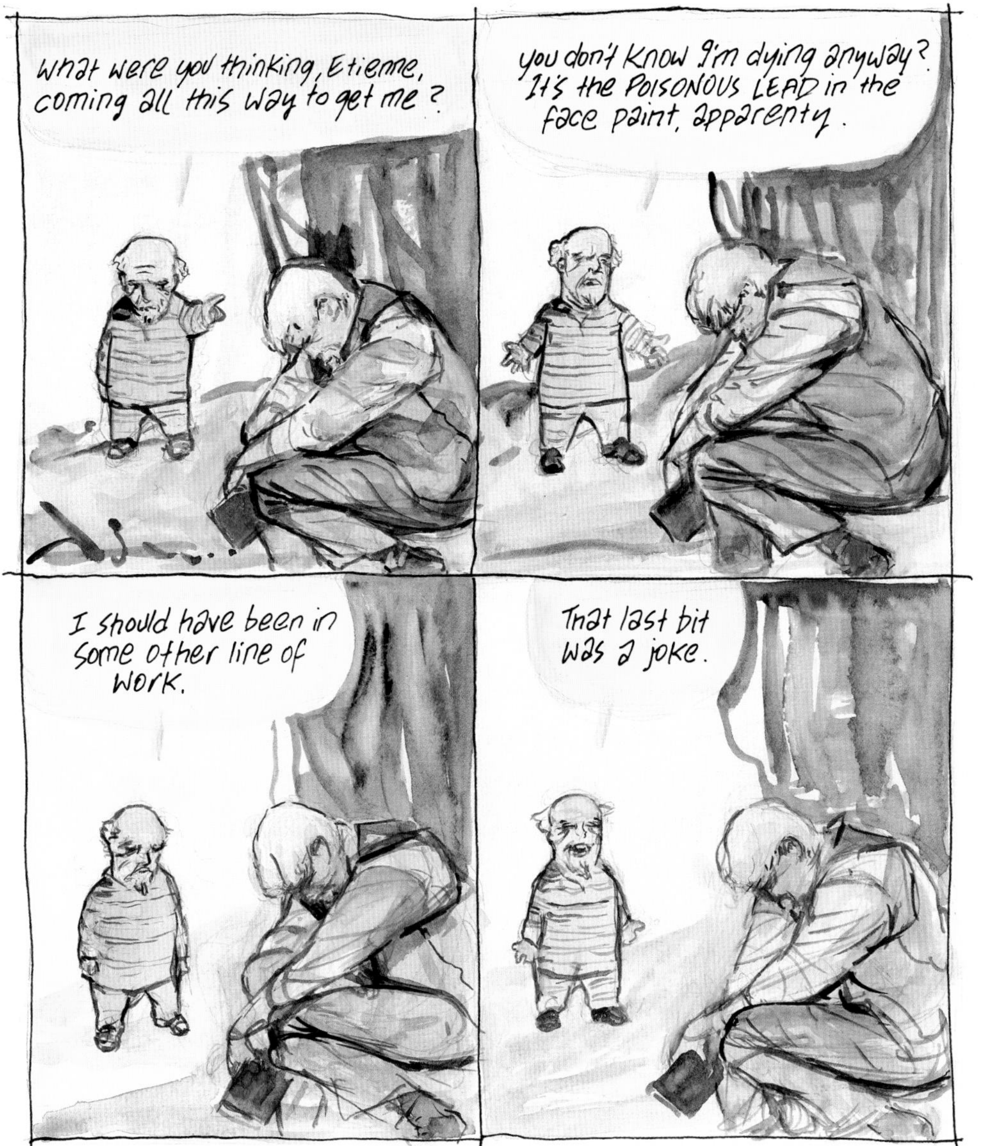
what were you thinking, Etienne, coming all this way to get me?
you don't Know I'm dying anyway? It's the POISONOUS LEAD in the face paint, apparenty.
I should have been in some other line of work.
That last bit was a joke.

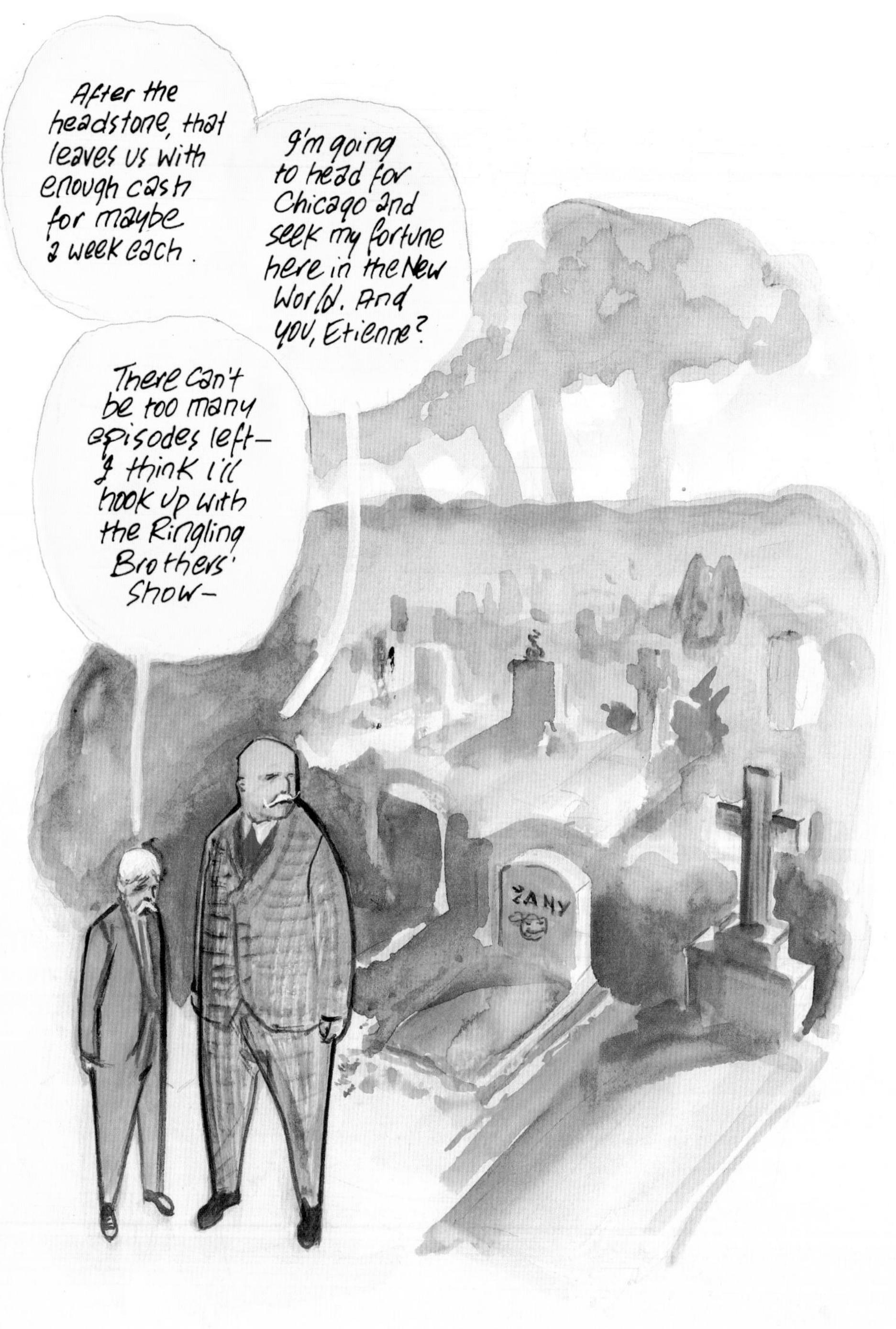
After the headstone, that leaves us with enough cash for maybe a week each.
I'm going to head for Chicago and seek my fortune here in the New World. And you, Etienne?
There can't be too many episodes left— I think I'll hook up with the Ringling Brothers' show—
ZANY

CLEVELAND

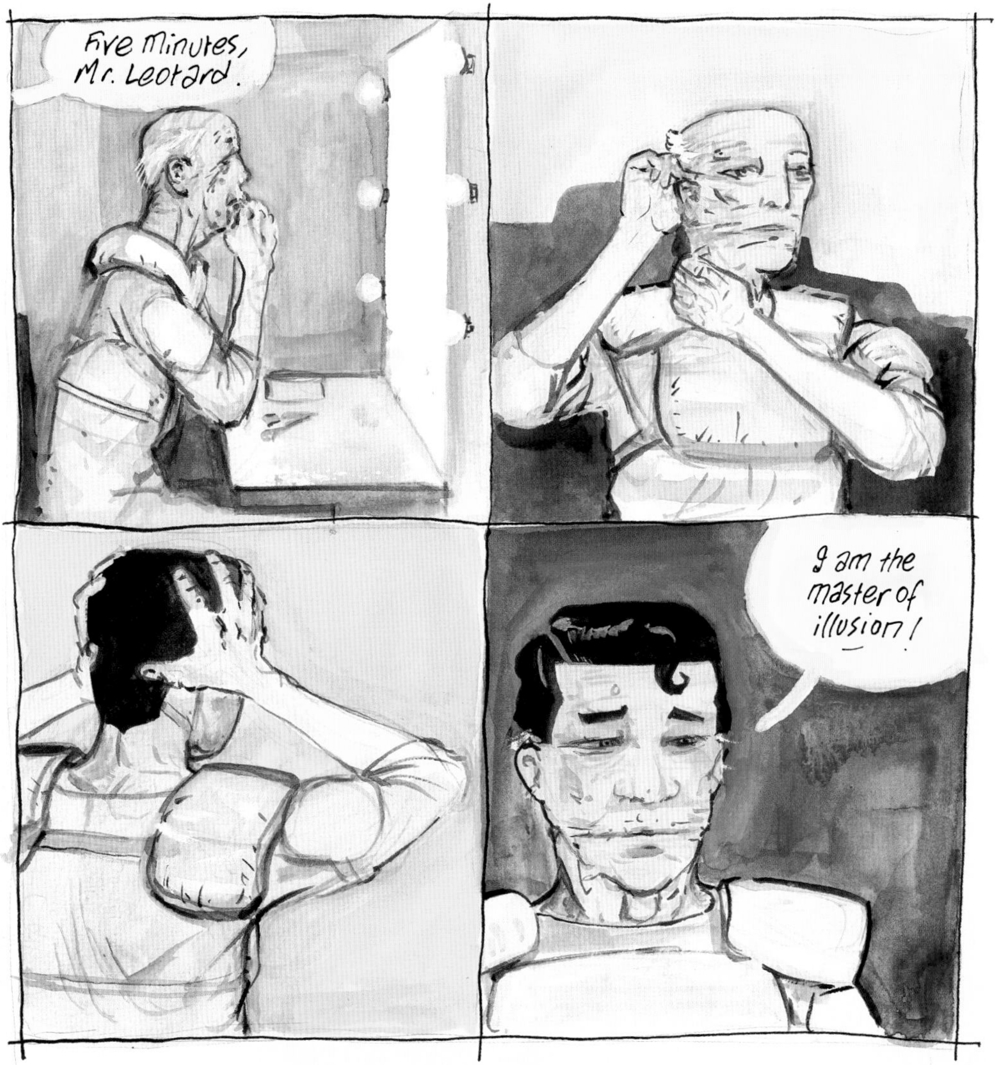

Five Minutes, Mr. Leotard.
I am the master of illusion!

RINGLING BROS

WORLD'S GREATEST SHOWS
THE LAST EPISODE

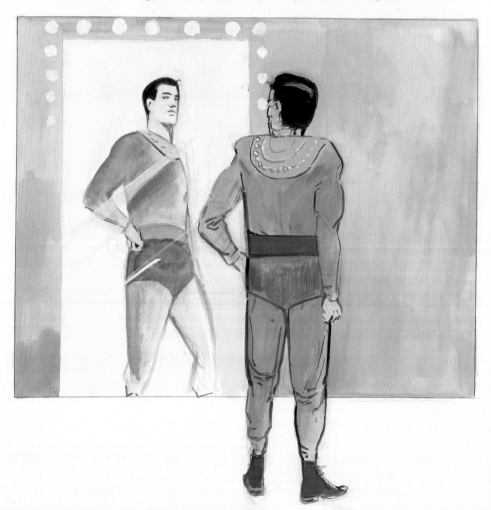

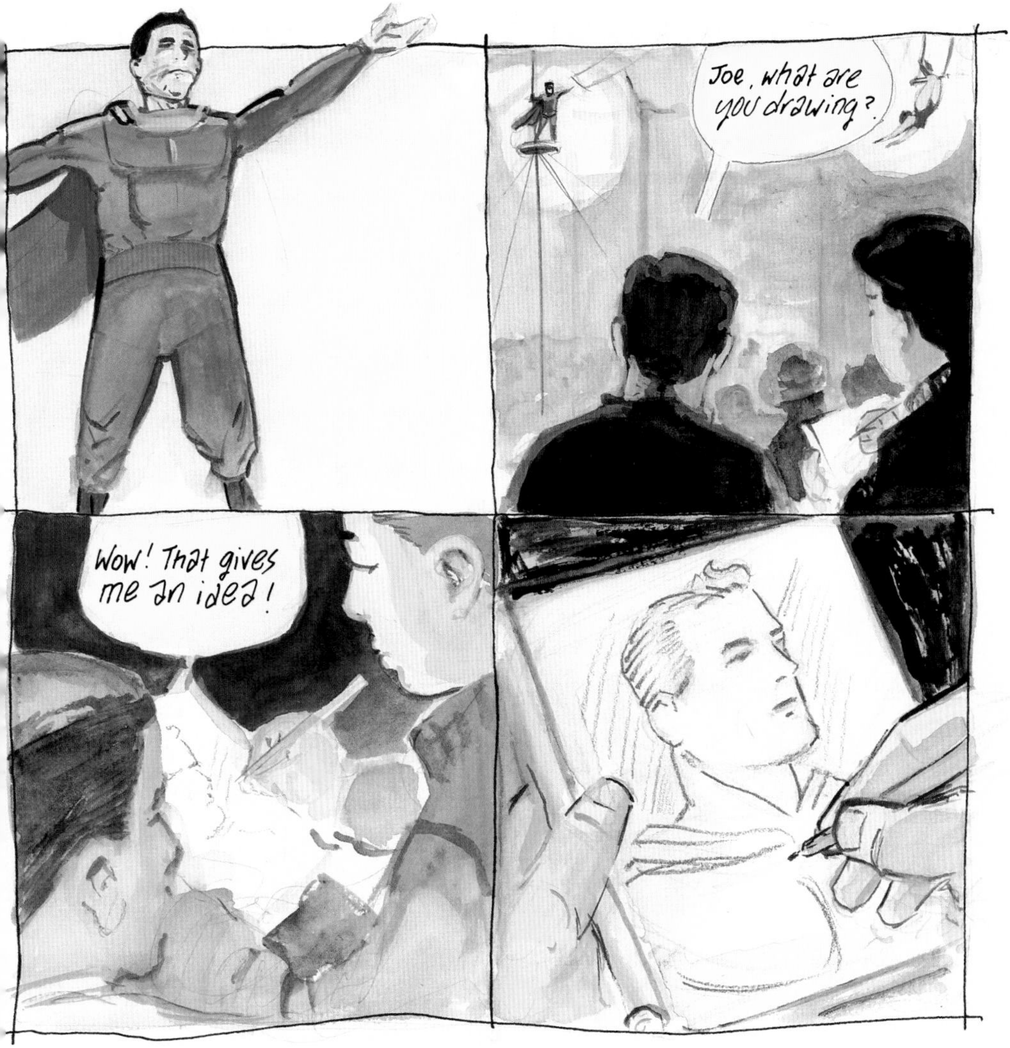
Joe, what are you drawing?
Wow! That gives me an idea!

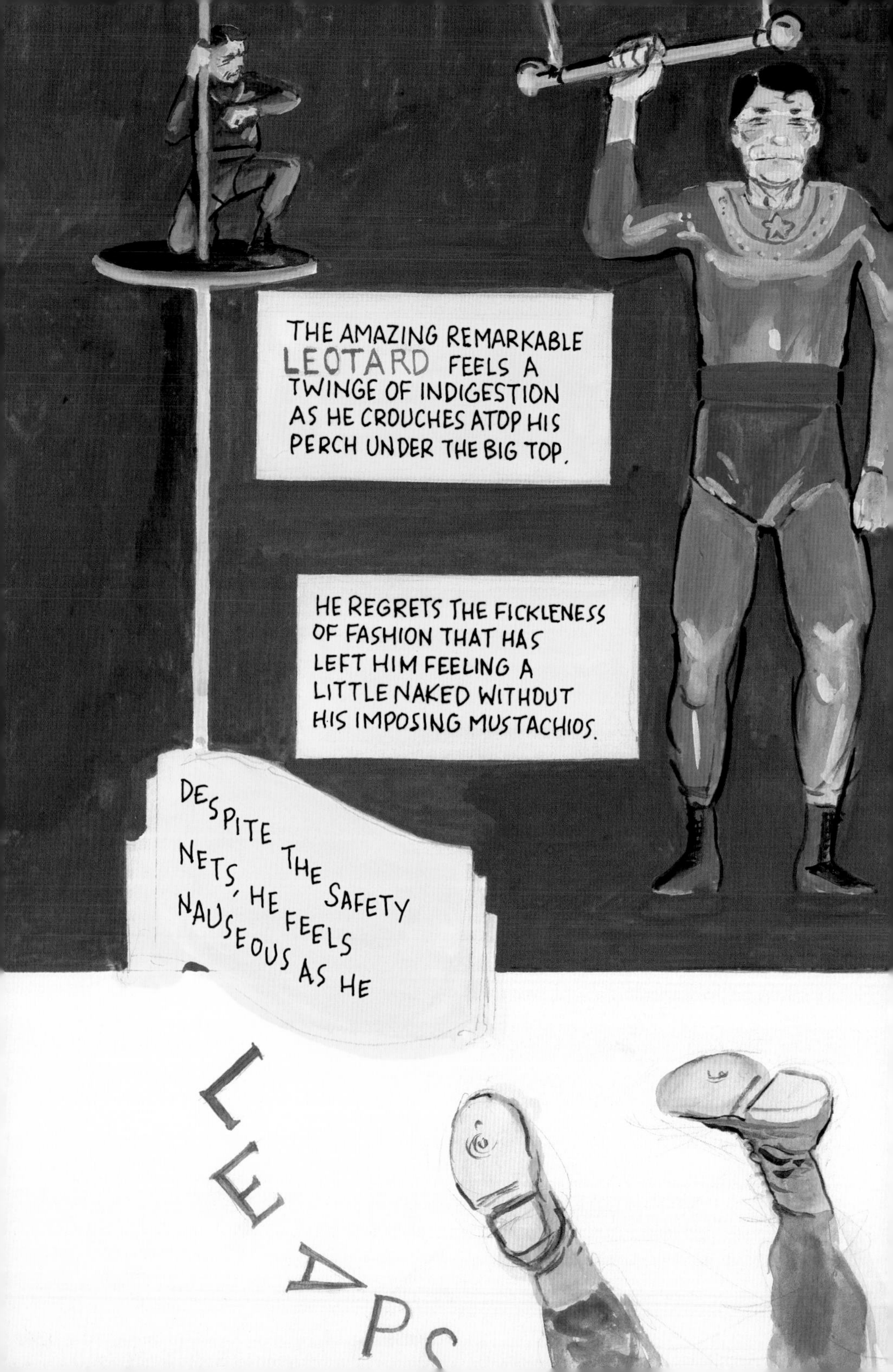
THE AMAZING REMARKABLE LEOTARD FEELS A TWINGE OF INDIGESTION AS HE CROUCHES ATOP HIS PERCH UNDER THE BIG TOP.
HE REGRETS THE FICKLENESS OF FASHION THAT HAS LEFT HIM FEELING A LITTLE NAKED WITHOUT HIS IMPOSING MUSTACHIOS.
DESPITE THE SAFETY NETS, HE FEELS NAUSEOUS AS HE
LEAPS

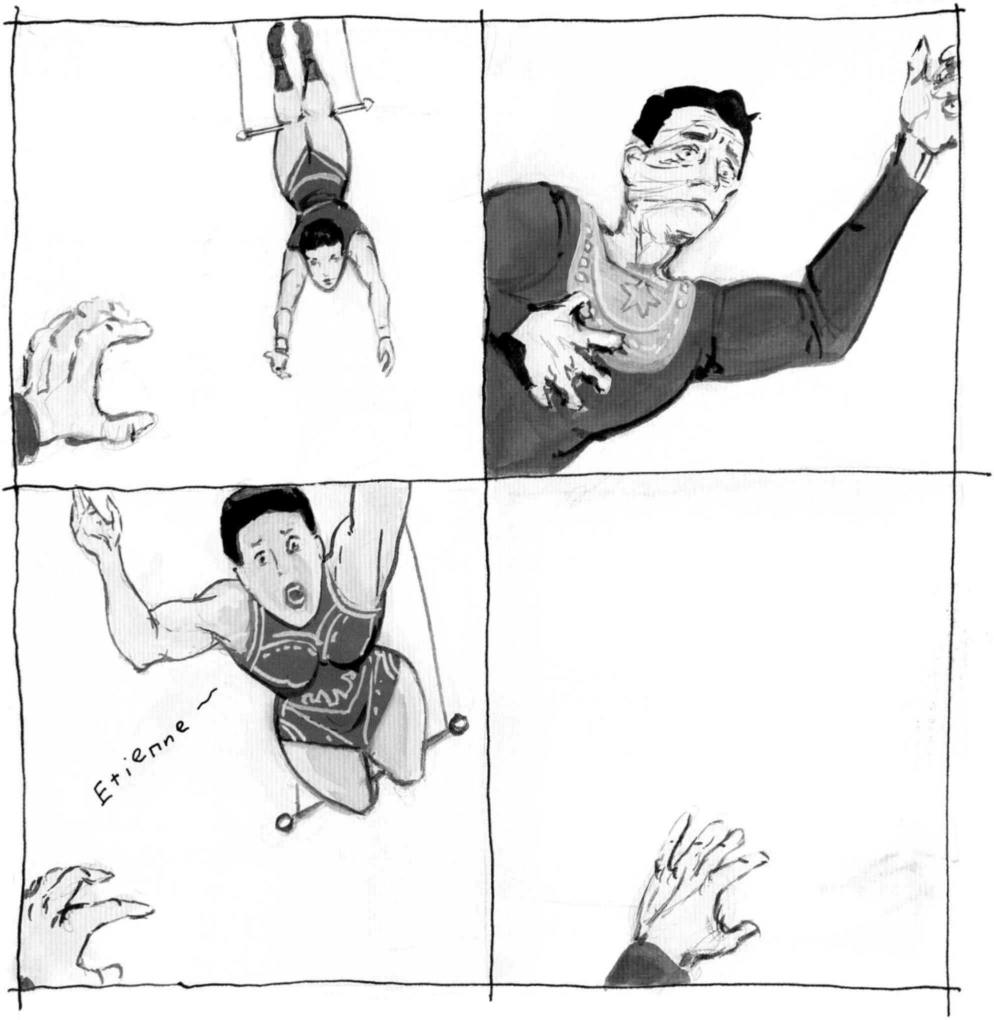
Etienne ~

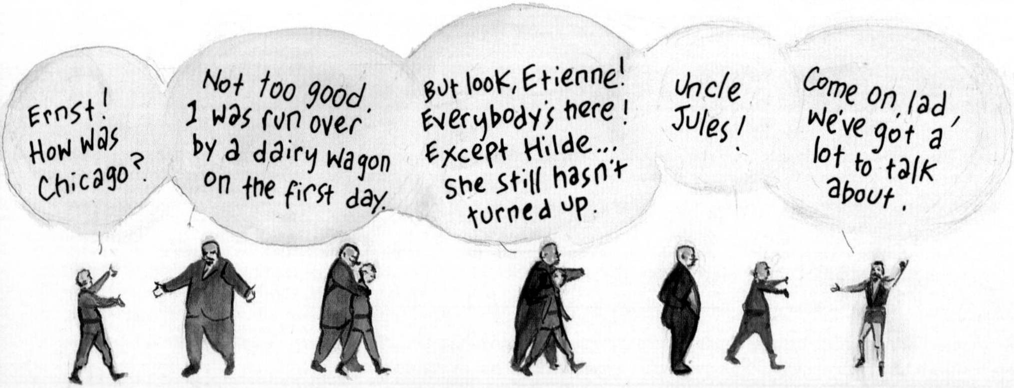
Ernst! How was Chicago?
Not too good. I was run over by a dairy wagon on the first day.
But look, Etienne! Everybody's here! Except Hilde... She still hasn't turned up.
Uncle Jules!
Come on, lad, we've got a lot to talk about.

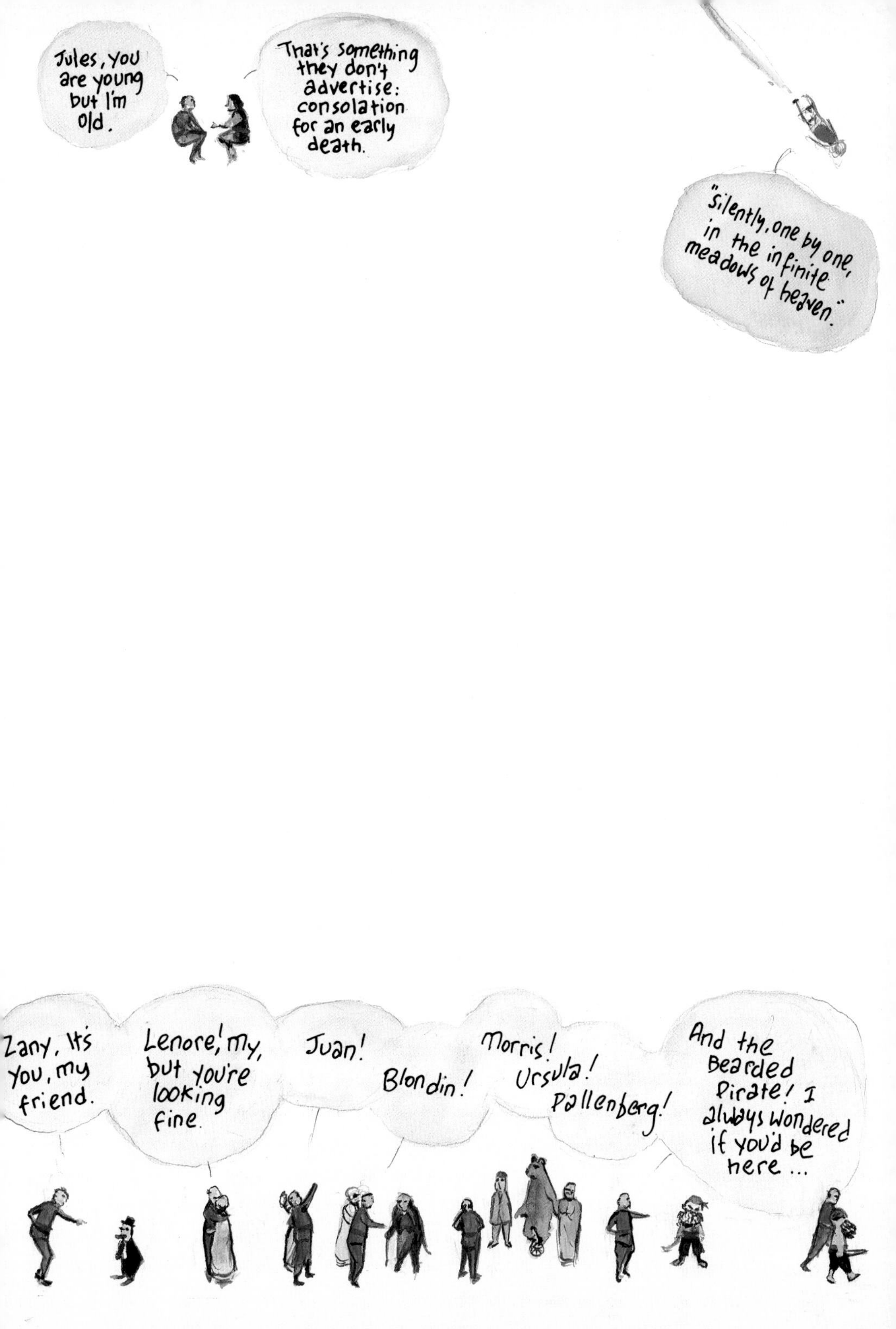

Jules, you are young but I'm old.
That's something they don't advertise: consolation for an early death.
"Silently, one by one, in the infinite meadows of heaven."
Zany, It's you, my friend.
Lenore! my, but you're looking fine.
Juan!
Blondin!
Morris!
Ursula!
Pallenberg!
And the Bearded Pirate! I always wondered if you'd be here...

Nothing occurs on this page